THE LAST KEY
TO SUCCESS

Secret Recipe of Company Building
Shared by Founders Under 30

GRACE GONG

TO ENTREPRENEURS AROUND THE WORLD!
AND TO MOM, DAD, AND RSS.

CONNECT WITH US AND CHECK OUT THE FUN STUFF SECTION ON
WWW.THELASTKEYTOSUCCESS.COM

ACKNOWLEDGMENTS

I want to thank all my founders and authors equally. You guys are just wonderful. Thanks to Patrick Slade for being the best person ever and giving me the ticket to go to the summit. Brian Powers for being so funny and the first person who signed the contract. Andrew Scheuermann for not killing me when I spell your last name wrong every day. Shruti Shah for letting me touching your hair. Courtney for being super nice. Kevin Chan for sharing the secret of Dior pants. Sarah Guthal for giving the best relationship tips. LV Jadavji for sharing the deepest secret about managing people. Danny for being such a great team sport, very supportive, with Tom! Wonderful team! Tim Hwang, president 2040. Joey, for photoshopping our book cover everywhere. Yehia, thanks for giving me an email address that eventually worked in Egypt. Mike Townsend for putting our book onto a podcast! Staff, real-life family guy. Rose and Laura are gonna be huge! Sercan for recommending the best mac and cheese burger place on earth. Tarun for getting together after me being five hours late in a traffic jam. Jessica for sharing your fabulous story. Thanks to Mary Jo for making education so interesting!

My lawyer Alan Haus, great contract! Thanks to Faisal, Mike, and Brian for the podcast.

Daniel Fishel for designing the awesome cover!

Nik Ingersoll, Mark Silberg, Cameron Titelman, Aradhya Malhotra, Amanda Curtis, Ty Stafford, Tai Tran, Erik Huberman, and Geo!

Everyone who helped edit this!

Last but not least, this book would not exist if my parents hadn't sent me to America to pursue my entrepreneur dream. And Ryan, for being so supportive and patient with me. I love you!

CONTENTS

CHAPTER ONE: ANDREW SCHEUERMANN...................................... 7
CEO and Cofounder, Arch

CHAPTER TWO: MARY JO MADDA 39
Senior Editor, EdSurge

CHAPTER THREE: SHRUTI SHAH 53
Cofounder, Move Loot

CHAPTER FOUR: PATRICK SLADE 69
Cofounder, PSYONIC

CHAPTER FIVE: BRIAN POWERS 83
Cofounder, TemperPack

CHAPTER SIX: TIM HWANG...95
Founder and CEO of FiscalNote

CHAPTER SEVEN: TOM BRADY 105
Cofounder and Chief Technology Officer, SkySpecs

CHAPTER EIGHT: LAURA D'ASARO..129
Cofounder and Chief Operations Officer, Six Foods

CHAPTER NINE: MIKE TOWNSEND 143
Cofounder and Chief Operations Officer, HomeHero

CHAPTER TEN: KEVIN CHAN...161
Cofounder, Maderight

CHAPTER ELEVEN: YEHIA ABUGABAL 171
Oncologist and Founder, International Cancer Research Center

CHAPTER TWELVE: COURTNEY GRAS 177
Cofounder, Design Flux Technologies, and Executive Director at Launch League

CHAPTER THIRTEEN: STAFF SHEEHAN 189
Founder, Catalytic Innovations & Former CEO, Dream 8, Inc.

CHAPTER FOURTEEN: TARUN GANGWANI................................ 203
Cofounder and Head of Product, Grok

CHAPTER FIFTEEN: JOEY PRIMIANI.................................... 223
Founder and CEO, Superfuture Labs, Previously Backplane and Cortex

CHAPTER SIXTEEN: LOUIS-VICTOR JADAVJI.................................227
Cofounder, Wiivv

CHAPTER SEVENTEEN: ROSE WANG... 239
Cofounder and Chief Executive Officer, Six Foods

CHAPTER EIGHTEEN: SERCAN TOPCU 253
Cofounder and Chief Marketing Officer, Tembo Education

CHAPTER NINETEEN: SARAH GUTHALS 267
Social Engineer and Entrepreneur, GitHub's Social Impact Team

CHAPTER TWENTY: DANNY ELLIS.......................................289
Cofounder and Chief Executive Officer, SkySpecs

CHAPTER TWENTY-ONE: JESSICA HENDRICKS YEE 313
Founder, The Brave Collection

INTRODUCTION

My favorite comedian, Judd Apatow, created a comedy book called *Sick in the Head*. In it he interviewed a number of famous comedians, including Jerry Seinfeld, Adam Sandler, and others. His purpose was to learn from these people about their comedy careers, their secrets to success, and the steps that led to their success. Thus, he learned the tricks of the comedic trade and was able to share them with the world.

I'm aiming to do something similar on the business side of life. The successful company founders who first came to mind were Elon Musk, Mark Zuckerberg, and Steve Jobs. After reading their biographies, I concluded that their successes are hard to recreate because they founded their companies over a decade ago or more. The resources they used and the market of those times are not really applicable today. So I decided to look to current entrepreneurs for current guidance. After ten years, some of our peers will become the next Musk, Zuckerberg, or Jobs. It's better to learn from people now to stand out in the competition ten years from now.

In January of 2016, I saw that some of my Facebook friends were on the list of *Forbes* magazine's "30 Under 30." I started to ask them how they started their companies. I also went to multiple start-up events and found that other people had the same questions. I decided to find over twenty successful entrepreneurs who created their own companies recently. They are all living in different places and come from different backgrounds.

I created a set of thirteen questions to prompt their responses. I asked them to address at least two of the questions in their responses to me.

Here's what I sent to them:

1. **How do you start a company?** (A holistic view of starting a company: What milestones do you need to set? How does someone get started by doing minor things that don't scale? What is the timeline for each step to be accomplished? How do you budget for your company? What was your starting point? Was it at school? A previous job? How do you plan to execute your idea? What were your working hours?)

2. **What are your resources, experiences, and strengths?** (Describe how you see your strengths and weaknesses. How do you deal with your weaknesses and maximize your strengths? How do you create your own startup environment and leverage your resources? What experiences or resources did you need?)

3. **Cofounders, teammates, and mentors.** (How did you meet your cofounder? Describe where you met them and how you feel about them. What challenges did you face while you were with them? When conflict arises, how do you resolve it? Who is your mentor? Who do you call when you need help?)

4. **Supporting yourself financially and mentality.** (How do you make money while creating your own company? How do you calculate your budget and stay within the budget? Who encouraged or supported you along the way? Who do you call when you fail? Who do you ask for advice? How did you meet them? How did your life change around the time you started your company? What was your personal

life like? How do you balance your life? What were your working hours?)

5. **Product.** (How did you come up with your product? How did you design your product? What goal did you have in mind? How did you set up your time schedule? Who did you hire? How do you test out your products in the market? How do you know which product to pursue and which one to cut? If you are creating a community, how do you find the audience and the contributors? How do you attract them to invest in your product?)

6. **Competition and trends.** (How do you find your core competency? What do you think is your core competency and your company's core competency? Are those two related? How do you do market research? Who are your competitors? How did you find your target audiences? How did they react to your product? What's your plan to compete or stay away from the competition?)

7. **Produce, operate, and manage.** (How do you produce your product? Do you outsource? Where do you find outsourcing companies? What problems arise with employees you manage? What are some challenges you are facing during company operation? Please talk about problems that really exist.)

8. **Raising money and a business model.** (How did you get the first round of funding to get the project started? How did you come up with the business model? Who supported you financially from the beginning? How do you minimize cost and maximize revenue? What are some specific things that you did?)

9. **Scalability and growth.** (What was a good market for you to enter? How did you discover it? How do you envision society and yourself in ten years? How do you plan to grow your company? You can also talk about what you thought when you started—it doesn't have to be a prediction.)

10. **Sales and marketing.** (What are some tactics you use to promote your company? What do you think is the best marketing tool for your company specifically? How do you promote yourself? How do you catch press attention? Did you send them emails about your company? How did you find them? How do you stand out on social media? What media do you use to target your audience? How did you find the best way to promote your company?)

11. **Visa and legal processes in a global market.** (How do you view the global market? What does the global market mean to your company? Do you have factories abroad or do you manufacture with others abroad? How did you find them? What was your visa status? How did you get a visa? Did you find the legal system challenging for your company?)

12. **Dealing with failures.** (How many times did you fail before you succeeded? What motivated you to keep going? When do you know if it is a good time to drop the project? When do you keep going? Can you give a specific example to prove your point? When was your lowest point? How did you overcome that point? What hurt you the most during the process of creating a company? What's the hardest thing about starting a startup? What's the best thing about creating a company? Did other people betray you? Did you run out of money? Did you have a break up during a company downfall? Did you lose people from your personal life during this period?)

13. **Values, self-improvement, and advice.** (What do you think is one quality that matters the most when you are creating a company? What advice would you give yourself if you were to start a company again? What's your advice for first-time founders? What do you think is the most important quality a person could have? What's your favorite book?)

After reading the engrossing responses that I got back, I phoned each person to discuss them. They were all wonderfully gracious with their time. After probing a bit, I chose the most interesting and unique parts of their business journeys. I encouraged them to include their visionary insights, to describe lucky breaks, and to share the tricks of their trades. I wanted to know their step-by-step guide to raising funds, and even what their pitch decks looked like. I even asked them to take pictures of their bookshelves and other places in their homes or offices. I was delighted with how much they shared.

I considered taking my manuscript to a traditional book publisher. Then I reflected on my goal of making current insights currently available. I considered what the customary bureaucracy and editing requirements of a traditional publisher would be. Of course, I concluded that I needed to get this to the public in a leaner, quicker, more entrepreneurial way. If nothing else, I have been inspired to this end by these entrepreneurs' stories.

I am also aiming to connect entrepreneurs around the world. This book is my first step.

I hope you enjoy these stories as much as I do, and I hope these insights will help drive your business successes!

Grace Gong
JANUARY 2017

CHAPTER ONE

ANDREW SCHEUERMANN
CEO and Cofounder, Arch

>>>> ABOUT ANDREW

Andrew Scheuermann is the CEO and cofounder of Arch (formerly called WellDone Technology), where he develops and connects devices for the industrial "Internet of Things." Arch is on a mission to make building smart physical infrastructure as simple and powerful as building apps on the smartphone has been for the last decade. Before cofounding Arch, Andrew did ten years of research on power and energy devices ranging from single-molecule machines, high-power switches, and nuclear weapons to hydrogen fuel cells, solar cells, and artificial photosynthesis cells, which are all-in-one devices that convert solar energy directly into chemicals and fuels.

From 2012 to 2014, Andrew was part of the early team that helped build StartX, the Stanford Startup Accelerator, which is consistently ranked as one of the top startup accelerators in the world. StartX's founders have raised over $2 billion in funding, and StartX itself has invested around $100 million across two hundred companies as of the fourth quarter of 2016. Andrew personally cofounded the StartX hardware program, led Stanford campus engagement, and cofounded an early-stage incubator called Mentor Labs that served over seventy companies. In 2015, he cofounded a startup called Deliberate that connected people from forty different countries in video conversations about important global issues such as climate change and social justice. Andrew earned a BS in chemistry and BA in economics from the University of Florida and an MS and PhD in materials science and engineering from Stanford. He has coauthored eighteen scientific publications, including work published in *Nature Materials*, where he developed a novel theory of leaky capacitors and applied it to artificial photosynthesis, breaking the world record for silicon photoanode efficiency. He was recognized by *Forbes* as one of the "30 Under 30" in Energy, and despite feeling that his career has only just begun, he is honored to offer his reflections thus far on how to build a great company.

S o let's talk about ideas. Great ideas are the core of a great startup, right? Wrong. There are only two essential elements to a great startup: people and passion.

While my journey is still in its early stages, I've had the opportunity to help hundreds of individuals and teams begin startups here in the core of Silicon Valley. I've also had the opportunity to start a couple myself, to experience both failure and success, and to be on a great journey with my current company, Arch. And I never would have guessed I'd be here ten years ago, heck even five years ago! So how do you start a company? If there's anything I've learned, it's that the process begins long before you become directly aware of your desire to start one. Many founders will tell you that they didn't plan to start a company before they did. That statement utterly confused me—even made me angry—until it happened to me.

STEP 1. AWARENESS: ENTREPRENEURSHIP IS FOR YOU

I came to the Bay Area in 2011, when I was in graduate school, at age twenty-two. I had a Navy and space industry dad and this was my ninth place to live after growing up in various cities across the southern United States—Alabama, Texas, New Mexico, and Florida. I was studying materials science, unsure of exactly what to do next, but eager to learn more and enchanted by the vibe I'd experienced on a visit to Stanford. Materials science isn't exactly the most common major leading to entrepreneurship these days, and I didn't think I knew anything about entrepreneurship when I arrived, but more on that later.

Summer 2011. My first weekend in the Bay Area, after selling everything and leaving Florida with only a guitar, fencing bag, and one suitcase of clothes. In my traditional style, I jumped on a train first thing and went to an iconic site to think about how I could reinvent myself: the Golden Gate bridge!

When I'd fully moved in, I was immersed in a culture of self-starters and entrepreneurship. This culture was everywhere and life-giving. As soon as I was aware of it, I knew I wanted to be a part of the idea economy and contribute however I could. I went to events of all types, I read the great books, I learned how to "talk startup" and understand more deeply what was being told to me. Most importantly, I learned how to "feel startup," how to get pulled into a seemingly good idea and think on it until late at night. It was addictive. But time and time again, true inspiration didn't strike.

HERE ARE THE KINDS OF BOOKS I RECOMMEND ALL FOUNDERS READ

MY TOP THREE BOOKS:

- *The Innovator's Dilemma: The Revolutionary Book That Will Change the Way You Do Business* by Clayton M. Christensen. Read this before you do anything else!

- *Zero to One: Notes on Startups, or How to Build the Future* by Peter Thiel and Blake Masters. This book is so good; it's on loan more than it's on my bookshelf!
- *The Lean Startup: How Today's Entrepreneurs Use Continuous Innovation to Create Radically Successful Businesses* by Eric Ries.

BIOGRAPHIES AND AUTOBIOGRAPHIES—
BUT REMEMBER, NO TWO PEOPLE WILL HAVE THE SAME STORY:

- Biographies of Steve Jobs.
- Biographies of Phil Knight.
- Biographies of Jeff Bezos.

BOOKS FOR UNDERSTANDING PEOPLE AND THE STATE OF THE WORLD:

- *The Righteous Mind: Why Good People Are Divided by Politics and Religion* by Jonathan Haidt. One of my all-time favorites.
- Books by psychologists like Jung.
- Books on democratic and decision making theory.
- Books on all the world's religions. The World Bible is an all-time favorite.
- *The Structure of Scientific Revolutions* by Thomas Kuhn.
- Pro tip: Read the books you are most afraid to read, the ones that will challenge the fields and ideas that are most dear to you.

TACTICAL BOOKS
(HOW TO GET THE JOB DONE REALLY WELL, ONCE YOU KNOW WHAT THE JOB IS):

- *How to Win Friends and Influence People* by Dale Carnegie. This book is epic.
- *The Alliance: Managing Talent in the Networked Age* by Reid Hoffman, Ben Casnocha, and Chris Yeh.
- *Harvard Business Review on Motivating People* by Brook Manville and Steve Kerr.
- *Inspired: How to Create Products Customers Love* by Marty Cagan.
- *Built to Last* by Jim Collins and Jerry Porras.
- *Good to Great* by Jim Collins.

I remember the first day I had an idea that seemed novel. I had just organized a small group event on my college campus for people interested in the same kinds of materials science and energy technology as I was—that is, solar cells used to electrolyze or break down waste gases like carbon dioxide into useful chemicals, a form of greenhouse gas recycling. After the event, I felt energized and alive, and I wondered why it wasn't easier to get people of shared professional interests together wherever you want. A friend, John, and I brainstormed, and we realized we could scrape scientific publications to build expert lists related to key words and perhaps help people locate others with shared skills and interests to organize such meet-ups themselves. Why not do this all over the world? Surely people everywhere had the same desire to connect with like-minded colleagues about topics of interest without needing big, complicated, and often boring, conferences set up for them. We spent all day thinking, and planning, and called up the only people we knew that were investor-like to get their thoughts. By the end of the day, we'd decided the idea wasn't yet clear enough to drop out of school immediately—that we even considered dropping out is just another an example of the way we assumed our story would have to look like stereotypical ones. We were, however, more eager than ever to keep searching.

KEY TAKEAWAYS FROM STEP 1

The first step is awareness. Entrepreneurship is for you! For me, personally, it took a giant hammer to the head (moving to the center of Silicon Valley) to realize it, but for you, it might be reading this book. The key thing to gain from awareness is motivation and a base set of skills. There's a lot to learn, but stay committed and you'll be surprised how quickly you pick it up.

Awareness is only the first step, so don't get frustrated that you're not there yet. I spent many nights closing my eyes really tight waiting for a "eureka" moment and not getting one. Even when I thought I had one, I wasn't ready to continue. I thought I needed money to rain from heaven right away, and when it didn't, my passion moved on. More on the two essential ingredients of a startup, people and passion, next!

STEP 2. EXPERIMENTATION: FIND A PROBLEM AND FORM TEAMS

After watching hundreds of entrepreneurs go through their journeys and walking at least parts of the entrepreneurship journey myself a couple times, I did my favorite thing. I drew a map.

Stages of starting a company

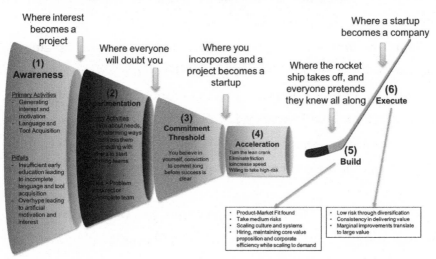

Stages of starting a company. This map depicts a typical funnel leading to a hockey stick, suggesting that many people become aware (Step 1) of entrepreneurship, fewer actually experiment (Step 2), and still fewer make a full commitment (Step 3). At postcommitment (Step 4), however, with the proper principles of acceleration, success is achievable, leading to the possibility of hockey stick–like company building and, eventually, the linear growth typical of later-stage companies.

The second step is one of the most exciting early steps, but also one where you risk stalling out. During the second step, you need to get hungry for a problem, not an idea, and surround yourself with extraordinary people.

What does it means to focus on a problem instead of an idea? For example, with my first startup idea—the scientific meetup—I had prioritized a specific idea (scraping scientific papers for keywords) over the underlying problem I was trying to solve (something about it being hard to meet up—I didn't even define my problem very well). As a result, when others showed me the idea had holes, I gave up instead of insistently searching for new approaches. Founders never give up, but they don't gain this tenacity from the sheer brilliance of an idea, as is often portrayed. Rather, they gain their strength by understanding the problem they want to solve more deeply than anyone else in the world, and knowing if they don't solve it, perhaps no one else will.

Thus, the first key ingredient of Step 2 is finding and developing passion for a specific problem you want to solve.

At this point in my journey, I hadn't found any such problem that would keep me up all night. What I did find next, however, was an amazing group of people who were already at work on solving a different problem that would deeply shape the next several years of my own journey.

In 2012, I had the incredible opportunity to join a group of fellow students spinning out a student club from Stanford to build a better entrepreneurship community. That club changed into a non-profit movement and would come to be known as StartX. StartX is now one of the top startup accelerators in the world. StartX was based on four key pillars: shared infrastructural resources, experiential education, mentorship, and founder community.

By getting involved in this group, I happened upon the other key ingredient of Step 2: finding and surrounding yourself with extraordinary people that can later serve as cofounders, partners, investors, mentors, and teammates.

Over the next two years, while continuing my materials science studies at Stanford, I spent every spare moment helping to build the community at StartX, being available to other founders building their companies, and learning and observing more than I ever thought I could in two short years. An underlying principle of entrepreneurship, true at every step, is accelerated learning. You must figure out how to hack your learning and do it in unconventional ways. If you learn the same skills as everyone else and spend time in the same places, observing the same things as everyone else, don't be surprised when you think the same way and can't magically come up with different ideas!

I myself spent a lot of time in Step 2. I was here throughout my time on the StartX team. In the second year, I found a problem I was very passionate about: helping the earliest-stage founders who were still students, not only founders who had already graduated. We had an overwhelming number of current students who wanted to join the program at StartX, but not enough resources and not enough mentors to help them. With a clear problem in hand, I put together a small team of dedicated volunteers, and we were off to do something big. With excess students eager for an incubator/accelerator but not enough mentors, we had a clear marketplace problem. We looked around and, through our network, found a group of over one hundred mentors who had grown out of the early Google team. They were operating independently and had the opposite problem, an excess number of mentors and not enough people to mentor. We formed an alliance and started an incubator called Mentor Labs that served over seventy early-stage companies with founders at the apex of Step 2 (experimentation) to Step 3 (commitment). More on the great things we learned next.

KEY TAKEAWAYS FROM STEP 2

Get hungry for a problem, not an idea. Don't focus on a specific idea; instead focus on the underlying problem that you want to solve in the world. Know that problem better than anyone else; go to bed and wake up in the morning thinking about it. Read voraciously. Commit to becoming *the* world expert on that specific problem. Pro tip: Don't pick initial problems that are too big or else gaining this expertise is impossible! Stair-step problem statements from small and manageable to world-changing, and commit to earning your way one step at a time.

Surround yourself with extraordinary people. After you've gathered your team, experiment on ideas together that address the problem. When an idea fails, take heart! Like Edison, you've just found one more thing that doesn't work on your way to a great idea for your underlying problem. You'll have a heck of a lot of fun, and with a passion for your problem and a focus on people, you're so close to starting something incredible.

STEP 3. THE COMMITMENT THRESHOLD: IN OR OUT?

Deciding to completely commit to a new startup is a complex decision. It depends on many other commitments in life, such as money, time, relationships, and more. But here's what it shouldn't depend on: a great idea.

Here's what you're probably thinking: "Really?! Are you telling me I still don't need to have that great idea?"

Yes! That's exactly what I'm telling you. The truth is, you won't know your idea is truly great until Step 5, when you're rapidly scaling, and you probably still won't believe it until Step 6, when you can connect the dots looking backwards. When you're experimenting with projects and standing at the precipice of the Commitment Threshold, you simply can't know if your idea will work. What you can know is that you've become a world expert in a specific problem, that you feel compelled to solve it, and that you've assembled the best team possible to walk the dark road ahead, bringing light to new possibilities. Remember: what you need is people and passion. Founders often say one of the biggest challenges is "managing your own psychology." It's kind of crazy to be all in on an idea that isn't actually very clear, but perhaps it's comforting knowing that's exactly what you must do.

I remember the day I went all in for my current startup, Arch. I came home triumphantly and announced to my fiancée that we were in and I'd just invested half of my life savings to redefine the next wave of computing. She wasn't immediately happy. In fact, she was quite distraught! I definitely should have consulted her more before making the jump—please do better than I did—but my decision shows how committed I was to the problem we had to solve and the strength of the founding team. We've never looked back.

Me and my wife, Saara, both scientists and entrepreneurs, supporting each other every day in our commitment to the mission of our respective ventures.

KEY TAKEAWAYS FROM STEP 3

Commitment comes before an idea is proven. It takes real bravery to cross the Commitment Threshold. There are many reasons not to commit, but waiting for a great idea should never be the reason.

Commit because of passion and people. When your passion for the problem calls to you every day and you have partners who you love and respect, who share that deep passion, you're ready. Just go for it.

STEP 4. ACCELERATION: TURN THE LEAN STARTUP CRANK

Welcome to your startup. Now the fun really begins. A startup is really a lean, iterating vehicle that is destined to become a company. Your mission is to understand all the inherent risks of your business (team risks, product risks, and market risks) and successively de-risk them with as little capital per risk as possible. The point of having capital is simply to have more time and more attempts to de-risk your business. Every time you do eliminate a major risk, the risk-adjusted value of the business goes up dramatically. In the venture world, eliminating successive risks often pairs directly with rounds of fund-raising. Seed rounds are all about having a great team and initial concept (de-risk the team with a general market focus and initial product concept). A rounds are typically about de-risking the product (it works, people love it, it's starting to sell), B rounds are about the market (it sells really well and it gets better with each unit sold), and successive rounds afterwards are about pouring fuel into a well-oiled machine that gets successively more efficient at turning capital into more capital. Venture-backed startups aside, the principle of de-risking is true for any business and a powerful way to think about what resources are needed to create a sustainable business that delivers consistent value to the world.

I name Step 4 "Acceleration" in part because of the rise of startup accelerators dedicated to helping startups do exactly that kind of de-risking. If you haven't read the book *The Lean Startup* by Eric Ries, definitely pick up a copy. The book focuses on software, but the principles it espouses are applicable everywhere. If you're not building software, it's all the more important for you to figure out how to be lean—plus you have an incredible opportunity to innovate, as we've learned by building lean electronics at Arch.

At Arch, we participated in multiple accelerators: Village Capital, Berkeley Skydeck, and of course StartX. The accelerators jump-started our own community and accelerated our learning. Just like raising capital, these programs aren't about building your company for you, rather they are resources to leverage as you accelerate your own startup to success. During our time at StartX, we connected with scores of founders who successfully launched their first pilots, found their first true enterprise customers, and raised capital from top investors. Information is gold, and having a trusted community is your ticket to getting information that you otherwise wouldn't have access to.

We had so many questions: What are the dos and don'ts of a first pilot? How do you talk to the likes of Microsoft? What kind of budget do technical product managers (or other customer groups) have for products like ours? How is their internal decision-making process structured? When should you talk to the enterprise research and development arm of a large enterprise instead of a product group or vice versa when trying to make a sale? Which investors are going to treat us like equal partners?

By the time we finished the accelerator programs and had dedicated ourselves to de-risking our initial concept, we had multiple pilots underway with incredible early results. We had connected devices deployed on rural water wells in Tanzania, monitoring water access to as many as 10,000 people; we'd been chosen for *Forbes'* "30 Under 30" list; we'd talked with more than fifty potential startup and enterprise customers and engaged with a few; and, after that, closed a massively oversubscribed seed round with some of the top investors in Silicon Valley.

At Berkeley Skydeck Demo Day sharing our concept and traction with industry partners, fellow entrepreneurs, and investors in Silicon Valley.

Each of those achievements took intense periods of acceleration, when we tried approach after approach, failing as quick as possible so that we could try something else. For example, with our financing our initial business model, based almost entirely on hardware, was met with skepticism. One long weekend, we huddled around the whiteboard and made a memorable list of all the potential business models that could apply to the problem we were solving and the technology we had. We separated them into two buckets first: "not a business" (like seriously, not a viable business) and "is a business." We got aligned to throw out the "not a business" ideas, which is harder than it sounds. When you care so deeply about certain approaches, reality can suck.

Then we divided our "is a business" ideas into "venture-backed businesses" versus "non-venture-backed businesses" and brainstormed the viable financing methods for each. Ultimately, we decided on a route that wouldn't require venture to be successful, a route we could do all on our own, but could certainly be accelerated by venture to make faster massive returns. It turns out, that's exactly the type of model you should have if you want to take the venture route anyway. Starting a business that is only possible if you get large outside funding is a losing proposition.

Don't give up. Fight for viable models. If there's true value in what you are doing, you must be able to define its worth to the people you are helping, and be able to mutually benefit to continue the good work. Once you start succeeding, then everyone will want to back you.

KEY TAKEAWAYS FROM STEP 4

Startups are vehicles to successively de-risk. Write down all the risks that stop you from delivering consistent value to your customers. Rank them by "most likely to kill your business" and start at the top. Figure out the most cash-efficient ways to take out risks and focus on one risk at a time.

Acceleration is about getting as many de-risking attempts per dollar as possible, and community really helps. Being in a community with extraordinary people (a repeated theme!) is an amazing way to accelerate your learning. Be as resourceful as possible. Definitely consider joining startup accelerators, but remember they are just a resource. This is not school anymore. Completing a program means nothing in and of itself. Treat accelerator programs just like investors—they're powerful partners on the journey—a journey that you must lead, de-risking your startup into a company that delivers consistent value to the world.

STEPS 5 AND 6: BUILD AND EXECUTE

The intersection of Step 4: Acceleration and Step 5: Build is best described by the beloved term "product-market fit." Step 5 is the magical time when a set of known and well-defined users really love the product that you've built and want to pay a compelling amount to get it. Better yet, those users represent a large market that can be expanded into, and the product has a foundation ready to scale. It's important to have an idea of what's ahead and complete the picture. In the map above, I use the iconic "hockey stick" to show Steps 5 and 6. It's funny because investors use a hockey stick to say they want exponential growth. In reality, only the heel of the hockey stick is an exponential, while the handle is a straight line—and that's typically what real companies do too.

Once a company achieves product-market fit, ideally you can throw money onto the machine and it just takes off. Key challenges are scaling culture, processes, people systems, and values, as the company grows so rapidly. Bad companies devolve into corporate inefficiency and choke, good companies devolve less, and manage to power through, but great companies build amazingly aligned teams, and nearly cult-like cultures that allow the resources, processes, and value to scale as fast as the company. For advice on how to build strong company culture, read the books *Built to Last* by Jim Collins and Jerry Porras and *Good to Great* by Jim Collins.

Great companies are able to maintain incredible operational efficiency while they spread their value proposition to the world. Eventually, the growth rate has to taper out and become linear. At this point the startup (a vehicle optimized around learning and iteration to find product-market fit) fully gives way to a company (a vehicle to consistently deliver value to shareholders based on known, and eventually multiple, product-market fits). This company provides a product or service to a well-understood market at a known and quantifiable value. It is growing at a quantifiable (and typically linear) value and, thus, can be somewhat more rationally traded, bought, and sold either through merger and acquisition or going public.

Rinse, repeat, and start something even greater the second and third time through!

KEY TAKEAWAYS FROM STEPS 5 AND 6

Product-market fit. Your goal as an early-stage startup is to build a product that customers love. Simultaneously, you must target customers who represent a large and underserved market, so that once your product fits a customer, it fits a market, and your company can begin to build for scale.

Great companies go for successive hockey sticks. Great companies have stair-stepped product roadmaps that typically involve finding multiple product-market fits on their way to dominating successively larger markets. By building such a roadmap you can embrace massive vision while still staying laser focused on the obtainable value proposition of your first hockey stick. Startups don't die from starvation, but typically from indigestion—that is, from taking on too much! Focus, focus, focus on true value to true users, and before you know it, you may be on your own hockey stick journey with resources and opportunities to take it to even higher levels.

The core Arch team in October 2016 trying to spell "Arch" and taking a quick break from shipping connected water-meter and soil-moisture sensors to our early customers.

SO WHERE ARE YOU?

Maybe you're in school right now, learning about a specific field, and trying to develop Step 2 projects on the side that could become startups. Or maybe you're in a Step 6 company right now, with consistent linear growth, and you are beginning to notice an important need that's not being served by anyone else, and considering taking a dive into a new project. Wherever you are, there is no better time than the present to get started on your own startup journey.

QUICK GUIDE TO NEXT STEPS AT EACH STEP

- **Step 1:** Dive deep into a core set of skills and get passionate about a problem. Find events near you (e.g., startup weekends, meet-ups, and so much more), read voraciously (see my book recommendations in this chapter), and get plugged in to your local startup scene. Get in the habit of observing every day: look for signs and redirects that suggest something isn't working, break down huge society-wide problems into underlying causes, and put a face to specific issues so you can get to know the people being affected and learn their stories.

- **Step 2**: Don't get too infatuated with the current version of your idea. Instead, invest your passion in becoming the world expert in the *problem* you've identified. Surround yourself with amazing people who complement your skills and see the world in different and complementary ways. When you can talk about the problem with expertise from a position of experience and knowledge with anyone, anywhere, and at any time, you know you're on to something.

- **Step 3**: Just do it. Seriously, if you know the problem you're after better than anyone else, you know no one else will solve it, and you've got great people around you to put ideas into action, please, just do it. The world needs you to take the dive. You'll never regret it.

- **Step 4**: Move as fast and efficiently as you can, and realize your job is to successively de-risk your startup and find product-market fit. Do anything you can to maximize your de-risking attempts at product-market fit with the capital you have. Consider joining accelerators and building community. You'll need the support!

- **Step 5**: Put down this book and go scale your company! Go back to the communities that helped you and give back. Your advice is invaluable and you may build key relationships to help you scale your business and to start the next one!

- **Step 6**: Get hungry again about the unserved needs around you—maybe it's time to start something new? Start refreshing yourself with new motivation and skills (see Step 1), start observing needs every day around you and sharing your passion with would-be team members (see Step 2), and consider taking the dive again! Do it within your current company by starting an internal initiative or consider a spin-out. Embrace evolution and never let yourself become satisfied with the status quo!

Rinse, repeat, and don't forget to pay it forward. Leave the world a better place than when it was handed to you. Long live the age of entrepreneurship.

➤ HOW HAVE YOU DEALT WITH FAILURES?

" **F** ailure is not an option." Have you heard that saying before? I had. In fact, in the schools I attended near Cape Canaveral, Florida, it was pasted all over classrooms and hallways. The quote, from the movie *Apollo 13* and true to NASA culture, underlies a pervasive sentiment in much of American culture, not to mention many other cultures around the world. We fear failure and glorify perfect records. From straight As to perfect laps, perfect pitches, and perfect photos, we strive for perfection. If failure is not an option, how can you dare to ever try something risky? And if you can't take any risks, how can you ever take on anything even slightly ambitious?

Fear of failure is death to innovation. To be honest, I have been terrified of failure for most of my life. I was a straight-A student, I have an NF personality (if you know Myers-Briggs), and I desperately want others to believe my life is perfect. I'm a smooth talker and can be debonair when I try, but beneath all of this, I've been a scared boy that wanted so desperately to be loved and to be able to contribute something meaningful to the world.

Fear of failure is deeply tied to our sense of self-worth and belonging. I remember when my grandparents visited us in Florida for the first time and saw the career that my dad, their son, had built for himself. My grandpa was born on the Mississippi River. He and my grandma were very poor, but wise and good people. My grandpa had a mind for math, and elevated himself to teach calculus and physics at the local high school, when they weren't tending the farm or painting houses. He gave my dad his knowledge and inspired him to new heights. My dad left the small town, joined the Navy to put himself through college, and worked his way up hour by hour to become a rocket scientist working on the International Space Station—a scientific feat that is, in many ways, the symbol of international collaboration and human exploration. Talk about an American Dream! So here my grandparents were, out of rural Illinois and visiting Florida for the first time, seeing what their son had become. I watched them look out over one of the large bays at the Kennedy Space Center, as my dad pointed out the International Space Station airlock and explained components and systems that he had helped design. Overwhelmed, they began to cry. The moment was beyond beautiful. All of us were deeply touched. I was also touched by that deep fear of failure we all try to stuff down as it whispered vehemently in my ear, "What in the world can you possibly do to make your dad proud?"

Fear of failure is hard. I struggle with it every day.

SILICON VALLEY SECRET SAUCE

Tina Seelig, a mentor, friend, and professor of entrepreneurship at Stanford, is a master of innovation theory. Early on, she shared with me the elusive yet powerfully simple secret sauce of Silicon Valley: embracing failure as data. You see, innovation is all about experimentation, and experiments are NOT meant to work every time. In fact, the most interesting experiments are the ones that fail in unexpected ways and thereby reveal something truly novel and intriguing about the world. Take the famous discovery of penicillin, for example. The discovery of that world-changing antibiotic started with an accidentally contaminated petri dish!

If only it wasn't so hard to see failures in life that way.

Tina encouraged me, like she has many others, to create something called a "failure résumé." If you're anything like me, it takes you hours to update a typical résumé, and even then you're never satisfied. Not so with my failure résumé. After I broke into this seemingly strange activity, I was writing page after page, surpassing my normal résumé three or four times in length with myriad stories of my shortcomings. It was cathartic and deeply revealing. What would your life look like if you viewed failure as data, as "learning what doesn't work," to more quickly and powerfully become a more complete person? Edison once said, "I have not failed, but simply found 10,000 ways that won't work." In coming to Silicon Valley and learning from incredible mentors like Tina, I've slowly been able to embrace a new reality. The truth is, as Chris Bradford put it: "There is no failure except in no longer trying."

THE PIVOT

Startups have a lovely word for this notion of "finding what won't work and continuing to try." It's called a pivot. In basketball, when you get stopped on the court, you plant one foot and pivot to try and find an open opportunity to shoot or pass the ball, to keep making progress toward the basket. Likewise, in life, from relationships and personal goals to innovation and entrepreneurship, many impediments will stop you dead in your tracks. You can give up, or you can pivot. Remember: real entrepreneurs never give up.

There's a common misperception that pivoting is just a nice way of saying "I give up" and trying something else, but that is simply not true! Pivoting in basketball is not giving up at all. Imagine if you traced the path of the ball on its way to the basket. The path would be winding, often heading in the opposite direction of the basket! Be assured, the players have not lost sight of the goal, and what looks like a pivot, or even a retreat may be the very move that sets up the winning shot.

One possible trajectory of the ball in a basketball game. Looking back at the winding path without seeing the defenders or situations, it seems like many failures before a surprising basket. "Pivoting" in startups is all about embracing small failures as data on your path to the goal.

I've pivoted many times in my own life, both within the companies that I've led and in my personal life as well. Throughout it all, however, I've had a pretty strong sense of the things I care most about. First among them is understanding and overcoming climate change through helping humankind better realize sustainability. When I first came to Stanford, I audaciously told my professor that I would "create the next GE" to overcome climate change. I think he tried not to laugh. Initially, I was convinced the best way to impact sustainability was to start an energy storage company. I invested years of my life into developing technology in this direction. Ultimately, however, there was no direct company in sight for my research. My PhD work had many scientific breakthroughs and I made novel contributions to the field. For entrepreneurship, however, my research did not lead to an immediate commercial opportunity. Frustrated after so much effort, I looked elsewhere.

Around the same time, I had the fortune of getting to know and becoming close friends with a group of energetic and passionate individuals who were on a mission to build a better community for early entrepreneurs. They were in the process of spinning out a student club from Stanford to become something much greater. They called it an "accelerator" to distinguish it from the incubators that were common at colleges and universities around the world. Intrigued by the mission, and even more so by the caliber of people involved, I joined as part of the early team and had the distinct honor of helping build what became StartX. At StartX, I channeled my passion for sustainability innovation in a new direction.

I asked the question, "Why is it so hard to start a hardware startup, such as the energy storage company I originally wanted to start?" I went down a road of questioning the implicit incentives, funding structures, and markets that make such innovation possible. We tried to found a "StartX Energy" to solve these issues and empower innovation in this incredibly important sector. But many of our efforts fell short. We failed, pivoted, failed again, and pivoted again, insistent that we could add real value and make a difference. Eventually, we founded a "hardware program" at StartX and channeled our efforts into helping a much wider scope of companies. Among the types of companies I would help most would be those in a new and upcoming wave called "IoT," or the "Internet of Things," companies making Internet-connected sensors and automation. What I learned would play a key role in my ability to start Arch down the road, but at the time, I had no idea just how important that would be.

After two years of helping build StartX, which created better mentorship for early companies and particularly programs for hardware founders, I again decided to pivot my direction. I wondered, maybe it was hard to start hardware companies in the sustainability sectors because people in general didn't know how important sustainability was. If people at large couldn't appreciate the importance of climate change and sustainable resource management, how, in a democracy, could we expect the government to properly incentivize the right kinds of companies and help better fund and incubate these ideas? Out of this vein I took a radical step, joined forces with a colleague named Keld, and started a government technology ("govtech") project called Deliberate. Our new mission was to facilitate social discourse on important issues, such as climate change, to engender a more educated and united people to support causes of great impact for the future. Like before, I tried many ideas in this new direction and failed, pivoted, failed again, and pivoted again. Despite recruiting several new potential team members and putting together an incredible group of mentors and supporters who believed in our goal, I remained unsuccessful in getting funding and we ultimately did little more than talk about our grand plans.

SPARKS OF INNOVATIONS: NEVER WHAT YOU QUITE EXPECT

About a month later, on January 7, 2015, shots rang out in France. That terrible event came to be known as the *Charlie Hebdo* shooting. As then-boyfriend (and now very lucky husband) of an amazing woman named Saara, who comes from a Muslim family, I was especially affected. I felt emptied by the senseless violence. I turned to Twitter to search for answers about why this was happening. What I found on Twitter that day was utterly disgusting, so disgusting that I counted my tweets, page after page after page, hoping this was a coincidence. After counting, I realized that well over 90% of all the tweets in my feed from both sides were full of hatred and misunderstanding, not the loving, peace-seeking voices I knew existed. The whole day, I was depressed at the state of our world and our generation's inability to do better. I wanted so badly to be able to connect with other good people around the world, feeling the same pain, who rejected the hate I'd read on Twitter.

Suddenly, I asked, why not solve that?

Before that moment, Keld and I spent months thinking and theorizing about how to get people to deliberate on issues of importance. This pivotal moment sent us straight into action, and ultimately, action is what really matters. We named our new project "World Dialogues" and set out to put people from different countries together in online video chats to discuss whatever was most pressing in the world. This project was a real departure from where I had focused in the past, but without a doubt, I was passionate about it, and the events in the world had catapulted us to do something real. We pitched our new idea across the Stanford campus and Silicon Valley and gained encouragement and support. Our mentors ranged from renowned thinkers on democracy, such as Larry Diamond and James Fishkin, to technologists, like Terry Winograd, one of the coauthors of Google's PageRank and PhD advisor to Google founders Larry Page and Sergey Brin. We built a simple minimum viable product and reached out to debate clubs around the world. In a few weeks, we signed up young people in over forty countries and held online video-conference discussions on issues ranging from education and human health to climate change, terrorism, and government surveillance. The work was hard, very manual, and we did lots of things that wouldn't scale in the way we reached people—for example, we spammed Meetup.com until we were repeatedly banned! Ultimately, we reached an extremely diverse audience and held many powerful video discussions with people I never would have met, sharing perspectives in incredible ways. Three months later, we'd been accepted to two renowned startup accelerator programs and received up to $100,000 in promised financing.

As we prepared to take investors' money, we entered the important deliberation: deciding whether we could rightly accept the funds and build toward an immediate financial return from such a platform. The investors, understandably, wanted to force me to say how we could monetize the attention and energy we'd tapped into across the world. We came up with several ideas for "deliberating" about products and doing leveraged market research via the new medium, but deep down, I knew this wasn't what we'd set out to do. Fundamentally, I had set out to try and make our world more sustainable. First, I thought I wanted to start an energy storage company, then I wanted to encourage others' innovation in key resources, food, water, and energy. That had morphed into helping hardware companies, which had morphed into helping educate people on why such companies were important. Finally, that had morphed into connecting people to talk about all kinds of important global issues, and now here we were, deciding if we should build a company to monetize the possibility of a video social network.

How exactly did I get here again?

After stepping back, I made the painful and difficult decision that this project, too, was something that "hadn't worked." Although, given our initial success, I was much less sure whether stepping back was the right decision. My goal had never been to start a company just for the sake of starting a company, however. Ultimately, I knew this was not where I was immediately called.

PIVOT BACK TO THE BASKET

The very next day—seriously, no more than twenty-four hours after making the decision to close and informing the would-be investors that we would not accept their money—a colleague asked me to lead his new startup with a fascinating international voice over Internet protocol angle. Sometimes, when it rains it pours. It's something I'll never completely understand, but sometimes you go months or years without a bite, and other times opportunity pours down on you like rain. The key is to be ready for it, and in this case, I took a step back. I talked with all of my mentors and the greater community and thought deeply about how I could best leverage the skills I had gained, leverage the community of support around me, and dig deep into my underling passion for a more sustainable world, to do something great. Three months later, after sifting through well over thirty distinct opportunities to embark on next, I was brought full circle back to my good friend and old roommate, Tim. Tim and I had done our PhDs at Stanford together and were roommates for four years, sharing our struggles and victories daily, and often thinking about how to change the world for the better. On the side, while I had been helping build the startup accelerator StartX and pivoting my way through the twisted path I've described here, he had been helping lead a nonprofit called WellDone designing Internet-connected remote sensors. WellDone's mission was to provide better clean water infrastructure for the developing world, but they'd been stymied realizing that as much as 40% of the infrastructure built by outside groups ended up broken, helping no one. If there was a cheap and affordable way to monitor such infrastructure, in the short term the infrastructure could be repaired, and in the long term incentives could be changed favoring sustainable development across the sector.

Tim recognized, however, that providing such cheap and affordable monitoring was simply not possible yet. There was a lack of robust, accessible, and affordable technology for the job. Consequently, he'd been deep at work trying to solve that issue by developing a framework for modular electronics that had the promise of dramatically reducing the cost and time to market of such sensors. Unfortunately, he had no way to fund the massive scale of the research and development operation needed to fully accomplish that goal.

One day, as we discussed what was needed to really develop such a technology, my experience helping so many companies in this new wave of IoT floated to the surface. At the time, those companies were mainly applying their sensing and automation technology to other fields, such as consumer technologies for fitness, sleep, and health—all very important areas, but not where I most wanted to focus. Talking to Tim, the connections and the opportunities began to crystallize. I saw the promise of what Tim was working on and how it could fundamentally empower and change the landscape for these companies. Furthermore, the way Tim had started building the electronics was ideally suited for the resource sector: food, water, and energy.

After so many seemingly unrelated pivots, the last four years suddenly aligned. The research that I'd done in energy was key, the experience at StartX in helping hardware entrepreneurs was essential, the insights I'd gained in a sector I thought was unrelated—IoT—were now absolutely crucial, and the hustling and fundraising chops I'd picked up with the prior failed projects had directly prepped me for the journey ahead. Thus, my next venture—with more preparedness, passion, and conviction than ever—was born.

LOVE IS KEY TO OVERCOMING FAILURE

Several weeks later, we cemented our plans to partner and go all-in on Arch. When I got home, my wife was understandably shocked when I informed her that I'd just invested half of my life savings. I definitely should have consulted her first. Ultimately, she understood that I'd been saving all the money I could since age fifteen to be able to take big risks just like this, and she supported me wholeheartedly. Scarily enough, Arch burned through all of this money before getting outside investment. We were not deterred. The support of my wife through such daring and harrowing times kept me going. I started this chapter by talking about how strongly our fear of failure is tied to our sense of self-worth and belonging. Truly, I tell you, there is nothing in the world as powerful as a loving and supporting partner to let you look potential failure right in the eye and stare it to the ground. And that goes for both my wife Saara and my business partner Tim. Both are marriages and essential to get right.

Fast forward a year, and Arch is a venture-backed company growing rapidly with real devices in the field connected to the cloud, large enterprise customers helping us develop our next wave of products, and an incredible early team dedicating every day to helping design the next computing wave. After deploying devices in Tanzania to monitor clean water in rural villages, continuing on Tim's earlier efforts, we were named to *Forbes* "30 Under 30" in energy, further accelerating our efforts to make IoT accessible to everyone. It's only a start, the very tip of the iceberg, but certainly an incredible journey so far.

I cannot yet tell you how this leg of my journey will go. Will it be again a precursor to something even bigger? Every great idea generates more questions than it answers. And every great venture generates more opportunities. Failure is data to be learned from, and I have learned an incredible amount since I changed my perfectionist ways and started daring greatly to do big things beyond my apparent abilities.

With Arch, the microfailures and micropivots continue. We have had to reset which customers we were working with and redefine our market approach; we have had to reset fundamental technical choices in our product to respond to the changing landscape; we have had to painfully reset certain mentors and advisors and at times reset the team when the dynamic turned sour and restart our culture when we realized we weren't seeding the team for success.

We're not giving up. Every day we grow stronger and more committed to what we're doing at Arch. You see, the real promise of monitoring and automation is to completely revolutionize the way we manage our resources. Automation makes us way more efficient, while monitoring does something altogether different. Monitoring gives us insight into how processes are actually working in locations both near and far. It creates transparency around the core industrial processes that drive our economy. And that transparency can tip the needle from an economy that profits from rapidly replaced products and staggering waste to a service economy based on sustainable infrastructure that keeps providing reliable and efficient work for years to come. The potential impact, economically and on the health of our planet, is incredible. Every day we wake up more committed than we were the day before because we realize that if we don't build this venture, we're not sure who will.

Ask yourself the same question: who will build it if you don't? If you really might be the only one, then you know what you have to do. Find every facet of what you're doing that doesn't work, find 10,000 ways it won't work, and never give up. Fail, which will give you data, then pivot, fail for more data, and pivot again. You must push onward because each and every one of us has the power to do something great, if we put aside fear and step into our legacy. And be assured, if you're reading this, this is your legacy. Put fear aside. Come and join us, join the revolution in entrepreneurship. We're waiting for you.

CHAPTER TWO

MARY JO MADDA

Senior Editor, EdSurge

>>>> ABOUT MARY JO

Mary Jo is senior editor at EdSurge, a media and community organization that helps schools find, select, and use technology to support all learners. Previously, she taught middle school math and science with Teach for America (Houston Corps '09), KIPP Houston, and the Archdiocese of Los Angeles, where she also served as an administrator, curriculum coordinator, and decathlon coach. Following her years teaching, she worked on the ScratchED team at the MIT Media Lab, and served as an Education Entrepreneurship Fellow at the Harvard University Innovation Lab while piloting an educational media startup. Mary Jo has a master of education degree from the Harvard Graduate School of Education and a BA from Northwestern University. Most recently, she was featured on the 2016 *Forbes* "30 Under 30" list for Education.

A t first glance, the word "competition" elicits groans—it's a reminder of our insecurities, the fear we feel when we realize that no matter how brilliant we think our idea is, we aren't the only ones who have identified a particular problem and are working to solve it.

But there's a comforting realization that any entrepreneur can turn to in those moments: competition is a natural and necessary part of the startup process. Your competitors are some of the most important people you will meet in the business of entrepreneurship. Why? They are the ones who will push you farther than your mentors and colleagues will—from the early days of your startup into profitability and beyond.

In the summer 2013, I was brought in to grow the audience at an educational technology (edtech) media startup called EdSurge; now I've been there for three and a half years and have helped grow web traffic by more than 300%. While that work landed me on the *Forbes* "30 Under 30" list, I really learned about entrepreneurship when I tried to launch a startup—and failed.

Before my days at EdSurge, I cofounded an edtech company called EDUtainment, a company that eventually shut down, and from that experience, I learned five things about identifying and handling competitors.

1. CONDUCT MARKET RESEARCH AND FIND YOUR TARGET AUDIENCE(S) EARLY ON IN THE PROCESS OF FOUNDING YOUR STARTUP.

Back in 2012, when my cofounders and I first discussed the original concept behind EDUtainment, we knew we wanted to address low performance on STEM (science, technology, engineering, math) exams among US students. I had seen such low performance as a teacher in my own sixth-grade science classroom. I imagined that creating high-quality content for the K–12 audience—science and math videos that rivaled *Schoolhouse Rock!* and Bill Nye the Science Guy, as well as curriculum to go along with those videos—was an answer to reengaging kids in STEM material. Whether it was *the* answer eluded my team and I.

Any good entrepreneur will tell you to know your audience, and that is the absolute truth. Your product is worth nothing if you don't have some clear indicators that there's a need for your proposed solution in the industry. Too often, I talk to entrepreneurs who want to create a product because they believe it's what the people need or want. But how do you know what the people need or want? Do you? Really? Better than those people themselves?

In the case of EDUtainment, and in the case of any startup, doing market research—acquiring data, quantitative or qualitative, to help you understand what's in demand—is a nonnegotiable. Even if one or more of your cofounders was a member of your market research's target demographic, one or two data points is a meager basis for the "why" of your product or initiative.

Market research doesn't have to be unrealistically expensive. Create a survey. Hold roundtable discussions and buy some pizza to get people to come. Reach into your networks for contacts you can interview. One of the best market research sessions we ever conducted involved just that—pizza, a bunch of teachers, and some regular face-to-face discussion about what makes good educational content.

2. RESEARCH THE COMPETITION FROM THE GET-GO.

Every startup industry has competition—consumer technology, e-commerce, even my own space of education technology.

Over the past seven years, the edtech world has exploded. Since 2010, investors have contributed nearly $2 billion to startups addressing the US K–12 market.[1] The number of startups has increased dramatically in tandem with this financial investment, with more than fourteen edtech-specific accelerator programs popping up since 2011. For the budding entrepreneur, getting into the edtech space can be intimidating. My first piece of advice for any startup is that before you begin, you must know your industry, or you must at least have an idea of what's being funded and what's being addressed.

As part of the EDUtainment ideation journey, we did our due diligence to find out what other content providers were doing in the STEM category. We looked into the old-school publishers of the world like Pearson, the newer players like Khan Academy, and relative unknowns who were dreamers like us.

Along the way, we found resources that made our market research a lot easier. Consulting startup hubs like AngelList or industry-specific resources like VentureBeat proved helpful. Investigating classes of startups from incubators like ImagineK12 and LearnLaunch gave insights into who was gaining some traction. And, as with all things, some good-old networking helped along the way—specifically gaining mentors at the Harvard Innovation Lab who provided us with insights into who would give our product a run for its money.

And don't just research those startups that still exist. Look for comparable startups to yours that have shut down or experienced problems. By studying companies that failed, you can learn what contributed to that failure and make a conscious effort to avoid those missteps. That is one piece of advice I received after EDUtainment's shutdown. In fact, for any of you looking to create startups around K–12 content, you might want to shoot me a note for some friendly advice.

---

1   EdSurge State of Funding Report, 2016, https://www.edsurge.com/research/special-reports/state-of-edtech-2016/funding.

3. FIND YOUR "SUPER USERS" EARLY ON, AND BUILD THEM UP AS YOUR CHAMPIONS.

Not everyone will love your product, and because of this, they might gravitate to your competitors. That's okay. Rather than trying to get every last user you can, find those early adopters who clearly connect with the problem you're trying to solve, and build them up as your champions.

Especially early on, these "champions" or "ambassadors" are crucial in brand building and getting your target audience. The beauty of finding these champions is that when you have a symbiotic relationship, where you help build up each other's practices or reputation, you accomplish what your competitors cannot—finding the people who are uniquely connected to your product above all others.

At EDUtainment, we wanted to wait on finding our champions— we wanted to create our platform and get some popularity before we elected to find those super users. Looking back, we should've moved more quickly. I've seen this "ambassador" concept work with a number of edtech companies, from the "Google Certified Teacher" program, to startups like the teacher-parent messaging app Remind, whose ambassador program is a common listing on educators' Twitter profiles and LinkedIn accolades. Likewise, I've seen startups hire these champions part time as social media coordinators, content creators, or brand strategists who share their thoughts with users.

Building up these champions doesn't have to be as organized as creating an "ambassador program" or hiring a new social media employee, but whatever you choose to do, it's wise to think about it sooner rather than later.

4. CONNECT WITH YOUR COMPETITORS IN-PERSON. AFTER ALL, YOU MAY FIND OUT THAT YOUR TRAJECTORIES ARE MORE DIVERGENT THAN CONVERGENT.

One of the biggest lessons I've learned from the past few years is the importance of humanizing your competitors by meeting them in person. In the education space, rarely do people go out of their way to create a company or startup just to bring another's down. Everyone usually wants to succeed, and the wisdom of the collective is much greater than that of any individual. As such, meeting competitors in person to talk shop and learn more about what they do, or hope to do, is a key component of dealing with competition—and improving your own organization.

The EDUtainment team accomplished this in two ways. First, to get to know other smaller startups like ourselves, we went to local live events and conferences where we knew we would find other content producers, including edtech nights at the Harvard Innovation Lab and the LearnLaunch conference.

And then, to get to know some of the bigger fish, we used our connections to hop on the phone with them, learn from them, and see if there were any opportunities for collaboration. Here's an example: an old friend of mine from college had worked with an open education resource website called CK-12. Upon hearing about EDUtainment, she connected us with the CK-12's CEO Neeru Khosla. During phone conversations with Khosla, we discussed the possibility of licensing some of our video content to CK-12 at some point down the road. Although nothing came to fruition, getting the opportunity to learn a little bit more about CK-12's needs made us realize a key truth—no company has it all figured out.

In several of these conversations with competitors, I came to realize that each of these organizations had slightly different goals from those of EDUtainment. While not every conversation or relationship between competitors goes well, to avoid speaking to competitors is simply a poor choice. You're both in this industry, so you're going to cross paths. At least offer a sense of cordiality or you risk losing out on some potentially useful information or camaraderie.

5. DON'T DWELL ON THE NITTY-GRITTY DETAILS OF HOW YOUR COMPETITORS ARE BETTER OR WORSE THAN YOU.

As I mentioned above, competition is a part of this game of entrepreneurship. And yes, it is a game, if you consider that some startups will "win" in the form of survival and some will "lose" in eventual shutdowns. From day one, EDUtainment had competitors, and we had them up until the day we shut down. All startups have competitors from the beginning, and they will continue to gain new competitors as the years progress. That is the game entrepreneurs enter into.

Dwelling on your competitors is a quick way to lose sight of why you're doing your work or what your research and know-how has led you to create, especially if it leads you to completely abandon your idea and instead imitate what your competitors are doing. At the same time, it's important to keep your wits about you. Some would say, "Sleep with one eye open." I say, have a tacit awareness of who and what is your competition.

Mike Kappel, a serial entrepreneur and the founder and CEO of Patriot Software Company, wrote, "Don't underestimate your competitors, especially the little guys."[2] In your case, you probably are the little guy, but there will be more little guys who will come after you. Competitors are a necessary evil in the world of entrepreneurship and acceptance of that fact is the first step in working in a crowded market.

---

2   Mike Kappel, "4 Ways to Deal with Competitors," Entrepreneur, April 25, 2014, https://www.entrepreneur.com/article/233379.

⏩ HOW DO YOU CAPITALIZE ON RESOURCES, EXPERIENCES, AND STRENGTHS—AND MANAGE WEAKNESSES?

I'm not your typical cofounder. For starters, I'm not actually a cofounder at the moment. For the last three and a half years, I've served as an editor at an edtech media startup called EdSurge, where we report on trends in the education technology market. During that time, I've seen a number of fun facts about the entrepreneurship world proven over and over again, including this one: every single entrepreneur—no matter how little funding they have, or how privileged they are in their network connections—has his or her strengths and weaknesses. Strengths can lead a startup to revenue, audience growth, and sustainability. Weaknesses, if not understood and addressed, can lead to failure.

But my understanding of that particular fact isn't something that I ascertained merely from my reporting. I experienced it myself—specifically, the failure part of the equation. And looking back, I've realized that several key resources would've helped push my team and me into success.

Here's what I've learned.

MO' MONEY, LESS PROBLEMS

If I could go back in time, I would have done more fundraising in the very beginning. Back in the year 2010, I was a sixth-grade science teacher obsessed with creating elaborate lesson plans and projects for my students. My idol, Bill Nye the Science Guy, danced around in the back of my head as I slaved away Sunday afternoons creating these lesson plans. The work was exhausting, but the product was worth the effort. The more I created, the more I realized that I wanted to generate even more colorful, learning-standards-aligned content for other STEM teachers across the country.

Throughout 2011, I began to ideate on the concept of an online platform containing media and curriculum that any educator could use in their STEM classroom—perhaps taking down the big bad textbook publishers of the world. I created a science character, Dr. MADD, who was the "host" of the medium. I drew up scripts and lesson plans. And I created a Kickstarter campaign in the spring of 2012 with a shrimpy $3,000 goal.

At the time, I didn't know why I wanted to do this "project," as I called it back then. Nothing could get off the ground with $3,000, especially into a seed-funding round, but I figured that $3,000 was quite enough to start up my platform, create ten to fifteen high-quality videos, and generate some merchandise. I suffered from a bit of foolish naïveté, I think.

When it comes to that big initial push for an idea, when you appeal to your inner circles for the bootstrap "angel investing" to get something started, setting your goals higher than what you might get isn't a negative. Rather, you *should* capitalize on the initial excitement that your connections and their connections have for your idea.

As much as I thought I could keep my costs low in the beginning, it's much harder than you think. And even with the buffer of my graduate school year as the time to experiment with the product, the issue of money (especially when it comes to student loans or a lack of salary) is always a cloud hanging over an entrepreneur's head.

THE IMPORTANCE OF A MENTOR

If I could go back in time, I would have found a mentor with experience. In the summer of 2012, my Kickstarter was underway. I was preparing to go to graduate school to get my master's degree, where I would meet others interested in education, and evidently, in entrepreneurship. In late July, I met two individuals who were interested in working on the project. One of them had begun referring to the project as a "startup." By the end of August, four individuals had joined the founding team, and I—somewhat blindsided by all this—found myself excited to see that others had interest and believed in the idea.

We created some videos, gained some fast accolades from Teach for America and the *Boston Herald* for the little work we had done thus far, and got accepted into the Harvard Innovation Lab. We officially named the startup EDUtainment, a word that I would later learn had negative connotations in the education and gaming community. Before I knew it, I was thrust into the realities of working on a startup, and on a team of five.

Challenges came in the form of trying to give weight to everyone's opinions without straying too far away from my original vision. I kept questioning myself: "But is my vision the right vision for this to succeed?" Handling the leadership it took to lead a team of five—where I was the only woman, no less—was not something I was prepared for.

In those moments, having a mentor, particularly a woman who had worked in education technology entrepreneurship, was a nearly nonnegotiable resource that I couldn't seem to find through my existing networks. Even as connected as the Harvard Innovation Lab was, most of the mentors were in straight technology and could only meet once or twice every six months.

It wasn't just a matter of limited network. At the time, I didn't realize that I so desperately needed guidance and advice from someone outside of EDUtainment. It seemed like only a nice-to-have back then. Some years later, I realized that it was, in fact, a need-to-have.

The utility of a mentor in a situation like mine is indisputable. Even though there are plenty of online resources, books, and YouTube talks about the ins and outs of founding a startup, you cannot beat face-to-face (even virtual) interaction with someone who's been there before. And while so many of the messages I see out there for entrepreneurs emphasize the "you" portion of "fake it till you make it," no one succeeds in the entrepreneurship world without learning from others.

DO THE PEOPLE ACTUALLY WANT THIS?

If I could go back in time, I would have balanced confidence with user testing and market research. EDUtainment stagnated when the team failed to reach consensus on a few key items. Should we stick with only STEM material for the first few years? Should we make all of our content free at first and then figure out a way to charge later? Who should be CEO? How are we already talking about who should be CEO when we don't yet have the product fleshed out?

Many of our issues came to down to questions of product. We felt that we were the best ones to figure out the product. I felt that I had enough background experience in teaching to make judgment calls about what the content should look like. But during our first user-testing sessions, when we sent our initial media content to educators and invited them to offer their thoughts, we quickly found that they didn't all jump with joy over the content.

The first batch of user feedback immediately sent the team into react-and-panic mode. Some members wanted to completely change the content. Some wanted to stick with what we had. There I was, in the center, unsure of what to do. And yet, looking back, our reactions seem almost comical given how little research we had actually done.

User testing is crucial to the development of the product. But sometimes, even the smallest amount of user feedback can result in a complete loss of faith and confidence in the product among founding members. In that moment, a strong leader is more important than ever. While things might be different now, at the time, I was not ready to be that strong leader.

In the summer of 2013, we lost three of the five founders, resulting in a pivot to a completely different product that I wasn't emotionally attached to. Ultimately, I realized that I couldn't continue with the work, and in late 2013, we shut the operation down.

FAILURE ISN'T A NEGATIVE

Back in 2011, I wasn't prepared to create a company or lead a team of five founders. Heck, I didn't even know what an entrepreneur was. I just knew I wanted to make great content for teachers who were tired of spending hours writing lesson plans.

I still haven't given up on that dream; Dr. MADD still lives deep within me. And while I've mostly focused here on a lack of resources, that idea that I haven't lost hope in is a strength. Perhaps the most important one.

I get tired of reading the same jargon and buzzword writings about entrepreneurship on the Internet, but there's one idea I can't help but agree with. Failure isn't a negative in this business. It's a positive, because even if you fail, you learn. And if you learn that you still believe you can make your idea into a reality, well, you're a little delusional. But you're also closer to success than you were before.

CHAPTER THREE

SHRUTI SHAH
Cofounder, Move Loot

》》》 ABOUT SHRUTI

Shruti Shah was a cofounder and COO of Y-Combinator-backed Move Loot, an online full-service marketplace for buying and selling used furniture. She has been honored by *Forbes* as one of their "30 Under 30" in Retail and E-Commerce, and by the Aspen Institute as an Aspen Ideas Festival Scholar in reimagining capitalism. Shruti's work with Move Loot was featured in numerous publications, including *Forbes, TechCrunch, Bloomberg Business Week,* and more. Before founding Move Loot, Shruti was a Teach for America corps member in Baltimore where she taught second, fourth, and fifth grades. Shruti earned her BA in political science with a minor in entrepreneurship from the University of North Carolina at Chapel Hill, and she earned her MS in education with a focus on urban education from the Johns Hopkins University.

There is a lot of guidance out there about starting a company. Classes, books, podcasts, and articles promise a roadmap for building the next Google. Nonprofit programs and government initiatives aim to make starting a business easier with tax incentives, grant funding, and coaching. While these resources can provide practical tools to get a business off the ground, they often leave out a critical piece of information.

Starting a business is *deeply personal*. It's a risk, with a distinct possibility that it won't work out. According to the US Small Business Administration, roughly 7 million small businesses start in the United States each year. Half of those businesses last more than five years, and only one-third last ten years or longer. Taking on that kind of risk requires that an entrepreneur both believe in an idea and develop a clear plan.

Aspiring entrepreneurs should ask:
- What problem am I solving?
- Why is the problem compelling?
- Why are my team and I the right people to solve this problem?
- What level of risk am I willing to take?
- Am I prepared mentally and emotionally if the business does not work?

Asking these questions is important, because starting a company is all-consuming. Work is not left at work and you will think about your company constantly. At times, the lines blur between founder and business, because as a founder, you will believe so strongly in the idea and will want to put everything you have into making it successful.

The information outlined in this chapter describes the process by which my cofounders and I launched Move Loot, starting with the idea generation and technical incorporation, and moving through the funding and launch. However, because entrepreneurship is deeply personal, I encourage you to see this not as a roadmap but as a menu of possibilities. We did not get everything right, and neither will you.

MOVE LOOT'S BEGINNINGS

In the summer of 2013, I left my job as a classroom teacher, moved to San Francisco, and took the plunge into company building with three friends. I had recently moved across the country and realized that the cost and time of moving all of my stuff from one coast to another was more than the items I would be moving. Thus I resorted to trying to sell my furniture before I moved. What I couldn't sell, I left on the curb. Upon arrival in San Francisco, I found myself at IKEA buying nearly identical furniture to what I had just disposed of. The entire process felt wasteful and expensive. I began talking about this experience with Bill, Jenny, and Ryan, my three friends, and later my cofounders, who shared similar frustrations during their moves from the East Coast to the West Coast.

After a few months of discussing the problem, we started to examine the market: How did people sell their furniture? How did people buy furniture? What was painful for both buyers and sellers? Where did the furniture that was left on the curb go?

We found that existing options weren't good enough—they were expensive, time-consuming, and harmful to the environment. When furniture is left on the curb, it most likely ends up in a landfill, making up the second-largest amount of waste found in landfills, behind food waste.

So, we thought, *Could we make selling furniture easy, encouraging reuse instead of disposal?* What if a trusted company came to your home, picked up the furniture, and sold it for you? Conversely, could we make it easy for someone to furnish a new house or replace an aging sofa? What if the furniture options were listed in one convenient online website?

THE TACTICAL

We tested the idea with more friends and family and held a few focus groups. After some debate about our business model, we decided that if we really wanted to make the startup happen, we needed to raise some money for a warehouse and legally incorporate as a business. We launched Move Loot on an Indiegogo campaign, raising $15,000 from friends and family to fund our first warehouse. For our model to work, we needed a warehouse to serve as a storage point for the furniture that we picked up from sellers, which we would later deliver to buyers who purchased it through our online marketplace. Our sellers would get a percentage of the sale and our buyers would be able to purchase quality second-hand furniture without the hassle of emailing individual sellers on third-party classified websites. However, before we could legally operate as a business, we needed to make sure we set up our business entity.

INCORPORATING

The "un-sexy" parts of starting a business are critically important for long-term success. In the beginning, take the time to properly set up a business entity. This often requires talking to a lawyer; in addition there are a number of online programs, such as Stripe Atlas and Clerky, that can help with the basic paperwork. Once the incorporation documents are filed, setting up a business bank account and searching for insurance become critical next steps. The best way to figure out who to work with is by talking with a lot of different banks and insurance brokers to understand their expertise and gauge whether they work with businesses like yours. As you begin to hire people, you will have to set up a system for payroll and accounting.

RAISING INITIAL CAPITAL

After working with a law firm to do the paperwork for incorporation, as I mentioned earlier, we decided to raise money through Indiegogo, a crowdfunding platform where anyone can contribute in exchange for small prizes. We filmed a video for our crowdfunding campaign page, and then we launched. We spammed our friends and relatives with emails about our new venture and posted information about what we were doing on social media. In two months, we raised $15,000. We found a warehouse in San Francisco's Dogpatch neighborhood, 1,200 square feet for $2,000 per month. We now had 1,200 square feet to fill, and we were four weeks away from launching our site.

Move Loot cofounders working in our first small
warehouse space.

BUSINESS MODEL

Would people give us their furniture in exchange for a promised portion of the sale? We tested this idea by finding people on third-party listing platforms who were trying to sell furniture. We told them that we would come to their home, take their sofa, and sell it. The approach worked. Customers were so excited to have us manage the process that they took a chance on a new business.

My cofounders and I rented a U-Haul truck and drove around San Francisco picking up furniture. We lifted sofas down long narrow staircases and carried dining tables through narrow doorways. We learned how difficult and frustrating moving furniture can be and we talked to our customers—people who shared our frustration with the challenges of buying and selling furniture—to learn more about how we could make the process of buying and selling furniture easier. Within two weeks, our warehouse was full of furniture. We spent a few long days tagging everything, preparing professional-looking photographs, and writing copy for the launch of our website.

Move Loot cofounder Shruti Shah standing outside our first rented moving truck. Photo Credit: Bill Bobbitt

On October 1, 2013, we launched our website—and we waited. By the end of the first week, someone wanted to buy a table. He was unsure about using our site, so he asked if we could bring the table to him, and he would pay cash. We agreed. We dropped the table off, placed it in the customer's home, and high-fived and hugged on the sidewalk out-side. Someone wanted to buy what we were selling.

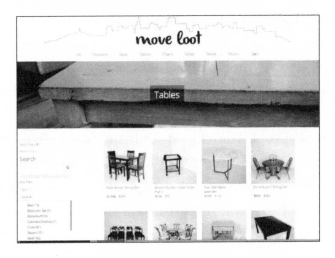

An early version of Move Loot's website.

The next few months presented more challenges. We couldn't simul-taneously move furniture, improve the website, manage support, and schedule pickups and deliveries. So we decided to hire professional movers, which came with a big price tag and propelled us toward a crit-ical decision. We needed to focus on growing the business, but doing so required cash—cash that we didn't have. Should we take out a bank loan? Grow more slowly? Try to raise money from investors?

GETTING INTO Y COMBINATOR AND WHAT TO CONSIDER WHEN THINKING ABOUT FUND-RAISING

On a whim, we applied to Y Combinator (YC), a tech accelerator in Silicon Valley that gives budding businesses startup capital and twelve weeks of coaching. A few weeks later, an email let us know that we would be interviewing with YC's founding team. We ended up sitting in front of YC's founding team in Mountain View, pitching the business we had launched just a few weeks before. We left the ten-minute interview unsure of what was to come, returning to San Francisco, and spending the afternoon walking around North Beach and drinking tea. Later that evening, as Jenny, Bill, Ryan, and I were settling in to watch a movie, my phone rang. YC cofounder Paul Graham was on the other end, offering us a seat in YC's Winter 2014 batch.

Move Loot founders outside YC's Mountain View
headquarters on Demo Day. Photo Credit: Jenny Morrill

Joining an accelerator like YC isn't the only way to build a business, but it made sense for us because we believed that we were tackling a problem in a massive market that could be solved with the help of technology—one that would require a lot of money and support from tech investors if we wanted to see it through. That said, this isn't the only way to build a business. Many successful businesses are built through bootstrapping—growing slowly and sustainably without a lot of upfront capital or, in some cases, founders can take out loan from a bank. Once you have a minimum viable product and have developed some traction with customers, think critically about the kind of business you want to build and how quickly you believe you can scale it. Your thoughts in this area should play a role in the type of funding you seek to support your business. As a founder, it's also critically important to think about what percentage of the business, if any, you're willing to give up in order to grow it. Taking money from investors means giving up a piece of your business and, in many cases, being held accountable to a quick timeline for growth. This financial structure doesn't work for every founder or for every type of business. There isn't one right path, so determining what path is right for you, and the type of business that you are building, will be critically important to the long-term success of the business.

YC helped us focus on what we needed to prove and why. It gave us the time and money to grow our business and prove that we were building a product and offering a service that people wanted to buy. After twelve weeks of visiting YC partners during office hours, attending Tuesday night dinners, and focusing on serious revenue growth (roughly 10% weekly), we pitched Move Loot before an audience of investors. Two weeks later, we closed a $2.8 million dollar seed round. We were able to rent another warehouse and continue to grow our business. It was the beginning of a difficult, terrifying, exhausting, exciting, and exhilarating journey.

KEY TAKEAWAYS

Building a business can be thrilling and fulfilling, but also risky and draining. If you're interested in taking the startup plunge:

1. Develop a clear understanding of the problem and the market (including the size and potential competitors).

2. Develop and begin testing the product.

3. Talk to customers and adapt based on feedback.

4. Determine the optimal path for growth for your business.

➤ HOW DO YOU CONTEMPLATE SCALABILITY AND GROWTH FOR YOUR COMPANY?

In 2013, Y Combinator cofounder Paul Graham wrote an essay titled "Do Things That Don't Scale."[3] This concept becomes ingrained in founders who go through Y Combinator. The essay suggests that many of the most important ingredients in a company's initial success are manual and cannot be duplicated by a machine. For us, doing things that didn't scale meant constantly talking to users, going out of our way to delight customers, and doing all of the moving, photography, scheduling, and customer support until we couldn't do them any longer because we had too many customers. Doing things that didn't scale allowed us, as founders, to better understand how people used our product—ultimately helping us find product market fit.

---

3   Paul Graham, "Do Things That Don't Scale," July 2013, http://paulgraham.com/ds.html.

In the early days at Move Loot, when incorrect items were delivered or the truck was late, we troubleshot in real time. We were the movers—showing up in a rented box truck with a new sofa, or painting, or kitchen table. We took photographs—setting up a makeshift studio in our warehouse space with a white backdrop—doing our best to highlight the merchandise. We scheduled each interaction—spending a few hours each day creating efficient delivery and pickup routes. When a customer had a less than magical experience, we would go out of our way to show our appreciation by sending cupcakes, flowers, or a thank you note.

In the early days of our business, these tasks felt laborious and, at times, overwhelming. None of us were trained in moving furniture, photography, or customer service. However, doing things that didn't scale gave us insight into how our customers used our product. It allowed us to see what they liked and disliked, and it gave us the insight to continuously improve our product and service. Doing things that didn't scale allowed us to scale our business.

EXPANSION

Scaling a business is hard, maybe harder than starting one. The business is off the ground, the initial money raised, but the company has not yet "made it." The founding team has a lot to prove and a long road ahead.

About six months after closing our seed round, we found a bigger warehouse just down the street from our first warehouse and hired a small team of operations associates, customer support staff, engineers, and marketers. After discussions with our investors, and strong growth in San Francisco, we made the decision to expand to our first new market, Raleigh, North Carolina. Our small team of sixteen grew to twenty-six. We would be working in different time zones. We needed to start to develop processes to enable better communication across teams.

We tried a lot of things—frequent check-in meetings, all-team meetings, communication norms, and different ways to set goals. As we expanded again, to Charlotte, North Carolina, and a few months later to Atlanta, Georgia, the team got bigger. With each expansion, it felt like we were breaking the process we had created.

In a year and a half, we took our team from 16 to 205—across seven cities. Before we raised our seed round, we spent long days at the warehouse, but once we really started to grow, it often felt like there were not enough hours in the week. The founders coordinated cross-team communication, doing what we could to make sure everyone was on the same page and feeling supported. We troubleshot when we ran out of space, or dealt with customer service challenges, and figured out how to constantly fix the technical and nontechnical processes that seemed to break with continued growth.

Our team was learning and, like the founders, they were constantly adjusting to their changing roles. Employees at a growth-stage company often change jobs quickly, giving up old projects when they are needed elsewhere. Growth can make a company feel unstable, and it is a human instinct to feel stretched by change.

Founders of growth-stage businesses should consider creating an open space for staff to talk about the changes. At Move Loot, we asked local managers to plan team activities that allowed each office to spend time together. We also had a monthly all-team meeting where everyone could hear a high-level update on organizational direction and ask questions about what was to come. Our executive team solicited company-wide input on projects, encouraging cross-office collaboration. None of these processes or activities was perfect; in fact we had much room for improvement, but they helped our rapidly growing organization feel a little bit more cohesive.

As a founder, scaling our business meant my schedule began to look different. I wasn't just an individual contributor anymore. Instead, I needed to both provide input about strategic direction and support the team in executing the strategy. My days were filled with countless meetings, check-ins, and travel. Learning how to manage a team of this size is a skill, and it takes time to develop, and I certainly made many mistakes. Here are some things to consider while a company experiences serious growth:

As a founder, get clear about the rate at which you think you can and should grow your business. This rate will dictate when you need to take on additional investment. Once you do decide to grow, start to think about what this might mean for you personally. Will you be managing a bigger team? How will your day-to-day change? What will you have to know that you don't already know? What can you do to help decrease knowledge gaps? A coach or mentor who can support you or give you training is important.

Talk openly about the changes a company might experience as the business doubles, triples, and quadruples in size. Roles may change. Some team members may have increased responsibility. Everyone won't know each other, and collaboration across teams, while important, will prove to be more difficult. Get ideas from your team about ways to make these transitions easier and talk to other founders about ideas that worked for their teams.

Develop team traditions (like a weekly happy hour or team lunch) and cross-team communication norms. Traditions and norms will help everyone feel like they are part of the same team, regardless of where they are working. For example, we used Slack, a messaging application, to share articles, photos, and relevant industry information so that people across teams could be in the loop.

Commit to continuous improvement. When things change rapidly, people will inevitably make mistakes. By building a culture of continuous improvement, one in which everyone is willing to acknowledge mistakes and challenges, you'll more successfully navigate the day-to-day and work toward building an even better and stronger business.

CHAPTER FOUR

PATRICK SLADE
Cofounder, PSYONIC

>>>> ABOUT PATRICK

Patrick Slade is the cofounder of PSYONIC, a biotech startup that develops advanced prosthetic hands at a low cost for patients around the globe. He is an honoree of the *Forbes* "30 Under 30" in Health Care, winner of the Cozad New Venture Competition, and the Samsung Innovation Prize. Patrick has improved the quality of life for amputees across the globe with his invention. Currently, he is a graduate student at Stanford, studying robotics and machine learning. His research is supported by the National Science Foundation and Stanford fellowships.

When people start a company, they come from many backgrounds and different levels of experience in business. Some, like myself, are product-oriented people, the ones who develop something in the lab or come up with the idea for a new invention and then attempt to commercialize the product. As a young person with essentially no knowledge of how a business is formed and operated, the most important thing for me was to be receptive and open to learning new things.

CONNECT WITH USERS

The first step in figuring out what your company will accomplish is talking and connecting with other people. Starting a business is not very difficult; anyone with a few hundred dollars and access to the Internet can form a corporate entity. The difficult part is finding a problem that other people care enough about to create a valid market for your product or service, connecting with others who also are interested in the same issues who can form a team with you, and investigating how to actually get your product into the marketplace.

The most important thing you can do, especially early on, is to find other people working in your area of interest and chat with them. In the first startup crash course we attended, we made a list of forty people who worked on prosthetics, would buy our prosthetic hands directly, or would help us build them. Since we were interested in developing revolutionary prosthetic hand technology, our list included clinicians, prosthetists, amputees, and distribution companies that sell hands in large quantities. To find these people, we did an exhaustive web search and created a massive list of everything we found. This research led us to famous prosthetists and upper-limb clinics spread all over the country. We leveraged all our research connections to get introductions to people on our list. Having these referrals was a benefit but, for the vast majority of people, we discovered we had no way to contact them other than a direct email or cold call.

We accelerated the searching and calling, finishing in a single week, which was the first difficult, but essential turning point for our company. Our research nailed down the difficulties that these patients and prosthetists were having with existing devices, giving us a core focus. We discovered a need for something completely different than our initial ideas, which dramatically shifted our business plan and technical work. Initially, we wanted to sell extremely low-cost, muscle-controlled prosthetic hands that we would 3-D-print ourselves and sell off the shelf for around $200. We found from those forty calls that there was definitely a need for a lower-cost hand, but the durability of the existing devices was also lacking, and a 3-D-printed version would be even worse.

With this in mind, we pivoted our product to be a low-cost hand, at 10% of the cost of comparable devices rather than the originally proposed 1%. The prosthetic would be made of tough rubbers and plastics to improve impact resistance and add compliance, like a real human hand. After making these changes, we found people were much more excited and supportive of the product, because they really wanted to have a device with these features. These features also gave us a wider range of potential patients, as we could now compete with the more durable, advanced hands as well as the cheap hook devices. The response was overwhelming, and we had a list of people who wanted to be notified when we would start selling the product.

FOCUS ON THE SIMPLEST PRODUCT AND BUSINESS

You need to have a willingness to take in new information and also the ability to stay focused on the "core issues" for your product to meet the bare minimum of the end user's needs. People often get sidetracked in adding unnecessary features that don't change the function or purpose of the product. These superfluous features can offer small benefits but ultimately require more effort and time, which detracts from your ability to rapidly test, redesign, and reach market as soon as possible. When calling the initial forty people, we had lots of ideas for cool add-on features, with different sensors to include in the hand. It was really tempting to make our hand into some Iron Man–like device with as many gadgets as we could pack in, but we quickly realized that the time it would take to add these wasn't trivial and would benefit only a few patients. When taking advice from others, nail down exactly what the end users desire and what will solve the core problem they face.

It's equally important to have specific goals when figuring out corporate direction. Everything is difficult—from selecting what kind of corporation to form to assembling an advisory board and issuing stock between cofounders, especially when you are inexperienced. The first thing we did when we became interested in entrepreneurship was take startup boot camp courses. These courses taught basics about the "The Lean Launchpad" method that was popularized by Steve Blank. The course had a great fast-paced, get-your-hands-dirty style that applied directly to the company we were starting. After the first hour of the course we drew up business models on sticky notes plastered all over the walls. The benefit of going to weekend boot camps is the ability to consult with mentors for feedback and figure out how the company will attempt to get the product to the end user, generate sustainable revenue, get materials, interact with employees, and ultimately achieve its goals in a short period of time. There are many places you can get the information taught in these courses: you can find them for free on sites like Udacity, you can buy books on these topics, you can leverage classes and camps at schools or in cities near you, or you can connect with more experienced business mentors directly. The important thing to remember is not to be afraid to reach out to people.

Whether it's cold-calling people to talk about our product, or asking professionals for advice in business or certain technology aspects, I'm constantly amazed at how friendly and welcoming people are when questions are posed in a polite and interested way. When we emailed or called anyone, we first introduced ourselves and told them that we were doing research in the interest of developing low-cost prosthetics to allow patients all around the globe to afford them. This passion and mission went a long way in getting advice and support. Talking to the lead prosthetist when he came to give an informal talk in our area started a collaboration that led to several trips and lots of testing with a nonprofit prosthetics group in Ecuador. The group didn't work with many upper-limb patients, but they were excited by our idea and enthusiasm and worked with us to connect with patients and resources to allow us to test our ideas.

CREATIVE PROBLEM SOLVING

At first we treated our product like research—we threw ourselves into the development and iteration process to get an initial model as quickly as we could. When it came to thinking about how we would test and manufacture our prosthetic hand, it was a nightmare. To produce batches of more than one thousand hands, we had to invest in injection molding tooling, which would be on the order of $50,000—essentially all of our funds at the time. Plus, the investment required us to sell a thousand or more hands to simply break even. We couldn't afford to pursue such a massive amount of initial production capability, so we explored more flexible options.

After talking with some design engineers and machinists we decided to rely on more in-house methods of fabricating these devices by rubber molding parts ourselves and achieving lower batch sizes with rapid prototyping. This increased the initial cost to make the hands but required essentially no tooling overhead costs. This process allowed production of any number of hands, from one to a thousand, at the same cost. This method may not be sufficient for all companies and products, but the lesson we learned is this: it is really important to investigate multiple avenues to prepare for varying popularity of your product. If you need to sell one million pieces to make a profit, that's probably a risky initial goal. A simpler target might allow you to get to market quickly and see if your product sells well before investing massive capital to mass-produce.

SUMMARY

The process of going from idea to company isn't easy or clear-cut for any business, but the general process is always the same: connect with people who work in the same area or would use your product, find out what their real need or difficulty is, come up with several potential solutions, iterate on these ideas and continue contacting others to validate them, and ultimately pursue the simplest design that solves the most essential parts of the problem.

As far as starting the company itself, the key is to reach out and use online resources, contact mentors, and participate in courses available through schools or cities. This training will give you the tools to figure out what kind of business model, corporate structure, revenue generation, and so on are best for your company. As the company matures, you'll continue the same cycle of contacting people to validate your idea, learning about business, and iterating on your product until you finally come to a result that seems feasible for the market.

➤ HOW DID YOU DEVELOP YOUR PRODUCT?

A dvanced, muscle-controlled prosthetic hands exist on the market; they typically cost between $30,000 and $40,000 and are only accessible to patients who have cutting-edge clinicians and prosthetists. We are able to match all the features of these existing devices by employing machine learning algorithms, which let our prostheses recognize different patterns of muscle activity from the user's residual limb. We use robust and simplified mechanical design to achieve desired grip forces, speeds, and the size and weight of a normal human hand. The difference is in the components we use and our process of manufacture, which allows us to produce our devices to sell at a price point around $3,000, which is the maximum limit covered by most public health insurance agencies. We will also have the first commercially available prosthesis capable of sensory feedback. Through PSYONIC's innovations, we will disrupt the status quo of the prosthetics industry and decrease prosthesis rejection and abandonment.

NEED FINDING

A common method to figure out what your "product" should be is to find a need. Our prosthetic hand was initially created through research at the University of Illinois at Urbana-Champaign. Through reading research papers, we discovered that there are 11.4 million people with upper-limb amputations in the world and 80% of these people live in developing nations. The access to devices and the quality of devices for amputees in developing nations is severely limited. Imagine living with a disability and knowing a powerful solution exists but not being able to get it because you don't have the money! We targeted this inability to receive devices by building low-cost and advanced muscle-controlled prosthetic hands. We chose materials carefully to avoid expensive custom parts and unnecessary additional cost. After meeting this goal, we iteratively designed, prototyped, and tested the hand versions to ensure that they met all the needs of these patients in their daily activities. Through this work we created an open-source prosthetic hand that can be downloaded from the internet, 3-D-printed, and assembled using only one hand from off-the-shelf components with a total cost of $100. Anyone located anywhere in the world with access to a 3-D-printer or mail can now build an advanced prosthetic hand completely independently, even if they are an amputee.

CONNECTING WITH KEY PLAYERS

Although the 3-D-printed product met the needs we had seen in research, it wasn't being picked up by many users. We thought the best way to see our technology make a difference on a large scale was to commercialize and sell a product in the traditional method of medical devices: through specialist clinicians called prosthetists. As I mentioned earlier in this chapter, the best way to find a need is by talking to people. We called dozens of prosthetists and amputees to hear about the most difficult aspects of using and equipping these prosthetic hands. The most productive conversations were those where we simply asked them about their daily routines and how they used their devices. This question led them to talk about the biggest challenges they faced without us needing to steer the conversation toward a need we thought might exist, and it let us know what improvements would actually have a positive impact on their lives. From this point we could really develop an idea of something people would give money to have right now.

This thorough, ground-level research is really important, so don't be afraid to cold-call people or send emails to anyone in your area of interest. Reaching out to strangers was definitely outside of our comfort zones. At first we tried relying on our existing connections to set up chats with people, but that led only to a handful of conversations. We quickly transitioned to mass-emailing our list of forty people. Less than 20% replied in the following days, so we decided that method was too passive. To take a more active approach, we started making calls during working hours with the intent of having an unplanned chat if they were available or asking for five minutes to schedule a brief meeting. At first these calls didn't go well and were awkward to initiate.

We found success connecting with many people, even some famous specialists, by calling or emailing them a brief note. We used a format similar to this: "I'm a researcher at the University of Illinois at Urbana-Champaign working on developing low-cost, myoelectric prosthetic hands. We work with researchers at the Rehabilitation Institute of Chicago who recommended you, based on your world-renowned custom prosthetics solutions. Would you be willing to have a fifteen-minute phone conversation about the key problems with upper-limb prosthetics that you would like to see fixed?" Mentioning the purposes of your work and what you hope to accomplish really motivates people to talk with you if they believe in the same cause. Positive comments about their work can also help. Be sure to acknowledge that they are very busy, thank them for their time, and make it clear that you know what you are talking about and have specific questions or topics in mind.

Mostly, the practice of talking to many people made us more confident in talking with people we had never met. The key we found was to give them a convincing reason why their answers to our questions would directly help us solve problems for these patients.

Once we showed interest in them and the level of detail in our knowledge about the subject, they were more engaged and positive, which resulted in conversations lasting an hour or longer. Using this method, we reached twenty-five more people on our list. This initial rush of calls was beneficial in sorting out the exact product we wanted to pursue, but even now we set aside time to continually make more calls to ensure we're constantly taking in information and staying on top of the problem our product should solve.

SIMPLIFY THE SOLUTION

Once you find the problem to solve, keep the solution as simple as possible and iterate quickly through several ideas to test a variety of solutions. You almost surely won't develop a winner on the first try, so keep moving through your ideas at a pace where you don't lose too much time if one product doesn't work out. We're currently on the sixth version of our prosthetic hand; we developed all six versions in the past two years. As the main person sitting at a computer for hours upon hours of designing and 3-D-printing these models, I know how easy it is to get attached to a product you've worked hard on. Even when you have a product that works in all the ways you want, it is essential to really take to heart what your entire team wants out of the solution and to be flexible to change. For example, I really didn't want to implement soft rubber fingers or palms in the hand, thinking the rubber would be too difficult to design and repeatedly manufacture, and the testing would be a nightmare. Ultimately, however, the amputees, clinicians, and even our team thought it was best to add these aspects to our design, so I scrapped dozens of hours of work and started implementing these changes.

Timetables for product development obviously vary widely between products. Just be clear in agreeing with all members of the team about realistic goals that will still push the product forward at a pace to meet long-term goals of product development. For us, creating a good timetable meant creating deadlines for each component of the hand so that the final version could be tested as quickly as possible. When doing mechanical work, we estimated how many days of design time were needed to fix a problem, such as fingers interfering with the palm. We added days for prototyping time and set a future meeting roughly halfway through that process, and another once the changes were complete. Since we developed these hands while in school, our timetables were in constant flux and the people on the projects rotated every few months. These outside forces caused us to create a larger team of well-rounded people who could fill in the different roles as needed and hold people accountable for meeting the deadlines they'd set. It's not an easy job to manage these timetables, but it is a necessary skill to be as efficient with money and resources as possible.

We've found that debugging and testing a hand with patients takes significantly longer than we expected, usually twice the original estimate. We now account for this and ensure there is plenty of time to get the product safely tested, analyzed, and improved before making commitments for production or testing of the next version. Having an accurate timetable becomes especially important as you finalize designs and invest money in manufacturing tooling and part orders. Bringing a product to market that is both safe and effective requires more testing and quality assurance work than just iterating through one-off prototypes.

RAISING FUNDS WITHOUT LOSING EQUITY

When we financed our project, we entered startup competitions and applied for grants to raise money without having to give up equity. Startup competitions often have small monetary prizes for finalists and larger prizes for winners. We honed our business plan, technical demos, and live pitches, and went on a circuit of these competitions, both to strengthen our business proposal and to try and gain some funds. You can find competitions with a web search for "general startup competitions" or field-specific events like "biotech" in our case. Major cities host several throughout a year. We competed in VentureWell, OneStart, and the Cozad New Venture Competition. Through the competition process, we received feedback from many business and technical professionals and dramatically improved our business plan in both detail and scope. We won around $40,000 to initially fund our work and used it for an array of costs from renting lab space to hiring employees, paying legal fees, and developing our technology.

Now we are pursuing much larger grants on the order of $250,000, most of which are targeting small businesses that develop technology through research, such as the National Science Foundation and National Institute of Health Small Business Innovation Research grants. We chose to use grants to raise funds because they are nondilutive, meaning the groups giving you money don't take equity from your company. If we had worked with venture capitalists or angel investors, they would have gained this equity (that is, a portion of our business) and would have wanted to shift our main focus to creating value in our company, and ultimately sell it to turn a profit on their investment. We are much more interested in seeing a slower-growing but larger-scale impact worldwide than in putting out a splashy product only for the US and European markets and then quickly selling to another company. Our technology has a chance to improve millions of lives and to make some profit—not the maximum amount that could be made by targeting the niche market of upper-income amputees in developed nations. We will give more people access to a device that enables them to live an independent life and do what they want.

SUMMARY

For a startup, putting out your first product is a make-it-or-break-it moment. To increase your likelihood of immediate and widespread adoption, find a compelling need that a lot of people really care about. This need can't be a superficial problem in your own life. It must be something you've found in a large market so that a lot of people care enough to buy your product. Validate this problem by contacting many, many people affected by or working to solve the issue you identified.

When first developing your ideas on how to solve the problem, rapidly move through many options. Stay open to what your contacts really want in a product. Be careful, because your instincts or personal attachment to a specific solution can cause difficulty and even derail the focus of a prototype. The same goes for building a strategy to raise money and manufacture your product: be open to many options and reach out to those who know more than you do.

In the end, it's all about helping improve someone's quality of life.

CHAPTER FIVE

BRIAN POWERS
Cofounder, TemperPack

>>>> ABOUT BRIAN

Brian Powers grew up in College Park, Maryland, where he enjoyed selling tickets to fellow kindergartners to go to the moon, as well as healthier hobbies like soccer and basketball. His speech therapist, hoping to coach Brian to finally say the "r" sound correctly, taught him the word "entrepreneur." Brian never doubted what he'd be thereafter, even if he couldn't yet pronounce the word. Buoyed by incredibly supportive parents and an overachieving sister, Brian started a junk removal service at St. John's College High School called Junk Runners and a rock band called Paper Planes with friend and current TemperPack cofounder James McGoff. Brian went on to study finance at the Wharton School of Business at the University of Pennsylvania, completed a year of investment banking at Moelis & Company, and then returned to the real world to take college project TemperPack full time with James and fellow cofounder Charles Vincent. Based in Richmond, Virginia, TemperPack designs and manufactures sustainable insulation that replaces plastic foam for the e-commerce food and biopharma industries. Brian now lives in Richmond, which after much practice he now can pronounce correctly.

Brian Powers has been named to *Forbes*' 30 under 30 in food and drink.

Throughout the dozens of presentations and calls we held, we found that professional and first-time investors share a fascination with startups, and a thirty-second pitch, success or not, rarely bores the listener. This discovery carried an important lesson: tell everyone about your startup. They won't be bored or put off that you're asking for money, and they'll likely refer you to other people who will be interested. One of those people might even give you the money you beg for.

If people thought our packaging company was interesting, chances are they'll find whatever you're thinking of doing fascinating by comparison. After all, our company is in packaging—not the sexiest of industries. TemperPack, which I cofounded with materials engineers James McGoff and Charles Vincent, makes sustainable thermal insulation that keeps food and biopharma products cold during transport. In other words, we replaced Styrofoam coolers with recycled plant fiber in cardboard boxes. In our presentations, after we used the "we think outside the box" joke, we were out of material to entertain. Nonetheless, investors found it worth their time to hear us out, and we got over the inevitable feeling of ridiculousness in asking for people's money.

Perhaps to compensate for a feeling of guilt for not investing themselves, they offered to help us in another way: referrals. Nearly every investor we talked to, even those who didn't invest, referred us to other investors. Put simply, the more we talked to people, the more people we talked to. And like the little leaguers we were, after each pitch, we got better—we just had to stay on the mound.

The first thing to know about raising money is that you shouldn't. Raising money is equivalent to chopping off your arm as a means to survive: by sacrificing part of yourself, you save the remaining majority. You should do everything possible to keep your arm by minimizing expenses—live at home with your parents, get customers to pay up front, partner with more established companies that will subsidize your research and development—anything to keep from spending money needlessly. The longer you wait, the more traction you will have. You'll be able to chop off less of your arm, and it'll be more likely that you'll actually survive, rather than lose all your limbs and die.

Eventually you'll reach that point where your business is really held back by lack of funds, and you must raise money to reach the next step. There's no halfway in raising money; you must seek it as a vampire seeks blood. If we could have sold our organs to raise money, we would have promptly covered the sales tax and gladly delivered them gift-wrapped. We hunted money from close friends, distant friends, and we even seriously considered raising money from exes, but worried the chopped-off arm would be literal rather than figurative.

Landing the first investor is always the hardest. Many startups look for that early big investor, but what worked for us was getting a friend who trusted us to put in an initial small amount to form the first couple snowflakes of a soon-to-be-legitimate snowball. Being able to say, "We'd love you to join the other investors in the round," sounds a lot better than "No one has said yes yet, but you could change that!" After you get that initial friend investor, go out to everyone and their mother. Again, everyone likes hearing pitches, so you're not inconveniencing them by presenting your dream of the future in the form of your company. Even when presented with the best pitch, investors are unpredictable, and thus you must engage with as many as possible to find the right fit. And the more you pitch, the better you get at pitching. The better you get at pitching, the better your business gets.

So far we've learned that (1) investors love hearing pitches, so you shouldn't feel weird about begging for money and (2) you should pitch to everyone because it's impossible to know who will actually invest and because you and your business get better each time.

But how and what should you present? Start with the problem that your product solves. Paint the world as a terrible, miserable place because of this problem. At this point, the investor should be thinking, "Yes, that's a big problem; I agree." Then, present your business. Address why your business solves or significantly alleviates the problem you began with. Then hit them with facts, data, graphs, and customer feedback that proves the viability of your solution. Your main presentation should be just six to eight slides with relatively few words.

You should, however, have much more material handy so that you're ready for the game of cat and mouse that comes with every serious investor. Here's how it goes: you present a simple vision of the problem, solution, and key facts supporting your idea. The investor is impressed but thinks he or she spots a hole in your idea due to some unaddressed point. Here's the catch-22 you have to solve as an entrepreneur: to intrigue the investor, you have to make it simple. To make it simple, you have to leave out some important details. When you leave out important details, your investors feel the need to quiz you on facts germane and arcane. During this quiz is when the beautiful appendix comes in. There's nothing more impressive than an investor saying, "I liked your pitch, but you didn't address what would happen in the event of [insert scenario], and I think that could be a big issue," to which you respond, "Actually, Mr. Investor, sir, if you turn to slide 43 in the appendix, we have some data on that, which you might find interesting." If you had put that same data in the main deck, your investor would have been overwhelmed. If you have it in your appendix, you've solved the catch-22 of keeping it simple while having all the necessary detail.

After you've gone through the deck, express the simple but unbelievably effective notion that you are incredibly passionate about this opportunity. Briefly list the sacrifices you've made and are willing to make on behalf of the company: low pay, turning down a great job, etc. Your willingness to sacrifice puts the investor on your side—at that point you're each sacrificing in the short term for the long-term benefit of the company—as opposed to the investor simply handing you money. After all, that money isn't yours, it's the company's, and it'll work for the company just like you do.

If you're young and you're raising a seed round, chances are it's from friends, family, and angels. That means you're not generally dealing with the Einsteins of finance. Keep the securities you offer as simple as possible. We issued straight, simple equity, but if you do issue a convertible note, be sure you can explain it in very simple terms. Complexity drives away early investors. To the extent the inevitable complexity arises, as long as you fully understand it, you can present it to investors in an understandable way.

When you finally do earn the trust of investors to raise money to build your business, it's important to immediately blow all of it on highly illegal activity and leave the country. Or for those of you who are more *responsible*, I would encourage you to at least celebrate in some way. As one of our earliest advisors told us, celebration breeds more future opportunities to celebrate. It's contagious.

After celebrating, constantly ask yourself, "How can I build equity value for investors so that they can get their money back times twenty?" It's a helpful lens that's often an even more powerful motivator than asking yourself, "How can I make myself richer?" The prospect of making yourself richer feels somewhat absurd as you do everything from the most menial tasks to the highest-level strategizing.

I'll conclude this section by pitching you on how you should pitch with exaggeration for emphasis:

The horrific problem facing society is that first-time entrepreneurs don't pitch to enough investors because they're too shy. This is a huge shame because investors actually like hearing pitches, are too unpredictable to be targeted in small numbers, and offer the opportunity to refine the pitch and the business. This lack of pitching causes entrepreneurs to become entrepre-losers as they fail at raising money and have their dreams utterly vanquished, leading the world to become the dark, undisrupted hellhole we find ourselves in at present.

But there's a better way. If entrepreneurs pitch as many investors as possible, they'll get better at it and improve their business plans, while also finally finding the right investors amid the horde of the unwilling. If 5% of the investors you talk with invest, and you talk to one hundred people, you have five investors, which is awesome, even if that means nineteen out of twenty said "no." The biggest point of this pitch, Ms. Potential Entrepreneur, is that I am extremely passionate about helping young entrepreneurs. I believe they can often make a far bigger difference building a business than operating within one, and that's why it makes so much sense for you to join the other entrepreneurs (my one other friend) and adopt this advice.

➤ HOW DO YOU OPERATE AND MANAGE YOUR COMPANY?

As much as they like growth, all entrepreneurs fondly look back on the days when it was just them running their startup. Beyond the romantic appeal of you against the world, there was the added benefit that you never had to worry about who would do what: you were the boss, the intern, and the janitor, all in one. A stressed-out, to-do-list-swamped jack-of-all-trades. You had to do everything and then some.

The best and worst part about success is that you now get to (have to) decide who does what. This decision presents a whole host of challenges that can seem like a distraction from the task at hand. Rather than just doing the thing, you must decide how, who, when, and why (HWWW). I worked for an investment bank for one year, where I learned that 80% of work is figuring out all the details of how the work is to be done. I can't imagine what the proportion for management consulting must be. The most liberating aspect of an early startup is how low this proportion is. In fact, when a startup starts, it's close to 0%. You pretty much do all the work without planning who should do it or how it should be done. You just do it. When work presents itself in the early days, such as a potential customer responding to one of your 1,800 emails to them, the work of figuring out the work goes something like this:

How? (1) Panic. (2) Calm down. (3) However you can with twenty dollars in your pocket, a MacBook from 2006, half a tank of gas, and a lethal level of caffeine in the bloodstream.

Who? Your secretary. Oh wait. You don't have one because you're alone in your company. So, *drumroll*, it's you.

When? Right now!

Why? Because good entrepreneurs get started by doing everything that may have the slightest good impact on getting your company going!

If you have partners, which you definitely should, like I did, then the HWWW is a bit more complicated even in the early days, but nothing close to the bewildering maze it can seem once your startup gains traction. When you have sales orders, the sheer number of steps involved would have even Rocky doubled over. When your team is up to five eager souls, the HWWW actually becomes a necessary process when each major task or project comes up. This basically entails your assigning work either to yourself or to one of your faithful first employees. You outline what needs to be done and how, who should do it, when, and why *it* needs to be done—more than the million other things that also need to be done. At this stage, you may not be the executor of the HWWW, but you are still the author. Your primary responsibility now is to do the work that allows the work to be done. For example, you don't necessarily prepare the document for the customer, but you do lay out what needs to be in it, when it needs to be done, by whom, etc.

There is natural guilt and pleasure that comes with assigning work to another: the guilt of not doing the work yourself—all the more biting because you know the benefits from the work will, in large part, flow to you and your equity—and the pleasure of not having to do it yourself. As soon as you have an employee or two, your default answer to the first W (who) should be anyone other than yourself. This new default brings a few benefits: (1) it frees you up to better determine the tasks that are most pressing and the associated HWWWs, (2) it trains your employees to be your clone—a somewhat terrifying but necessary feat—and (3) it allows you to check their work. Checking your own work is important, but until another checks it, it's not really checked. Horror stories abound from even top companies and scientists due to seemingly minor mistakes in Excel, unseemly typos in PowerPoint, or worse, issues with product. Each piece of the work should follow these steps: (1) planning the HWWW, (2) carrying out the work, and (3) checking the work, done by someone other than the executor of the work.

The benefits of dividing and conquering must be weighed against the fact that you're the work-monster entrepreneur who didn't get into the startup game without a healthy pitcher of elbow grease to pour on the gears of innovation. But you must outgrow this mindset. You personally can grow, but not as fast or as large as you want your company to grow. You must add bodies and use them.

The HWWW you author in your five-person startup provides the direction your employees need to do their work. But when you start to get closer to ten employees, you can't write all of the HWWWs required or check them properly. Now you can't do the work and you can't even do all of the work to plan the work. This is a humbling realization, but a crucial one. A business mentor once told me, only a bit sarcastically, that the goal of your business should be for you to have absolutely no idea what you're even selling. At that point, you've set up a highly scalable system independent of you. To achieve this system, you should protect your time like it's your cute puppy. Remember, every investor, customer, supplier, and employee is trying to steal your puppy. You may let them pet it at times, but ultimately it's your puppy and you want to raise it rather than give it away. A good gauge for whether you're on the right track is this: Are you doing the same tasks you were last month? Each month you should have lists of what to do and lists of what *not* to do. Anything routine should be on the not-to-do list as soon as possible. Paying bills, paying employees, talking with customers about orders, low-level hiring, etc., should all be delegated to employees you trust.

Your ability to delegate depends on you having good people who can be your clones or, even better, souped-up versions of you. But how do you get them? Here are some tips:

- Hire recent graduates for most managerial positions—they are half the price and 80% as good as more seasoned people.

- Hire a head of operations who is better than you are at operations—they will be able to train the recent graduates to get them to 110% better than people who are more seasoned but poorly led.

- Present to all hires the reasons your company will be the biggest in your industry. This will get them excited about your vision rather than just seeing the startup for the small company it is at present.

- Hire only people who want to be there. Good hires typically have other options (often at higher pay), but they choose to work for you because they view working on your startup as a life adventure rather than just a job.

- Offer equity to the first ten strategic hires. It doesn't have to be a lot, but it really makes them feel like they're entrepreneurs as well, which is the perfect way to inject your innovative DNA in their clone minds.

Even with the best people, things do not get done properly without systems. Routine, like practice, begets professionalism. It also allows for better monitoring of progress, as you can more easily compare results, such as accounting or customer acquisition, from one period of time to another. The best systems, or standard operating procedures (SOPs), share these qualities:

- They are coauthored to some extent with the people who are to follow them.
- They are written down.
- They are followed (rather than ignored).
- They are enforced—someone holds everyone accountable.

To summarize, to do anything in the business, a manager clone authors the HWWW according to an SOP and then checks the work. All done? Nope. Last step: feedback.

Feedback is rife with the potential to hurt feelings, both those of the giver and the receiver. The best way to alleviate hurt feelings is to use a matter-of-fact tone and to focus a bit more on the positives than the negatives. Try using the compliment sandwich, whereby feedback begins with specific positive points, followed by the opportunities for improvement, and finally general appreciation for their overall good work. People hate criticism when it hurts their pride. Protect their pride, but tell them exactly what they need to improve on.

If your company makes widgets, your goal is to reach the point where you, personally, don't make the widgets. You don't even figure out how to make the widgets, or even ensure the widgets get delivered on time. Your job is to hire manager clones and coauthor SOPs with them that ensure you're the best widget company on earth.

CHAPTER SIX

TIM HWANG
Founder and CEO of FiscalNote

>>>> ABOUT TIM

Tim is the founder and CEO of FiscalNote, a real-time legal analytics platform that uses AI and natural language processing to help global organizations take control of their government risk and understand the law. The company now powers some of the world's largest and most influential law firms, legal departments, and governments. With Hwang's technology and over $34 million in funding from the likes of Mark Cuban, Jerry Yang, Steve Case, NEA, Renren, and others, FiscalNote is revolutionizing access to legislation, regulations, and court cases for organizations around the world.

Prior to starting FiscalNote from a Motel 6 in Silicon Valley, Hwang worked in politics. He began at age sixteen as a field organizer for the Obama 2008 campaign. One year later, he was elected to the Montgomery County, Maryland, board of education, overseeing a budget of over $4 billion for 22,000 public employees. Tim was also president of the 750,000-member National Youth Association and the founder of Operation Fly, Inc., a national 501(c)(3) organization that served inner-city children in underprivileged areas around the country.

At age twenty-four, Tim was profiled in *Forbes'* "30 Under 30," *Inc.'s* "30 Under 30," CNN's "Top 10 Startups," *Business Insiders'* "Top 25 Hottest Startups," and many others. He is a graduate of Princeton and currently deferring Harvard Business School. He is also a World Economic Forum Technology Pioneer and a member of the Economic Club of Washington, DC.

S tart with a Passion. I don't entirely remember when my fascination with government took hold. My earliest memory of the excitement and energy of our political system was during the presidential election of 2000 between Vice President Al Gore and Governor George W. Bush. As the returns came pouring in, I defied my parents' wishes and stayed up all night counting the Electoral College votes and soaking in the analysis of Florida's tumultuous battle. I had barely started elementary school at the time, but the passion and energy with which people spoke of both candidates that evening sparked a lifelong interest in the inner workings of politics and government.

Throughout middle school and high school, I began to slowly immerse myself in politics. It started off innocuously enough: running for student government, getting involved in local congressional races, volunteering at the local court. Every experience created a deeper desire to get engaged, whether it was talking with voters about their concerns about our education system or listening to stories from minorities who felt like their options were growing limited. As I grew older, I knew that I wanted to be doing political work.

Sometime in high school, several friends pushed the idea of working for then-senator Obama's presidential campaign. Back then, Senator Obama had been gaining momentum after his speech at the Democratic National Convention. There was growing excitement in the country—though it was still a long shot, given the dynamics of the primary. Even then, many of us took the plunge and joined the campaign, building what we would call the fastest growing startup in American history. Working in the field and on data operations, sleeping in pews and on top of pizza boxes, we applied our passion and work ethic, soaring to an election victory. Later on, I used these experiences to run for the

Montgomery County, Maryland, board of education (the thirteenth-largest district in the country) and serve as an elected official myself. Before that, I knew on Election Day that this was what I was passionate about.

NO RISK, ALL REWARD

Inevitably, I believe that the start of a great company comes from the drive of an entrepreneur in solving challenges that they are fundamentally passionate about. Even though I had been engaged in the political process throughout my entire life, I entered university in 2010 disappointed by the partisan gridlock that gripped government from that time period on. It was then that I began searching for alternatives, and tech became an obvious answer. To me, technology promised a fast track to implementing change in areas that I cared about, from health care and education to political transparency and rule of law.

With this in mind, I grabbed two of my friends from high school and we decided to start a company together. Digging into what we were passionate about, we decided to look intimately at the problems organizations and governments faced in understanding changes in the federal government that impact them. Back when I served on the board of education, the challenges facing our school system were not readily understood. Whether it was the barreling changes in No Child Left Behind and Common Core or budgetary and curriculum constraints, institutions were often left in the dark regarding the political process. Helping institutions become more politically savvy seemed like the perfect problem to solve. We decided that we would build an Internet company that would pull together all the laws and regulations impacting organizations around the country and use artificial intelligence to analyze the impact that they would have on these companies and institutions.

We bootstrapped a couple thousand dollars and some grant money and moved to Silicon Valley the summer of 2013. At the time, we were all twenty-one years old and had no idea what we were doing, but we knew that this was a problem worth solving. We also gambled, as young entrepreneurs, telling ourselves that there was no better time to start a company than in our early twenties. With no mortgages, no family commitments, and no crushing levels of debt, we were lucky and privileged. Because the risk of failing was low and the reward was potentially high, we simply jumped in and got started.

PUTTING IN THE WORK

Much of the early days of FiscalNote was spent on only three things. Number one, we needed to build a proper prototype to validate our solution by putting together a web application that would initially serve as a search engine for all of the country's legislation in all fifty state legislatures and Congress. Number two, we needed to validate the distribution model and messaging in the market by cold-calling as many prospects as possible. And number three, we needed to bring in the core team to help us execute properly by testing the labor market for people's interest in working for our mission. With those three priorities in mind, we set out to work like we'd never worked before.

We set up shop in a Motel 6 off the highway in Sunnyvale, California, and began designing, coding, cold-calling, and recruiting. We worked relentlessly—seven days a week, fourteen hours a day—to get the company off the ground. We were racing against ourselves to prove that this could be done and we knew that if we could not prove the market within a couple of months we would have to close up shop.

In the first month, we completed a basic web application and search capability over all state legislation in the country. We then spent the vast majority of the time recruiting and speaking with prospects about the value of a solution like this. We faced challenges in building a platform as audacious as we had hoped and spent much of our time refining the minimum viable product for completion—all this while balancing a precarious cash situation and trying to come up with the words to describe our solution in front of customers. Upon reflection, the company was simply willed into existence by a handful of college kids who were passionate about solving a problem.

Four months into the company's founding, with all three of our priorities validated, we set off to raise a round of seed capital to get the company off the ground. We reached out to Mark Cuban, who immediately responded and was interested in getting a deal done. The round was closed within a month with Jerry Yang and New Enterprise Associates all pitching in $1.3 million. We later raised capital from folks like Steve Case as well as Renren, many of whom who reached out to us about the exciting work we were doing.

Realizing our company needed to be close to its customers, we moved our headquarters to Washington, DC, and never looked back, keeping that same work ethic and drive as we scaled the company to multiple offices and hundreds of employees around the world.

▶ HOW DO YOU OPERATE AND MANAGE YOUR COMPANY?

STARTING WITH CULTURE

One of the first things we did at FiscalNote, even before our product vision was fully fleshed out, was sit down all together, early employees and founders, to define the kind of company we would be. What would our philosophy be on work-life balance? What kind of employees would we look for? What would our vision of the ideal workplace look like? Thinking about these questions made much of the secondary processes of starting a company much easier as we laid down a set of values that would serve as the guiding principles for decision making.

We decided we wanted to be a company that looked for people who were incredibly invested in being better at everything they did. We decided we wanted to be an open and creative workplace that valued risk taking and experimentation, even if the risks and experiments did not always pan out. We decided that we wanted our employees to feel like they were owners in the business—a family-run business across the board. We wanted people to be detail-oriented and responsible for the work they were in charge of. We wanted our employees to feel like they had a transparent view into all workings of the company. With early hiring successes and failures within the organization, we constantly talked about—and refined—our values and our culture even after we started the company.

With our core values in mind, we began to build the initial framework for what our company would look like. By defining our values first, we were able to distribute decision making throughout the company to as many people as possible by giving them all guidelines for how to operate. When we hired individuals, we made sure that we built in the right processes for ensuring that prospective employees would feel empowered and comfortable in such an environment. When we built our products, we made sure to push transparency and experimentation. When we started to scale up our business development organization we pushed ownership as a mentality and personal responsibility within industry verticals. These core tenets enabled our employees to have clear guideposts for how we wanted the organization to grow.

MANAGEMENT TRAINING

Once your company reaches around forty employees or so, one of the realizations you come to, fairly quickly, is that oversight is not scalable without investments deep into the organizational structure. Earlier in the organization, we could communicate values and processes simply by grabbing everyone in a room and talking about what needed to get done. As we scaled our company, however, we made the conscious decision to invest much of our time in creating and conducting management training, which all our managers were required to go through.

With the premise that management is a technical skill, we taught our managers the basics of everything from how to properly run a meeting (where we spend most of our days) to driving performance and accountability within teams of highly creative and independent team members. Investment in your management becomes even more important at 150 employees, where senior executives become less reliant on personal relationships (and remembering names) and more on the expectations that have been set between managers cross-functionally. Many of the challenges with scaling come from keeping people accountable and aligned, even in the midst of ever-growing teams and complexity.

There is a saying that goes, "Most employees don't leave companies, they leave managers." By standardizing management across the company early on, we set a uniform expectation of management and were able to rein in the inevitable attrition that comes from a fast-growing company while driving our culture and values in a repeatable way. To this day, I credit much of our growth to the investments that we have made in setting a uniform expectation of how management is conducted at FiscalNote.

ADAPTABLE PROCESSES AND COMMUNICATION

One of the things we do at FiscalNote that represents the ever-changing nature of fast-growing tech companies is our all-hands meetings. When we were fewer than ten people, we would grab people in the office at 10:00 a.m., seven days a week, to go over progress and exchange ideas. Of course, as anyone who runs a startup knows, this meeting strategy quickly grew unwieldy and inefficient. But how do you preserve that sense of camaraderie with the need to drive efficiency? Do you have such meetings weekly? Monthly? Quarterly? We eventually moved from weekly meetings to biweekly with quarterly off-sites for all our employees. And yet this meeting schedule will most likely change within the next couple of months.

At FiscalNote, we've learned to constantly be adaptable, both in our processes and in our communication. The company at ten people was radically different at two hundred, and it appropriately needs to adapt alongside growth. Every process and form of communication needs to be revisited at each stage in the company's growth. There will be a need to drive predictable release cycles between the development and distribution sides of the organization—from product development to performance evaluation.

This is the real fun part in building a startup: learning every day and facing new challenges as you scale and grow.

CHAPTER SEVEN

TOM BRADY

Cofounder and Chief Technology Officer, SkySpecs

>>>> ABOUT TOM

Tom Brady is a cofounder and chief technology officer at SkySpecs, a company based in Ann Arbor, Michigan, that develops software and services for enterprise drone deployments. His cofounder, Danny Ellis, is also a contributor to this book. In 2016, *Forbes* named Tom one of their "30 Under 30" recipients in the Manufacturing category. Tom has worn several hats at SkySpecs, ranging from chief financial officer and bookkeeper to the leader of the company's product development efforts. Since starting the company, Tom has held two fund-raisers, two product launches, written thousands of lines of code, and played a lot of foosball.

Prior to founding SkySpecs, Tom earned his bachelor's and master's degrees from the University of Michigan in aerospace engineering. While at the university, Tom was a team leader for the Michigan Autonomous Aerial Vehicles (MAAV) team. During Tom's time with MAAV, the team developed a drone that could autonomously perform inspections that are dangerous or expensive for a human to do on structures such as wind turbines, bridges, or cell towers. The founding team of SkySpecs worked together on MAAV for three years before eventually launching SkySpecs in 2012. Tom enjoys brewing beer, scuba diving, golf, good food, and Michigan Wolverines football.

t takes money to run a business. For established businesses, this operating capital comes from selling a product or service for more money than it takes the company to deliver that product or service. But where does this money come from when you have a startup company with no product to sell and nothing but a dream to its name? If you're unable to bootstrap[4] your company to a point where revenue funds its growth, bringing investors into the business becomes an unfortunate necessity. The process pretty much goes like this: convince rich people (more commonly, people who represent rich people) to exchange cash for stock in your company. This stock allows them to profit from your growth, and ultimately sell their stock for more than they bought it for. Eventual buyers for this stock are either the public in an initial public offering, or another company if you get acquired. Simple, right? Why, then, have hundreds of people—myself included—felt compelled to write books on the topic of fund-raising? It really comes down to this: the less you screw up in the process, the more an investor will pay for your company's stock, and the more you get to keep for yourself.

Let me reiterate. People write ENTIRE BOOKS on the topic of fund-raising. I, however, am going to make you an expert on the topic in 6,000 words or less.

Well, maybe not.

Truth be told, I know very little in the grand scheme of things. Intellectual humility, by the way, is a key trait for an aspiring entrepreneur. It's one I've come to value immensely, both in myself and in the people I hire. Here's what I do know: every person you meet in life brings

---

4   To "bootstrap" as a startup is to grow the business via sales, and not via raising funds in exchange for stock. Bootstrapping is unique among hyper-growth startup companies because, in many cases, investors and founders want the business to grow faster than would be feasible from sales alone.

unique experiences and knowledge to the table. It's your job as an entrepreneur (and frankly, as a human being) to peel the layers back to understand and value another person's knowledge and experiences. So consider this an easy exercise in understanding another human being, because I'm going to tell you exactly what my unique experiences are and what knowledge I have.

Here's what we'll cover:

1. Raising money from people you care about

2. Evolving a business model through rounds of fund-raising

3. Raising money through business competitions, grants, and government programs

So, dear reader, join me as I regale you with tales of our fund-raising journey at my company, SkySpecs: the successes, the times we screwed the pooch (more of the latter than the former, I assure you), and some of the things we've learned along the way. No need to take notes; I've written it all down for you here.

RAISING MONEY FROM PEOPLE YOU CARE ABOUT: HOW THE SHIT GOT REAL

This is the part of the story where an author would typically inject some anecdote about their experience to establish credibility. But since I'm floundering through this whole startup experience just like you probably are, I won't bore you with the details of why I'm so amazing or why you should listen to me. Instead, I'll get right to it. Danny Ellis, Sam DeBruin, and I founded SkySpecs in March 2012. At the moment I am writing this, SkySpecs has raised 2.25 rounds of funding and I now own a very small piece of the company that has been my baby for the last five years. I'll get back to why I say "2.25," and not "3" rounds of funding a bit later.

A "round" of funding is an event in which a company accepts funding from one or more investors, usually with the same terms (there are exceptions, often for "lead" investors), to accomplish some agreed-upon set of milestones and objectives. If you aren't familiar with the naming distinctions between rounds of funding, that's okay; they're basically arbitrary, but here are some guidelines. Pre-seed rounds are usually for companies that have nothing but an idea and need cash to build a prototype. Seed rounds are typically for companies that have a bit of traction with their product, perhaps a working prototype, which they'll be starting to test with customers. Series A companies generally have proven product-market fit and are looking to scale up. From here, the rounds just increment as the alphabet does: "A," "B," "C," and so on. With each new round, the startup is presumably starting to look more like a business. Some companies get creative and call their rounds "A prime" or "B2," which doesn't mean much except that they aren't ready to move up to the next letter yet. Keep in mind these are just rules of thumb, and investors in different industry sectors have different expectations. Heavy technology companies often get away with raising a "Series A" before having proven product-market fit, for example. Biotech and pharmaceutical startups can sometimes end up raising "D" rounds and beyond before their product even has FDA approval.

Our first round of funding, which was the 0.25 of our 2.25 rounds, was a "pre-seed" round in December 2012. This was nine months after Danny and Sam, my cofounders, and I started our company. We received a $25,000 investment from a professor we studied with during our freshman year of college at the University of Michigan. I was twenty-two years old and in the second and final year of my master's degree when she made her investment. Our professor was the kind of woman who stayed in the engineering lab until two in the morning for her students. She ordered pizza, brought juice boxes around on her lab cart, and was adamant that we got our daily fix of fruit and granola bars. She was truly our knight in a shining babushka. With her $25,000 check in hand, we ran to the bank and made our deposit. This was, by far, the most money I'd ever seen in a bank account. "Look at all those zeroes!" we thought. The amount of money seems inconsequential now, but with this first investment, an enormous sense of responsibility came over us. Someone else believed in us enough to put her own livelihood on the line to support us. The metaphorical shit had just gotten real. My cofounders and I are eternally grateful that our professor took that very first bet our company. Frankly, I'm still not sure what she saw in us.

The vessel for this pre-seed investment was a convertible note. This is essentially a loan from an investor, which upon some trigger event, can either be paid back or converted to company stock, usually at the investor's choosing. The most common trigger events are (1) the company raising another round of funding; (2) the company being acquired; or (3) the note "expiring" (commonly one to three years after its issuance).

The entrepreneur and investor don't set a stock price when issuing a convertible note. Rather, they defer this discussion to a later date. In exchange for the inherent risk associated with investing in an early-stage startup, the investor is typically compensated by receiving a discount on the price per share when their loan converts to stock. This discount can be a flat-rate discount, for example 20%, but can also be instantiated with a "valuation cap." A valuation cap essentially sets a maximum conversion price for the stock that the debt will ultimately turn into. With a valuation cap, an investor says, "I will pay no more than $X for each share of stock when my loan converts."

The best way to explain this is with a quick fund-raising scenario. Let's say you raise a $500,000 seed round on convertible debt terms. We'll use 20% discount, 10% interest, and a $5 million cap for the example. It turns out these are typical numbers for this kind of investment. Say your company absolutely crushes it and your app goes viral. It's one year later and you are raising your next round of investment from investors who are willing to pay $10 million for a 25% stake in your business. Let's see how the company ownership (the "capitalization table" or "cap table") plays out—with and without the valuation cap included.

SCENARIO 1: NO VALUATION CAP

- Series A investor gets 25% for $10 million.
- It's been a year, so interest has accumulated on the convertible note. Seed investor's $500,000 plus 10% interest is $550,000.
- Seed investor gets a discount. A 20% discount means they can buy 25% more product.[5] Product, in this case, is stock in the company. Twenty-five percent more than $550,000 is $687,5000.
- From here all things are equal. Series A investor got 25% for $10 million, which is 2.5% per million invested—or 0.0000025% of the company per dollar invested. Therefore, the seed investor gets $687.5K times 0.0000025%, which is 1.72%.

SCENARIO 2: VALUATION CAP OF $5 MILLION

- Seed investor's $500,000 principal plus interest is $550,000.
- The math behind the valuation cap is that it's as if you had just done a priced round with the pre-seed investor in the first place, except with the interest accumulated. Recall that the cap placed on conversion was $5 million. Therefore, if you were looking

---

5   If you have four dollars, you can by four one-dollar products. However, if you have a 20% discount on those one-dollar products, that means each product costs you only eighty cents. With a discount, you can now buy five of that product with your four dollars. Five is 25% more than four.

only at the result of the pre-seed investment, the pre-seed investor would get $550,000/($5 million + $550,000) = 9.9%.

- The Series A investment dilutes both the seed investor and the founders. The Series A investors still get 25%, so the founders and the seed investors are diluted by 25%. The founders' and seed investors' percentage ownership of the company will be 75% of what it was previously.

- Seed investors final ownership is 9.9% × 75% = 7.4%.

Take a look at the difference in how the capitalization table shook down for these two scenarios:

	SCENARIO 1	SCENARIO 2
SEED INVESTORS	1.72%	7.4%
SERIES A INVESTORS	25%	25%
FOUNDERS	73.28%	67.6%

Valuation caps are just one of the many, more dangerous, nuances an entrepreneur should be educated about when negotiating a term sheet.

By February 2013, the proceeds from our $25,000 pre-seed investment were long gone, and our company was still nowhere near ready for a serious fund-raiser. Between February and August 2013, we racked up a little over $90,000 in grant funding. It was just enough to live off ramen while we limped along in developing a prototype, which we'd ultimately throw away and regret spending our time on. Living off ramen is, of course, hyperbole, because who really lives off that stuff? Maybe living off ramen is a construct of Silicon Valley because it's so expensive to even travel, let alone to live there. To any of you Silicon Valley entrepreneurs who are living off ramen, come to Michigan. We'll feed you.

Truthfully, most of us at SkySpecs also stayed employed half-time as graduate student instructors to pay our rent. As the end of the school year drew near, and we were preparing to graduate, it became clear that we were going to need to bring in a more serious round of funding if we were going to take this business anywhere.

I don't recall how many investors we pitched in our seed fundraiser, but it was more than we thought it would be, and it took a lot longer than we expected. If I could do it again, I think I'd ask each investor how tall he was, and then find the sum total height of white guys wearing blue shirts. What can I say? I like statistics. One of these white guys in a blue shirt was Nick, an advisor of ours who Danny had connected with before SkySpecs was even founded. Danny was practicing his pitch with Nick for an upcoming pitch competition with faux investors, in which we could win some token amount of cash. By the way, during fund-raising you're going to get a ton of nos from investors, so you may as well try a few of your let's call them less than desirable pitches on people who aren't going to judge you for it. In most cases, as we did with Nick, you'll get some helpful feedback.

By the spring of 2013, when our fund-raising efforts were in full swing, Nick had signed on with Invest Detroit as an entrepreneur in residence (EIR). EIRs are usually entrepreneurs that have already built successful companies. Often, their goal is to join one of the startups the investor invests in. Nick connected us to Adrian, one of the partners at First Step Fund, which is more or less a fund within Invest Detroit. After a few months of due diligence with Adrian, First Step Fund led SkySpecs' $600,000 seed round in August 2013.

SkySpecs' seed round was what you might call a "family, friends, and fools" round, and we certainly had a well-balanced mixture of each. In our seed round, there were a total of twenty-six individuals and groups that invested. Our largest check in the $600,000 round was for $120,000. The smallest checks were from family members investing only $5,000. Set aside, for a moment, the complexity of getting twenty-six signatures and twenty-six checks rounded up. We later discovered that answering to this many people would be quite burdensome. Often contractually, and sometimes just because you feel obligated to, you'll find yourself needing to keep your investors informed about how their money is being spent. For you, this this might mean making *a lot* of phone calls. For me, this means Danny (who is our CEO) receives *a lot* of phone calls. This is one of the underappreciated and often unnoticed responsibilities of the CEO and his or her executive team—to shield the rest of people who work for them from distractions.

Further complicating matters, investors typically have the contractual right to vote on any new financing activity for the company. For us, this meant that when we raised our Series A investment, a little over two years after our seed round, we had to get express approval to bring in new investors from a bunch of current investors who didn't completely understand the terms of the new investment. How can you blame them? After all, there was well over 200 pages of documentation associated with our Series A investment.

It may not be obvious why one would need permission from previous investors to bring in financing from new investors. *Shark Tank* didn't cover this detail, did it? Let's say it's your first round of funding and your company has 1 million shares outstanding, distributed only among the founders. When an investor proposes an investment by saying, "I will give you $500,000 for 20% of your company," they are inherently placing a price on all the existing stock in your business. To be precise, they are saying each share of the existing stock is worth two dollars.[6] If your company accepts the investment, $500,000/$2 = 250,000

---

6   $500,000 for 20% implies a "post-money" valuation of $2.5 million because $500,000/$2.5 million = 20%. This means there was a "pre-money" valuation of $2 million ($2.5 million minus the new investment of $500,000), and therefore each share of stock was worth $2 million/1,000,000 = $2. "Pre-money" and "post-money" refer to the valuations of the business before and after the money from an investment lands. Naturally, the valuation goes up when there's a big cash influx because there's literally more cash on your balance sheet.

new shares are created, giving the new investor 250,000 out of the new total of 1,250,000 shares outstanding in the business. Note that I did not say you give the new investors 200,000 of the currently outstanding 1,000,000 shares to get them their 20%.

Therein lies the reason that you need to get permission from your current investors to bring in new investors. When you bring in your next round of investment, you aren't just handing over more of the founders' stock to the new investors. Everyone, including the old investors, gets diluted when new investors come in. Let's say your next group of investors offers you $5 million for 33%, implying a "post-money" valuation of $15 million, a "pre-money" valuation of $10 million, and a share price of eight dollars. You accept the offer, thereby creating $5 million/$8 = 625,000 new shares. Recall that your old investors still hold 250,000 shares of stock. Combining the original founders' stock, the original investors' stock, and the new investors' stock, there is now 250,000 + 1,000,000 + 625,000 = 1,875,000 shares outstanding. Your old investors, who previously owned 20%, now own 250,000/1,875,000 = 13.3% of the company. Clearly, once a founder brings in an investment, they can't answer only to themselves anymore. Additional parties now share in all your wins and losses alike.

Old investors getting diluted by new ones isn't some law of fund-raising; it's just how these things usually play out. Anti-dilution provisions in an investment contract can protect investors against such dilution, but guess who loses if they don't get diluted? You do. Entrepreneurs and their legal counsel should be wary of these anti-dilution clauses. In many cases, these provisions can be innocent and justifiable. For example, it's quite common for an anti-dilution provision to trigger in the event of a "down-round." A down-round is a round of funding in which the new investors assign a lower value to the company than the previous investors did.

But wait, this doesn't seem fair, right? We are in this together with our investors! That mindset is all well and good, but you should also think about this from the perspective of the investor. Without this provision, you could bring in a round of funding from one investor, and then go out and find another "investor" who invests in such a way that severely dilutes the other investor in a matter of days. This outcome would not be fair. At the end of the day, most investment terms exist to protect investors and entrepreneurs alike. You just need to be exceedingly deliberate about what the documents actually say. When things go well, you'll never look back at those contracts, but this is my take on it: plan for the worst, and hope for the best.

Because investors share not only in your wins but also in your losses, doing business with family or friends can be tricky to navigate. You likely have people in your life who are willing to go beyond their means to support you and your endeavors. As an entrepreneur, you should be honored by their faith in you, but also very cautious. When dealing with family and friends, swallow your confidence for a moment and think of your startup more as a monetary black hole, rather than as a business opportunity. The money will go in, but there's no guarantee whatsoever that it will ever come back out. Reiterate this constantly with family and friends who are considering investing. If you have family and friends who either tell you outright or who you believe are not ready to lose their investment forever, it's your job as an entrepreneur to find a loving way to deny their investment. This investment protection is exactly what the Securities Exchange Commission (SEC) is trying to capture by allowing significant accountability benefits to private companies that deal only with "accredited investors."

In 2016, for individual investors, accreditation required either a net worth of more than $1 million or an annual income of more than $200,000. The idea behind the SEC accreditation is that people who meet these criteria are "sophisticated" enough (the SEC's terminology, not mine) to know what they're getting into when making their investment.

There are a few things you can do to ease the pain of raising a round of funding like ours. First, you should set a minimum investment amount and stick to it. Our minimum investment was $5,000, but I'd recommend selecting an amount that is higher, unless your prospects are truly limited. Second, set up recurring updates that you can automatically send to all your investors so they can stay in the loop without you making twenty-six phone calls each week. To simplify voting, depending on the maturity of your investors, you might also consider requesting that smaller investors assign your lead investor as a proxy, allowing the lead investor to vote on their behalf. Finally, try to get your investors to agree to typical drag-along provisions. For example, they can agree to approve an upcoming round of financing if a majority of the other investors in the round have agreed to do so. Not only will these precautions save you a ton of time, they will make new, often more sophisticated investors more interested in working with you and your current investors.

EVOLVING A BUSINESS MODEL THROUGH ROUNDS OF FUND-RAISING

Founders with significant others should come to terms with something immediately. During fund-raising, you're going to need to see other people. These new interests will make you feel very vulnerable when you're around them. They'll be able to provide for you. You'll have better luck if you can play a little hard to get. But you mustn't have sex with them. They're going to be your new investors, after all. You've heard the analogy before: picking your investment syndicate is a lot like dating. Just as dating is an opportunity to learn about yourself, as much as it is an opportunity to learn about a new person, fund-raising presents an open door for you to learn about your future investors and their needs, as well as what your company is about and what it stands for.

At SkySpecs, the time of our rounds of funding was pivotal for our company's evolution. Fund-raising forces you to tell your company's story. You'll have to answer questions like where you've come from, what makes you special, where you're going next, and how an investor's money will help you get there. Without crystal-clear answers to these nearly existential questions, how can you possibly expect an investor to join you on this journey? With any luck, you won't be desperately seeking investment to keep ramen on the table. It's in these moments of vulnerability, though, that you'll be most prepared to change your way of thinking. These are moments for individual and company growth, and they'll force you to iterate on your story and evolve your business model. That's what happened with SkySpecs.

I'll start from where we are today and work backwards and for-wards in semirandom order until all the dots are connected. You've probably heard the term "SaaS" (pronounced sass), or "software as a service." SkySpecs is essentially a "drone as a service" company. I guess you'd pronounce this *daas*, which is awkward when said out loud, but seems fine for my story. Our "daas" company develops software and services for enterprise drones: things like wind turbine inspections, bridge inspections, or cell-tower inspections. We provide automated drones to do these sorts of processes that are dangerous or expensive to do with a person. Our business model has changed approximately ninety-seven times throughout our nearly five years of existence and 2.25 rounds of financing. Like a couple of apes throwing shit at a win-dow, we had to try a few different things before anything stuck.

When SkySpecs was taking on its first investment in 2012, drones were just beginning to gain popularity among consumers and were still several years from being the least bit useful in most commercial settings. In fact, it wasn't until January 2013 that the DJI Phantom 1 hit the shelves. That's the small white one that everyone and their mother thinks of when they hear the word "drone." Companies like DJI and 3DRobotics were beginning to change drones from a niche hobby, enjoyed mostly by dorks, to a global phenomenon. Before this time, if you wanted to fly a drone, chances are that you were paying a lot of money for it, or you were building it yourself. Prior to the birth of Sky-Specs, when we were still university students working on unmanned aerial vehicle research, and even well into the first two years of the life of the company, we fell into this "do it yourself" camp of drone users. We were literally building everything. A flight controller, electronic speed controllers, repackaged batteries, and carbon fiber enclosures—nothing was beyond the purview of our custom drone integration efforts. We were the typical "solution looking for a problem." We knew we wanted to make an autonomous drone, we just didn't know who would care yet. By the way, it's important that you know who cares about your product and *why* they care.

EVOLUTION 1: HARDWARE RETAIL TO HARDWARE RENTAL

I'm not sure if the term "product hubris" has been used before, but if it hasn't, I call dibs and hereby coin it. SkySpecs had a very bad case of product hubris in its early days. Departments of transportation, utility companies, amusement parks, police forces, fire rescue—we thought everyone was going to buy our drones. If we built it, they would come, or so we thought. Without truly understanding even a single customer, we were trying to build a platform for *all* of them.

My statements above are not intended to discourage you from building a "platform." Platform companies and technologies can be extremely valuable due to their broad applicability and their resilience to being dethroned by competition. However, even with platform products, it's a good idea to build the product for just one person first, and then expand to a more broad appeal.[7]

Fund-raising forces you to think critically about your business. More specifically, investors will ask you poignant questions that will force you to think more critically. This was exactly the case for Sky-Specs as we prepared to raise our $600,000 seed round in 2013. These investors, along with pretty much every investor we've ever spoken with, had a few things they asked for in initial diligence. One of those things is *not* a business plan. Please, for the love of God, do not write a business plan. Any investor who is asking you for a thirty-page business plan is the wrong kind of investor to work with a startup. Sorry, it's old school.

We *were* asked for a financial model and three-to-five-year projections. Regarding financial projections and models for early-stage startups—they will be absolutely, unequivocally, truly, and terribly *wrong*. And that's okay! Investors aren't looking at your financial projections to actually forecast your future. They're looking at them to understand what your assumptions are, to see whether you understand the variables that will make or break you, and to understand how well you've thought through how your business will operate at scale.

The scene: Lightning fills the sky, a crash of thunder, the clouds break, and a heavenly light beams down on the Kindle, paperback, or hardcover copy of this book, in which you've been so unfortunate to meet me.

---

7 One of my favorite books on the topic of building for a specific customer before building for all of them is Geoffrey Moore's *Crossing the Chasm: Marketing and Selling High-Tech Products to Mainstream Customers* (2006). I highly recommend it.

BEHOLD, TOM'S 10 FINANCIAL MODELING COMMANDMENTS:

1. Thou shalt know thy numbers.
2. Thou shalt lead with thy assumptions.
3. Thou shalt not argue with investors about the results of math.
4. Thou shalt bring all disagreements back to the assumptions.
5. Thou shalt not be too confident in thy financial projections, for they are wrong.
6. Thou shalt plan for the worst, and hope for the best.
7. Thou shalt not have an unbalanced balance sheet, for thou shalt look like an ass.
8. Thou shalt not present financial models with a negative cash balance, for that is impossible.
9. Thou shalt not include pennies in thy financial model.
10. Thou shalt not email financial projections until such projections are discussed in a meeting with an investor.

Amid fund-raising, Danny and I, along with pretty much everyone else in the business at the time, were discussing our financial and business model. We concluded that we would be leaving a ton of value on the table if we were to sell our automated drone systems outright. After all, you could satisfy all our industry's inspection needs with just a handful of drones. A recurring revenue model was necessary. With that, our business model changed from one of hardware sales to one of hardware rental. We were going to charge by the hour, or by the asset, for people to use our drones and conduct inspections. It was with this business model that we charged forward in our seed round. We never sold a damn thing during the time we were funded by our seed round, but that was our plan nevertheless.

EVOLUTION 2: FROM HARDWARE RENTAL TO SUBSCRIPTIONS

There was a combination of circumstances that forced us to once again rethink our business model, not the least of which was that our seed round was pretty much gone and nothing was working. Perhaps this was another one of those moments of clarity forced upon us by a moment of desperation and vulnerability.

It was the summer of 2014. By this time, we had mastered the entrepreneurial art of making money disappear and having nothing to show for it. Given that we would soon be out of cash, we needed a way to generate excitement, and maybe even a bit of revenue, extremely quickly, or else we'd be applying for jobs in the next six months or less. We posed this question: "What is the *bare minimum* amount of technology that it would take for someone to do an inspection?"

Entrepreneurs should constantly be asking *why* they're doing something, and when the answer is, "because we always have," the alarm should sound. Let's just say SkySpecs was a bit slow on the uptake. We had spent the better part of two years developing an almost entirely custom drone; meanwhile other companies in the drone industry had commoditized *most* of what we had been spending our time on. Product hubris strikes again.

The answer to our inquiry, and what we determined to be our "minimum viable product," was a collision avoidance system for drones.[8] We figured that if you could make a drone crash proof, then you could pretty much put the controls in anyone's hands. Any Joe Schmoe would reasonably be able to use a drone to inspect a wind turbine or other machine, provided that our onboard systems would keep them and the drone safe. Our business model would be subscription based. We'd

---

8   There was no such thing as an off-the-shelf collision avoidance system for drones back in 2014, so our thought process was semi-novel at the time. Fast forward two years, and most new DJI drones come equipped with a collision avoidance system. Ideas are cheap.

provide the hardware for our collision avoidance system for free, and drone operators would pay a monthly subscription fee to keep their drone crash proof. It was almost like an insurance policy, but much less reliable!

The collision avoidance system would be called "Guardian." It was a drop-in (I use that term very liberally here) module that you could attach to any off-the-shelf drone to make the drone automatically see and avoid obstacles in its environment. The concept was pretty neat, in my *totally unbiased* opinion. Over the next few months we developed a prototype, made a YouTube video, and "launched" our product at the TechCrunch Hardware Battlefield, as part of the Consumer Electronics Show. Guardian generated so much excitement that it would prove—after almost two and a half years as a company—to be the medium by which we'd see our very first commercial traction. After our launch video and pitch at Hardware Battlefield, just north of forty companies signed up for our "Early Adopter Program," basically a beta program that allowed early-development access to the Guardian system. This was a major turning point for the company. We started to understand what it meant to be focused, and what a minimum viable product really was.

Danny (our CEO) on stage at the Hardware Battlefield pitching the first version of Guardian, our collision avoidance system, atop a drone. Ain't she a beaut'? (The drone, not Danny.)

In connection with our new direction with the Guardian product, we were accepted into TechStars and won a $500,000 business competition in November 2014. I'm quite bullish on business competitions for companies at a particular stage in their growth, as I'll describe later. With the $500,000 in funding, we were positioned to survive for another year—a luxury that would permit us to get through our Early Adopter Program and set ourselves up for a strong Series A in the following year.

EVOLUTION 3: FROM SUBSCRIPTIONS TO SERVICE

We shipped our first three Guardian units to early adopters in the spring of 2015. Our first three customers were relatively small professional drone operators with existing customer bases in industrial inspection and cinematography applications. The initial feedback was—*meh*. I think it was a combination of the fact that installation of our Guardian system was still too complicated and that collision avoidance isn't something you know you need until you need it. None of our customers ever even used the product.

We inherently knew that our big opportunity wasn't with these smaller companies. It was—we thought—with large, industrial engineering firms that would have dozens, or even hundreds, of drones in their fleet. We struggled, however, to sell Guardian to these kinds of customers.

Here's how the conversation would usually go (I'm ad-libbing a bit):

Customer: Hi. This is Blah-dee-blah with big company Blarg-blarg. What's up?

SkySpecs Sales: We have a drone force field. You don't want your drones to crash, right?

Customer: Well, yes, absolutely. We'd love that, but we have a few other questions.

SkySpecs Sales: Go right ahead.

Customer: What batteries do I buy? What drone do I buy? What cameras do I buy? How do I get clearance to fly? Who can I hire to fly this thing? Where does the data go? Et cetera. Et cetera.

Industrial customers wanted collision avoidance, but they needed so much more to make commercial drone use a reality for their business. Armed with this new understanding, SkySpecs pivoted its third and, tentatively, final time to become a service business. We now offer an entire software-enabled inspection solution for enterprise customers. Although our product offering has changed, our core customer segments and business model have remained consistent ever since.

RAISING MONEY THROUGH BUSINESS COMPETITIONS, GRANTS, AND GOVERNMENT PROGRAMS: THREE NOT ENTIRELY USELESS WAYS TO SPEND YOUR TIME

You'll find that many entrepreneurs and investors scoff at the idea of participating in business competitions. After all, you're supposed to be building your business, not playing house with a bunch of other wannabes, right? At SkySpecs we had a different, much more positive experience with business competitions. I'll share a serendipitous outcome from our business competition days, and then I'll get off my soapbox.

Remember how I said that early on in our days as a company, we didn't know who would care about our autonomous robots? Well, we thought state and federal Departments of Transportation were going to care a great deal about this awesome drone we were building, so much so, that we hypothesized they would fund us with grant money.

Here's the funny thing about the Departments of Transportation, or any government agency, for that matter: they can't just *give* you money. They need to put out what's known as a "request for proposals," or an RFP, that allows anyone with a budget and a plan to bid on the project. You can be an integral part of the construction of that RFP, but nothing is guaranteed once it's out in the world. SkySpecs had maneuvered its way into advising on one such RFP for drones to inspect bridges. We thought we had it in the bag, but we ultimately ended up losing it. One day after we received notice that we had lost the grant, in the wake of this devastation that had befallen us, we were pitching in a business competition geared toward clean technology.

We got involved in this business competition by pure serendipity. An advisor of ours had suggested we apply. All we had to do was tell the competition organizers that we would be inspecting wind turbines instead of bridges. Boom, now we were clean tech! Winning this competition led to so much more than the $50,000 grand prize. It triggered a butterfly effect in our company that would make Ashton Kutcher proud (apparently, he's the lead actor in *The Butterfly Effect*). What started as an application on a whim led us to connect with people at the Michigan Economic Development Corporation, one of whom was organizing a sponsored booth for startups at the American Wind Energy Association (AWEA) trade show.[9] At AWEA, we met a company whose affiliation and commitment to future work with us pushed our Series A investors over the top. To this day, our company is focused entirely on automating wind turbine blade inspections. We have paying customers and we're positioned to dominate the industry we landed. It can all be traced back to that room where our advisor convinced us to apply for a business competition by telling us, "Well, you should just inspect wind turbines." Dammit, Norm, you were right. I should note that, while I am bullish on business competitions for new companies, not all business competitions are created equal. They come with different entry requirements, classes of competition, and structure and stipulations for the prizes.

For competitions with smaller prizes, they are often grants that come with zero obligations. These are the kinds of winnings that you can use to buy yourself a seat at the World Series of Poker and no one will have much to say about it, except that you're a bit of a douche for doing so. Larger prizes justifiably come with more requirements. For example, the $500,000 competition SkySpecs won in 2014 was a $100,000 grant, along with $400,000 of convertible debt investment with rather friendly terms. Because this competition was partially funded by the state of Michigan, SkySpecs was also required to remain a Michigan company for some time, or else the cash would need to be repaid (this

---

9   Trade shows will often charge you an arm and a leg for a bottom-of-the-barrel booth off the beaten trail, or your first-born child for a nice booth in a central location, so a sponsored booth was a big deal. We wouldn't have gone to the trade show without this support.

wasn't an issue for us, as we're quite happy where we are situated). In some cases, the prizes from these competitions aren't cash but can be equally valuable. Marketing firms, lawyers, accountants, and other service providers will often donate in-kind services as an award for the winners. These sorts of prizes allow entrepreneurs to work with a prepaid service provider, while the service provider works to gain the entrepreneurs future *paid* business. As you can see, the differences in prize form and function are driven largely by how the competitions are funded. Before you get too involved with a business competition, make sure you understand what you're competing for. Remember, if it sounds too good to be true, it probably is.

Business competitions have more to offer than just funding. They also tend to be a central gathering place for entire communities of entrepreneurs, investors, and advisors. The networking opportunities at these types of events are abundant. Entrepreneurs should also be practicing their pitch delivery every chance they get. Business competitions are a relatively judgment-free environment in which to do so. Put yourself out there, folks. You never know what crazy opportunities will come up.

CHAPTER EIGHT

LAURA D'ASARO

Cofounder and Chief Operations Officer, Six Foods

>>>> ABOUT LAURA

Laura D'Asaro is the cofounder and chief operations officer of Six Foods, a company that works to normalize insect consumption as a sustainable source of protein. Laura's journey in social entrepreneurship began at age fifteen, when she raised $14,000 through her lemonade stand to build a playground for her community. At nineteen, she cofounded Wema, Inc., an education nonprofit in Kenya. At age twenty-three, after graduating from Harvard, she cofounded Six Foods with Rose Wong (another founder featured in this book).

Laura's inspiration for Six Foods stemmed from being an off-and-on vegetarian, struggling with the moral and environmental aspects of eating meat. While traveling in Tanzania, she ate a caterpillar from a street vendor and realized that insects could be the sustainable source of protein she was looking for. Laura sent an article about insect consumption to Rose, her roommate at Harvard. Their experimentation resulted in a cage full of escaped crickets hopping around their dorm room, but eventually Six Foods was born. In addition to founding her company, Laura has broken multiple world records to raise money for charitable causes, including crawling one mile in the fastest time and creating the longest book domino chain.

Laura D'Asaro has been named to *Forbes*' 30 under 30 for social entrepreneurs.

When people ask me how I can afford to live in downtown San Francisco, I smile, because it is actually the cheapest rent I have ever paid: $300 per month to be exact. Don't get me wrong; there are caveats. First, I live with seventy other people; second, I sleep in a bunk bed. My housemates are mostly people in their twenties and thirties, who come from all over the world. People have described my living situation as a dorm for adults, and it is not without its downsides. Sometimes I walk downstairs and discover the floor is sticky from late-night partying or there are dirty dishes in the sink. There is also the constant frustration of only having a tiny drawer in the refrigerator. However, despite all of the drawbacks, I don't doubt for a second that living where I do is one of the best decisions I could have made.

Let me back up and explain how I got here. When my cofounder and I first started working on Six Foods full time, money was the obvious challenge. She turned down a full-time job offer at Microsoft, and I moved across the country to be with her. When you are trying to make a living by getting people to eat bugs, investors don't exactly throw money at you—they're not so easily convinced that you have discovered the next big thing. We knew we would face a long battle, trying to persuade Americans that insects really are the food of the future. However, we believed that the fight would be worth it.

When I was a vegetarian, the health and sustainability benefits of insects-as-food won me over, and I was convinced these benefits would win over others as well. For example, to make a pound of beef, you must raise a cow, which takes over 2,000 gallons of water, whereas raising a pound of crickets only takes about a gallon. From land usage to greenhouse gas emissions, insect protein is orders of magnitudes better for the environment than any animal protein sources. By putting cricket flour into a fun and accessible form, we felt like we finally had a way to get people excited about eating insects, but that change wasn't going to happen overnight. Over the last three years, we both have taken on a lot of small side jobs. We have tutored, babysat, walked and watched dogs, and helped with college essays. Through everything, we have come up with three main strategies to survive on an entrepreneur's budget.

1. LIVE WITH OTHER PEOPLE

Living with other people is good for a few reasons. First of all, there is power in numbers when it comes to reducing your rent. If you live alone in a studio, you are definitely going to pay more than if you live with one roommate, and even more than if you share a four bedroom. My cofounder currently lives with seven people. The other advantage to living with a lot of people is that you can ask them to help with or test whatever you are working on. When my cofounder and I needed help with Facebook ads, we turned to one of my seventy housemates who had a full-time job creating social media advertisements. When we had an issue with our website, I had fifteen coders on hand who were happy to help. After living in my "dorm for adults" for just over a year, I now have over 150 friends with their own skill sets and networks to come to the rescue when we need them the most.

Living with other people also means there are everyday things that you don't have to worry about. Need an extra egg? Can't find your laptop charger? Someone has you covered. When my phone was lost, people were eager to let me borrow theirs. And this "live with other people" thing really extends to the larger lesson of the sharing economy. More and more companies are instituting family plans, and you don't have to be related to qualify. Over the last few years I have used everything from shared cars to bicycles, Netflix accounts, music services, and cellphone accounts to make these services affordable.

2. COMBINE YOUR JOB WITH SOMETHING ELSE

When I started this company, my first job was babysitting. I love kids and the work paid relatively well. But by the time I took the bus to a job, babysat, and came back, the work took much longer than I planned. Although I was paid for two hours, the work took at least three hours out of my day. Not to mention that by the time I got back, I was exhausted, often covered in sticky substances, and I didn't feel like working on my company at all. On top of all that, I still had responsibilities at home and friends who wanted to hang out.

When a position opened to join a housing co-op and help manage it, I jumped on the opportunity. Suddenly, my life became so much simpler. There were other benefits, too. Because I got paid to work at the place where I live, I was forced to create stronger relationships with my roommates than I otherwise would have. Before, I had to go out of my way to hang out with friends; now I had seventy right where I lived and worked. Movie nights, playing board games, or just cooking or eating a meal together gave me the stability and social life that I had been missing.

Tying your second job to an entrepreneurial goal can give you the motivation to succeed. For example, a friend took on a second job doing social media for a professor, and she was able to apply what she was learning to her own business. Take on jobs that help you. Do you like to exercise? Instead of spending an hour at the gym and then going to work a second job, why not get a job making deliveries on your bicycle? Want to learn Excel better? Take on a job where you will use Excel. Second jobs can be a great opportunity to add to, instead of take away from, your own business.

3. SET A TIME LIMIT

When you first start a business, the goals can be a bit amorphous. Your aim may be to grow the business as big as possible. For us, the objective was to normalize eating insects. These big, amorphous goals can take a long time to achieve and, for someone struggling to make ends meet, they can seem infinitely long term.

I suggest making a finite timeline. For us, the timeline was one year. We made a deal with our parents—they would help support us for a year. We promised to find a way to support ourselves after that time or move onto "real" jobs if we couldn't. This short timeline was helpful in two ways. First of all, it gave us the pressure we needed to succeed. Like many things we take for granted, the prospect of not having the opportunity to continue our work made us more determined to succeed. Second, giving yourself an end date makes the sacrifices more tolerable and makes you feel like you are working toward an end, one way or the other. We were lucky that we had our parents to help us. We have friends who literally lived on rice and beans or ramen for extended periods of time when they were first starting out, and it can be emotionally exhausting to not know how long you will have to survive like that.

FINAL THOUGHTS

There is no doubt that starting a business is hard. However, there are ways to get through the financial issues that face so many companies in the early stages. I honestly believe that having to take on a second job and living with seventy people ultimately made our business stronger and more successful. The early stage is a time to test your idea, your dedication, and your willingness to step out of your comfort zone, and if you are able to do that, then you and your business can come out stronger for it.

▶ WHAT ARE SALES AND MARKETING TACTICS THAT HAVE WORKED FOR YOUR COMPANY?

When I was seventeen, my grandmother died of cancer. I learned then the harsh reality that caring about your cause or idea in itself isn't enough to get others to care. It sounds obvious, but somehow, up until that point, I believed that passion and hard work would get me pretty much anywhere. After my grandmother passed, I was trying to find some meaning in it all and a way to do something to help, so I joined Relay for Life, a fund-raiser for cancer research. It is a twenty-four-hour event at a local running track to celebrate those who had had cancer with games, speeches, and a luminaria.

Leading up to the big day, teams competed to raise as much money as possible for the American Cancer Society, so I started asking friends and family for donations. After raising a few dollars from my mom and dad and some money from a couple of aunts and uncles that caved to my begging, the response to my fund-raising was pretty quiet. I wasn't getting anywhere and I was starting to feel pretty guilty about bothering my friends for money.

During this time, I was flipping through a world record book at a bookstore and I started dreaming. Every kid wants to break a world record, and I had one in particular in mind: the fastest time to crawl one mile. My older brother had gone through some physical therapy as a child. One part of his therapy required him to crawl to increase his coordination. As his little sister, I had of course followed along. Therefore, I thought that I had a slight advantage over the average person. I could break the record at the event and maybe help bring more awareness to cancer research.

I started training. I made a website that linked to my Relay for Life donation page and I wore a sign on my back while practicing. What happened shocked me. Complete strangers started to care. People stopped me every day on my crawls and asked what I was doing and how they could help. The local media even did a piece on me and the donations started pouring in. I couldn't wrap my mind around what was going on. By the time I broke the record at the relay, six months later, I had raised $5,000 for cancer research.

Laura D'Asaro breaking the world record for the fastest one-mile crawl.

That was my first glimpse into the power of PR and marketing, but at the time I didn't see it as marketing at all. I just wanted to find fun and creative ways to get people excited about doing good. I took this philosophy and applied it to helping out my local food bank. Instead of doing a canned food drive, I organized a Halloween candy drive, collecting one thousand pounds of Halloween candy for local food banks and getting the attention of the local news.

While my ideas drew attention to my causes, they also helped me stand out during the college application process, and I was accepted at Harvard. However, it wasn't until years later that I was really able to put a name to what had happened. During my sophomore year at Harvard I came across a theory that became my life philosophy, called the Fun Theory. For example, in a subway in Stockholm, Sweden, proponents of the Fun Theory asked the question: Can we get more people to take the stairs by making it fun? To test the theory, they made each step into a piano key, so when people walked up or down, they made music. And the answer was, yes! After the piano stairs were installed, 66% more people took the stairs than the escalator. The idea behind the Fun Theory is that fun is the easiest way to change people's behavior for the better.

I used this theory to promote the reading program at my local library by helping them build the world's longest book domino chain. My friends and I promoted recycling at Harvard by using move-in boxes to build a giant box fort. Then we resold the boxes for move-out in the spring.

Promoting recycling with a giant fort made of moving boxes.

Over the years, I keep coming back to the Fun Theory as the corner-stone of marketing and have learned three main lessons from trying to implement it.

1. THINK BIGGER

An easy mistake is to focus too closely on your brand or mission. At Six Foods, early on we made the mistake of focusing way too much on bugs. Our mission is to get Americans eating insects, so we felt like everything we did had to be about bugs and eating bugs. We posted recipes about eating bugs to our blog, tweeted facts about where in the world people eat bugs, and posted an infographic on Facebook about all the bugs you are already eating without knowing it. The posts were interesting enough, and we got a few followers, but we just weren't getting the response we were hoping for. We realized the reason pretty quickly: the harsh reality was that, again, people didn't care. Eating insects, in and of itself, was not something people really wanted to read about. Unless our audience was entomologists, the average person probably lost interest after about the second entry. We weren't creating content that our audience could connect to. We had to think bigger.

Answering this question is about thinking beyond the mission. What values or ideas does your company embody that a larger audi-ence can connect to? We came up with the themes of being different and helping people see the world in new ways. Based on these themes, we created content and came up with the slogan "Forget Normal. Eat Bugs." We could then connect our brand with people all over who were doing cool things off the beaten path, and suddenly we had a lot more to write about than bugs.

2. TAKE YOUR MARKETING OFFLINE TO STAND OUT

Today, it is easy to feel like you can run your whole business from your computer; but real interactions with real people can be more powerful than online marketing. I was reminded of this lesson recently, on my way to a trade show.

At these shows, I dress up in a cricket costume to bring attention to our brand, but getting the costume across the country was posing an issue. At the airport, after checking the suitcase that held the body of the costume, I was left with the cricket head. I didn't want to pay fifty dollars for a second checked bag, and airline restrictions allow only one carry-on. However, there were no rules about hats, so I wore my cricket helmet with antennas through the airport. I wore it in the line before we reached security, put it through the X-ray machine, and wore it all the way to the gate. I continued to wear it on the airplane.

I guess you don't see too many crickets while flying. In the sterile environment of the airport, I really stood out. People wanted to take pictures; they wanted to know what I was doing and why I was dressed the way I was. The helmet even made an impression on fellow travelers attending the trade show. For days after, I had people coming up to me at the show, telling me they had seen me on the plane.

From this experience, my business partner and I launched an idea. What if I wore the cricket costume all the time? I started wearing it on the streets, to the club on Friday night, to the gym, and even on dates. Everywhere I went, people laughed, took pictures, and wanted to know more. We realized that these days people are bombarded with advertisements on their computers, but they are often delighted when you can transform their day in some small way by making it more fun and exciting. These positive experiences can really help your brand stand out.

These days, people search out things to take pictures of, that they can share with their social media networks. The great thing about creating live content is that your fans help share it. They do the social media work for you. Having someone share a picture of themselves with me in a cricket costume is one hundred times more powerful than our brand sharing a picture of me in a cricket costume.

My cricket helmet at the airport.

3. IF YOU WOULDN'T SHARE IT, DON'T POST IT

This is a simple test for a social media post, newsletter, or really any marketing effort at all. Before your content goes live, ask yourself this: If I saw this online, would I share it with a friend? If the answer is no, then it isn't good enough. Period. The point of marketing is to make people WANT to pay attention to what you are doing, and shareability is a good test of that.

We realized that despite our Philosophy of Fun, too often we were failing this test. For example, for Halloween, we posted a pumpkin with our triangle Chirps for eyes and a mouth instead of cut-outs. It was cute, even pretty, but it ultimately failed the test. The problem again went back to lesson one: think bigger. The pumpkin with my product for eyes was too self-promotional without having a bigger theme people could connect with. Next Halloween, I plan to trick friends with a giant spider attached to a remote control car. It's still about bugs, so it connects, but it will be something people actually want to see.

The pumpkin that no one cared to share.

THE TAKEAWAY

The line between advertising and entertainment is blurry. The best advertising gets people excited about even the most boring topics. Look at airplane safety videos. In just a few years, they have gone from a normal presentation to videos with musical ensembles, animation, and even all-star athletes. Airlines found out that the best way to get people to watch the video—and keep people safe—is by making something that people actually WANT to watch. Getting people to want to engage with your marketing material has to be your goal as well. The best way to get people to try your product is to connect it to something they care about. Red Bull decided their audience likes high-flying stunts, so they sponsor extreme athletes. Ever notice how many puppies and babies there are in ads? This idea of connection is the reason why. Figure out what your audience likes. Get out there, hit the streets, do something crazy, and make a difference by having more fun.

CHAPTER NINE

MIKE TOWNSEND

Cofounder and Chief Operations Officer, HomeHero

⟫⟫⟫ ABOUT MIKE

Mike Townsend is the cofounder and COO of HomeHero, a home care provider that leverages smart technology and human compassion to extend the health system into the home. After graduating from the University of Connecticut, Mike moved to Singapore to work as a design engineer for Brookstone (owned by the Singaporean corporation OSIM), then as a mechanical engineer at Exelis Corporation designing radar defense and surveillance systems.

Mike began his startup career by founding ZingCheckout in 2011, which was later acquired by BigCommerce. He then founded Flowtab in 2012 with Kyle Hill, which didn't work out, but made Kyle and Mike a team. Together they founded HomeHero in 2013. Under Mike's leadership, HomeHero has provided over one million hours of care to thousands of families and raised $23 million in venture capital since its start. He was named to the 2016 *Forbes* "30 Under 30" list in Health Care and actively speaks at health care and technology events worldwide.

Mike hosts *Around the Coin*, a podcast discussing startup news, marketplaces, and behavioral philosophy. He is an active writer on *Medium* and is a contributor to American City Business Journals. Mike is a competitive Ironman triathlete and is training to break the world record for the fastest marathon while dribbling a basketball. Mike enjoys meeting other highly motivated entrepreneurs and brainstorming ideas to make the world a better place.

Our product is a service, specifically the service of a caregiver in the home helping a patient in their most vulnerable time of need. We hire caregivers, "Heroes," and use custom web and mobile applications to help send them to a home to provide care in the form of transportation, meal preparation, companionship, etc.

We have a ten-person product and engineering team that focuses on three audiences:

- Families: We create products that help us deliver a better home care experience.
- Heroes: We focus on making home care a fulfilling and exciting career for our caregivers.
- Health Systems: We build tools for hospitals that improve care coordination and patient outcomes.

Our work is never one-dimensional, though—we must also build software that is intuitive for our care management team and other partners to use.

OUR APPROACH TO OUTSOURCING

Our team has a few contracted engineers in Argentina who work remotely. Our outsourcing tools have certainly changed over the years. In the early days, when the company was just Kyle and me, we would use Skype and deploy code directly to the production server. Today our engineers use tools such as Slack for communication, Tower for version control, and Sublime for text editing, which makes working together very easy and highly effective.

We are all humans, hard-coded with the desire to seek a deeper purpose in our work and to feel that we are contributing to something bigger than ourselves. Unlike our other employees who work out of our office in Santa Monica, California, our Argentinian engineers are remote most of the year, so we pay particularly close attention to integrating them into our culture and making them feel a part of the team. For example, we have a tradition that every Friday at 5:00 p.m. we do Friday Trivia over the #team channel in Slack.

The start of "Friday Trivia!" on Slack

This is a time to take a break and chat with each other as friends. This tradition helps build a culture of equality, fun, and camaraderie no matter where you're physically located.

As part of our culture, we believe in building a caring and engaged team. Every year we bring everyone in the company, from all over the world, together for a company retreat where we highlight individual and shared accomplishments over the past year—and have a little fun as well. After our first year, in December 2014, we decided to go on our first offsite retreat as a team. We found a twelve-bedroom mansion on Airbnb in Truckee, California, which fit our team perfectly. We rented a big, white cargo van and drove everyone from the Reno airport out into the country.

The HomeHero team on retreat in Truckee, CA, 2014

The retreat was two days full of activities designed to inspire creativity and brainstorming. The first night, we all gathered around the beautiful fireplace and everyone shared a childhood story that was special to them. This was an incredible experience that had us all laughing and crying. Everyone really opened up.

This time together and away from the office also allowed us space to define our mission and ourselves. We collectively developed our core company values—which are now posted all over the office.

Office wall displaying four of our company values

This statement of values serves as a foundation for hiring and working at HomeHero. We spent a lot of time digesting and defining our brand as well as our core differentiators. It was very valuable to allow people in each department the opportunity to learn about the challenges that each person faces in their role.

The subtle and incredibly valuable aspect of this experience came during the time everyone spent together working on non-work-related tasks. We cooked together and spent evenings drinking and discussing the future of technology and health care, as well as existential questions. In hindsight, I think the bonds we created during this time allowed us to function as a tight team years later.

OUR APPROACH TO HIRING

Deciding whom to hire is the most important thing a founding team does. Founders heavily influence culture, but at the end of the day, the people you bring on the team have the biggest impact. We take a conservative approach to hiring and weigh our options carefully before opening a new position. We spend an incredible amount of energy on recruiting, and we interview 125 candidates for every one that we hire.

When we interview candidates, we spend less time on the specifics of their past and think more about their potential, culture fit, and ambition. The team you have today will be solving problems that look a lot different in five years, especially in the earlier stages of the company when challenges change more frequently. A team that learns together and builds upon each other's strengths usually wins in the end.

The challenge is, how do you decide what questions to ask in the short time you have with a person so you can make the important decision of whether to invite them to be part of your team? We generally break down interviews into a few sections and pay closer attention to the tiny indicators that tell a story.

First, we think about the **pre-interview phase**. Did this person apply through a job board or get an introduction from someone we trust? It's always more powerful to have a simple email introduction from someone in our network than it is to apply through a job board. It's a simple way to differentiate yourself by creating a sense of value through our mutual connection. Networking is important.

The introduction phase, the exchanging of pleasantries in the beginning and the end of a meeting, is the most underappreciated time in business. This is true for every interaction, especially interviews. People are off the record with their guard down, thinking casually and honestly. This is the time to learn what motivates the person, where their passions lie, which dictates many of their life decisions. It's an art to get to know someone quickly.

The background phase: Generally I prefer to start interviews by saying, "So, tell me about yourself." The question is open ended and interviewees will lean on the experiences that have had the most impact on their life. Notice how they value experiences, whether they give credit to others over themselves, and use the phrase "we did this," versus "I did this."

Then, I use two types of questions to get more information:

- **Situational questions**: I like to dive right into specific questions about challenges the company is facing to learn how they would solve them.
- **Personal questions**: I like asking simple questions such as what a person's hobbies are.

References: I've found that references from past coworkers tend to tell a better story than references from past managers. When talking to references, try to ask generalized questions that have no positive or negative answer, such as, "Do they like to work quickly to hit deadlines ahead of schedule or work carefully to ensure the delivery of near perfect work?" The majority of the time, references won't speak negatively about a person because they have a relationship so your challenge is to discover their strengths, weaknesses, working style, and values by framing questions in a subjective light.

Aim at the heart: The success of a person at work is most impacted by the level of dedication and energy they apply. Inspired employees do great work consistently, because they feel a deep connection to the mission of the team and the role they play within it. The goal of the interviewer is to understand what drives the candidate, what kind of impact they want to have on the word, the skills they want to learn, and the legacy they want to leave. The magic here is to find the questions that get to someone's heart and get them to open up.

Once, journalist Cal Fussman was told his scheduled interview with Mikhail Gorbachev would be cut down from sixty minutes to ten. Fussman opened the interview with this question: "What's the best lesson your father ever taught you?" Gorbachev answered with a story about when his father got called up to fight in World War II, and he began to reflect on his childhood and his life. Ten minutes later, when the publicist interrupted to stop the interview, Gorbachev said, "No. I want to talk to him." Fussman later realized, "If I hadn't aimed my first question at his heart, the interview would have been over in a few minutes."[10] Instead, because Fussman asked the right question, he got a great interview.

---

10   Cal Fussman told this story for his 2016 talk for the Shine Movement (theshinemovement.org) titled "From the Heart," available at https://www.youtube.com/watch?v=uDpfLCXhXaA.

APPROACH TO MANAGING EMPLOYEES

At HomeHero, we constantly remind ourselves of our nine company values and make a conscious effort to live by these values in our daily lives. We hold reviews, or "360s," with each employee one month after they join the company and every six months thereafter to ensure they are both as happy and productive as can be.

These meetings are especially important, as they help catch issues when they are small. Usually when we feel unhappy with something in our work environment, it's because of something very small and changeable: how someone acted toward us without realizing it, or a lack of appreciation for the work we did, for example. It's so important for employers to make the effort to stay in touch with the morale of each employee in order to bring out the best in each person.

At HomeHero we also have team meetings, held every other Tuesday for one hour, where our whole team gets together in person. The meeting kicks off with one of the founders, Kyle or me, giving a recap of the business over the last two weeks and any changes coming down the pipeline. We break the meeting into three parts:

1. **Founder update and company vision**: What's new with the company?

2. **General department updates**: What things are affecting other people in the company?

3. **Acts of gratitude**: What exceptional things have team members done?

Unlike many tech companies, HomeHero has a very diverse team, which is a major asset for us. Having people with different cultural and ethnic backgrounds helps provide unique perspectives and insight, which in turn helps to improve the overall patient experience.

Like every other company, however, HomeHero has employees who go through life changes and decide to move on to do other things.

I often think back to a story my father would tell me. My father's boss would actually encourage him to take interviews for other jobs. His boss would say, "If you found something you'd rather do, you should do it because life's too short to be working somewhere you're not happiest. On the other hand, if you don't find anything better, you'll have a much deeper appreciation for the job you currently have." So, rather than try to restrain people from seeking other opportunities, we encourage them to explore every potential path in life with the confidence that they'll appreciate HomeHero even more.

Problems that do arise between employees most often stem from an emotional threat or inadequacy. Disagreements most often happen at the end of the day when mental attention is lowest and people feel tired and hungry. Sometimes Kyle, my cofounder, and I argue about trivial things like how to structure the titles of Google Drive folders or what kinds of art to have on the wall at the office. The best time to practice debate techniques and argument styles is when the stakes are low. Trust is the key to building an environment where people can push each other and intensely debate ideas. If there is trust that the debate is not personal and people are open to all ideas, then the best solutions will surface.

OPERATIONAL CHALLENGES WHEN TRANSITIONING TO FOCUS ON ENTERPRISE

HomeHero has come a long way and faced big challenges, just like any other company. From an operational perspective, our biggest challenge was our transition in 2016 from an emphasis on direct-to-consumer marketing to a focus on larger enterprise contracts with health systems.

For our first three years, we built an incredible experience for patients coming directly to us, and we focused our product and operational attention on that alone. When we launched our Enterprise model, our entire business changed—we began selling to health systems.

In April 2016, Cedars-Sinai Medical Center, one of the largest and most prestigious hospitals in the country, invested in HomeHero to explore opportunities to help patients immediately after they are discharged from a hospital stay. Because Cedars-Sinai was our first major health system, we had big opportunities on our plate—ones that came with big challenges.

To become a trusted hospital partner, we achieved full HIPAA compliance, transitioned our Heroes to W-2 employees, hired a chief nursing officer, chief medical officer, and a team of clinical case managers—all within a four-month window. These transitions presented huge challenges for our team, and I'm incredibly proud about how efficiently we were able to make them.

➤ HOW HAVE YOU DEALT WITH FAILURES?

B efore HomeHero, I was involved with a number of different projects and companies. Some worked out as planned, while others didn't. When things do not go as planned, embrace the obstacle and use it to your advantage. I reject the idea that anything is either a complete failure or success. Everything you do is valuable and can help advance you to your next goal. Each project is an opportunity to learn, to meet new people, to build a reputation, and to discover the next step in your career.

In August 2010, I moved to California to work for an aerospace company called Exelis, where I was a mechanical design engineer designing and developing radar systems. During my two years there, I worked nights and weekends inside a coworking entrepreneurship studio called CoLoft. It was my time at CoLoft that propelled me into entrepreneurship. I met incredible people, including both of my future cofounders and the majority of my close friends. Putting yourself in a supportive environment where people share your ambitions and values helps make the transition process much easier. We spent evenings pitching each other and whiteboarding out possible business ideas. We had big dreams and encouraged each other to go after them. My first startup idea was called AirPair, which would allow people to choose their seatmate on a flight. AirPair never took off, but we learned how to incorporate, build the first version of the product, get press articles, and get in the door to pitch to airlines and investors. It put me on the entrepreneurial path and led me to the next project.

We are all hardwired in the limbic system of our brains to resist change, specifically big change like starting a new company and leaving behind stable income. To help reduce change anxiety, it's helpful to build as much momentum as possible. Reading blogs, writing answers on Quora, meeting people on Twitter, listening to entrepreneurial podcasts, reading or listening to books, taking coffee meetings with people to pitch ideas, and trying to absorb as much of the culture as possible will give you momentum to make a commitment.

However, it's always tough to know when to quit your day job and commit to starting a startup. I think the decision should be most heavily weighed on the people you have on your team. When you find brilliant people that complement your skill set and are willing to dive in to solve a real problem, you should probably go for it. If you're working in another field, it's more important to jump in, take the opening, and press on than it is to wait for the perfect opportunity. This is the case for anyone who achieves long-term success. Your first project and first few years get you in the game; they allow you to learn the rules and cut your teeth. From then on, it's just a matter of perseverance to make things happen.

Coloft, 11:00 p.m., November 2012

When I started working with Nate Stewart at ZingCheckout, a web-based point-of-sale startup, I knew we'd make a great team, so I decided to dive in. We worked together day and night to grow the business, selling to local merchants during the day, and working on product and software in the evening. We hustled hard to raise angel funding and moved the company to Austin, Texas. After a few years, we sold the company to BigCommerce.

After ZingCheckout, I moved up to San Francisco to work with Kyle Hill on Flowtab, a mobile drink-ordering app. Flowtab allowed you to order drinks in bars and have them delivered directly to your table with all payment being handled in the app. We removed the need for you to stand in line at bars and made the experience of ordering simple and effortless. We walked door to door to sell bar owners on how Flowtab would drive customers to spend more money. At one point we had twelve bars in San Francisco installed with Flowtab, and it felt like we were juggling one hundred balls in the air at once.

Flowtab

$5 Drink Voucher

Flowtab is a mobile app that lets you order
and pay for drinks from your phone.

Promo code: _____
www.flowtab.com

Flowtab promo code

We took ten Lyft rides a day to pass out Flowtab free drink promo cards to the drivers so they would give them to passengers on the way to the bar. Each bar had a different payment system, a different work-flow, different quality of cell phone service, and different clientele. Each night was a battle to educate customers on using the app. It felt like never-ending stress, going out each night to promote, finding bugs in the product, and spending the next day trying to fix the bugs.

Flowtab launch party, 2012

The lowest point in my startup career was at Flowtab, when we had a few weeks of money left. We decided to host an event just before the Super Bowl to get a bunch of new users at our biggest bar, McTeague's Saloon in San Francisco. We promised a free drink to each person at the bar who tried Flowtab. The night started off with ten of us and progressed to hundreds of people fighting to get in the bar. At our peak hour, the system crashed, and people couldn't order through Flowtab. Kyle and I were going crazy, trying to push an update to the code from the back room, and every second felt like a day. Our connection was slow to nonexistent and it felt like we were letting everyone down—our customers, the bartenders, and the bar owner. People were yelling at the bartenders, blaming them for the issues. Eventually, we ended up paying people directly for the cost of the free drink we promised.

In the days that followed, we realized that the economics of the business were untenable. The high bartender turnover, low Wi-Fi connections, inconsistent workflows, and point-of-sale technical challenges made the cost of acquisition too high to justify the business model in bars. Instead of letting that realization end us, we created a graph of every alternative vertical we could go after. We decided selling to stadiums gave us the best chance for success.

We sprinted to call every stadium in California, setting up meetings with the University of California at Berkeley, the San Francisco 49ers, and San Jose State University, all of whom expressed genuine interest in running trials of Flowtab in select seats, but they said they couldn't start until the following season. Unfortunately, that was over six months away and we only had a few weeks of cash left.

At the same time that all this was happening, Kyle's ninety-eight-year-old grandmother was getting sick and needed a caregiver in her home in Seattle. Her needs pulled Kyle away from our business for hours every day so he could help her with recruiting and hiring in-home health care. It felt like we were pinned in the corner and our only option was to give up and go find jobs. Instead of conceding defeat, we decided to do the opposite. After Kyle experienced firsthand how difficult it was to find and hire a caregiver for a loved one, we embraced the challenge and decided to do something about it. Thus, HomeHero began. After *TechCrunch* covered the story of Flowtab, we decided to open-source everything from our pitch deck to our software code on www.flowtab.com.

In the years after publicizing our story at Flowtab, we've gotten hundreds of emails from people around the world working on similar ideas, looking for advice, and thanking us for sharing the knowledge and lessons we learned. Most startups don't end up being acquired or having an IPO, so it's especially important to think about how you can make the most from your experience.

Publishing our work at Flowtab created more exposure for the successes we did have, which was leverage going into our next project, HomeHero. Always remember the luck platform: the x axis is how good you are at what you do and the y axis is how many people know about how good you are. The area under the graph is how lucky you are going to be in life. Even if a startup doesn't work, you can level up by learning and pivoting to the next thing.

The most important aspect of your career is the relationships you make with the people you work with. Market conditions change all the time, and most startups are an experiment in the beginning. When you find great people and work well together, you may work on projects that fail, but you'll persevere over the long run. Kyle and I maintained a great relationship through the ups and the downs and went on to raise $23 million from some of the top investors in Silicon Valley.

The HomeHero team, Christmas 2016

Maintaining a positive attitude regardless of the circumstances may sound cliché, but it's the most powerful tool you have. Stoic philosophy, which was practiced by Edison, Roosevelt, Rockefeller, and Washington, can help you focus on quieting your ego and controlling your reactions in various situations. Developing the ability to separate yourself from the outcome of a project is also very important. If a project fails, you yourself are not a failure.

During the process of creating a company, everything hurts if you let it, but the trick is reducing the negative things that impact you psychologically. Your bank account will drop, the time you spend with friends will decrease, and it will seem like there is no possible way things will work out. The hardest part about a startup is maintaining consistent positive focus on the long-term vision while balancing it with short-term needs. When your company is small, you will feel every bump in the road, which will be draining.

The irony is that the best thing and the worst thing in a startup aren't much different. The volatile and unpredictable nature of a startup is both incredibly exciting and terribly stressful. It becomes easy to fixate on specific goals and outcomes (like raising money, hiring key people, hitting growth metrics, etc.), and when things go the other direction, it's our natural reaction to carry the weight of that impact personally. I believe in the stoic outlook here: detach yourself from the outcome of the situation, imagine the worst possible outcome, and realize that anything better than that is great.

It's especially important to have outside hobbies and challenges that take some of the pressure off the startup. I choose to compete in Ironman triathlon competitions, which makes running a startup seem not so hard. The outside activities help create a sense of balance—when one is up the other will be down and vice versa.

CHAPTER TEN

〉〉〉〉 ABOUT KEVIN

Kevin Chan is a serial entrepreneur currently working on Maderight, a Y Combinator- and StartX-backed startup that is democratizing ethical manufacturing in the fashion industry. He has been honored by *Forbes* as one of the "30 Under 30" in Manufacturing. Cadillac chose Kevin for its Daring Greatly campaign, as one of twenty-five innovators, creators, and pioneers who are trailblazing in their field. The White House named him a Champion of Change. His work and views are regularly featured in top industry publications from *TechCrunch* to *Business Insider* to *The Business of Fashion*. Kevin also advises a number of startups and is a mentor at StartX, LAUNCH, and Cardinal Ventures. He received his degrees in computer science and business administration at the University of California, Berkeley.

S tart with a plan, but be prepared to throw it all out of the window. Going into my senior year at UC Berkeley, I knew exactly what I wanted to do and I had my next ten years planned out. I was going to work at a hedge fund as a quantitative trader right after graduation, get married at age twenty-five, become a fund manager by age thirty. More importantly, I'd be so rich that I could finally support my shopping addiction. What else was I going to do? After all, I had spent the past three years double majoring in business and computer science specifically to acquire all of the skills I needed for this career.

Fast-forward five years and I have yet to spend a day working at a hedge fund. In fact, I've never even had a "real" job. I'm very single—the only thing I'm married to is my business. And I'm definitely not rich. But it's all okay. In fact, it's better than okay, because I'm happy with where I am today.

So what happened?

I bought a pair of jeans. More specifically, I bought a $600 pair of jeans. Even more specifically, I bought the Dior Homme AW06 19cm MIJ Raw Indigo Selvedge 28. Let me break it down:

- Dior is the brand.
- Homme means "men" in French.
- AW06 stands for Autumn/Winter 2006, which lets you know that Hedi Slimane designed them.
- 19 cm is the measurement of the leg opening laid flat.
- MIJ means Made in Japan.
- Raw means unwashed.
- Indigo is the color.
- Selvedge means that the fabric was woven on a vintage loom that creates a clean edge.
- 28 is the waist size.

Why should you care about these jeans? Well, you probably shouldn't. But I do. The point is not to teach you about overpriced designer jeans; rather, the point is that everyone is passionate about something. My passion is fashion, and it took buying a pair of jeans that I couldn't actually afford for me to finally realize it.

DO WHAT YOU LOVE

Because my passion is fashion, the first company I started after college was a men's fashion brand called ASPECD. The initial idea was to sell custom-made shirts online, because what man wouldn't want that? We would have a website for customers to enter their measurements, and choose their fabric, and—*BAM*—a few days later, a perfectly fitted shirt would show up at their doorstep. Pretty genius, right?

How hard could it be to get started? We'd been to China and met tailors who spent their entire lives mastering the craft, so we knew they produced the highest quality shirts at a fraction of the price of tailors in the United States. We believed that all we had to do was create the website and the company would be a success in no time. Customers would line up out the door of our online store!

We spent two weeks perfecting the website. Meanwhile, we read somewhere online that using your own service might be a good idea, so we decided to do exactly that. When it was finished, we used our own website to order custom shirts for the entire team. Not to brag, but it was truly a beautiful website. It had a slick user interface that was ahead of its time. But that was about as good as it got. The process of buying shirts for our team created all kinds of complications:

Problem 1: Everyone on the team measured each other, but every time we checked the measurements, they came out differently—no one could get them right.

Problem 2: Shipping the packages cost more than the shirts themselves.

Problem 3: Rather than showing up at our doorstep within days, delivery took four weeks.

Problem 4: The shirts looked ridiculous; they fit worse than shirts we could purchase at a local department store.

These problems posed an uphill battle that we were not equipped to face. Back to the drawing board! But this time, we were guaranteed to succeed, because we were smart guys who'd just learned a major lesson: *Thoroughly test your assumptions before wasting time building your product.*

ITERATE, ITERATE, ITERATE

The next iteration of the brand had the same mission of providing guys with better-fitting shirts at an affordable price. This time, we took the approach of not changing the shopping process. Rather, we'd enhance it. We created in-between sizes so customers would have more sizes to choose from. On top of that, the service would personally alter the shirt to customize it to your body shape.

For the next two years, we ran with this iteration and gained mild success. We were able to go through four seasons of designs without going out of business. In the fashion industry, this is fantastic! Fashion is a competitive field, and most new brands fail in less than a year.

There was only one major issue: design and development took about six months, so we had to reinvest every bit of revenue we made back into the company, which meant we weren't getting paid. Our financials showed something along the lines of the founders not being paid a living wage until about four years in, assuming the business continued to grow at its current rate.

Fortunately, while running our brand, we had other brands begging us to help them with manufacturing and logistics.

THIS IS HOW MADERIGHT WAS BORN

From the beginning, we've likened Maderight's business philosophy to that of selling pickaxes during the California Gold Rush. Thousands of people every year are drawn in by the glamorous facade of the fashion industry, but very few succeed in creating their own brand. It's similar to how hundreds of thousands of people migrated to California seeking elusive gold in the 1800s. Starting a brand is sexy—the way gold is sexy. The biggest moneymakers of the Gold Rush, though, were the people who sold the pickaxes. Maderight is the unsexy but necessary tool that all brands need. From prototyping to manufacturing to logistics, Maderight manages a brand's entire supply chain, so that brands no longer need to coordinate between multiple vendors across different time zones and languages.

The evolution of my passion and my business doesn't end there, though. While traveling around the world to develop connections with garment factories, I discovered an even larger problem. It was one I'd never contemplated. Perhaps you've seen headlines about sweatshops and factories employing child labor. The reality is actually much worse than what we see in the media. Forced labor, unsafe worker conditions, underpayment, and general exploitation are the norm. These were just the factories that were willing to show me their operations. Now think about all of the factories that are working under the radar. What must conditions look like there?

Running Maderight opened my eyes to the injustice happening on a global scale. It has helped me to develop a personal mission to give as many people as possible the opportunity to lead a better life, whether through a job or access to better education. Maderight's mission has also evolved from simply democratizing manufacturing to democratizing *ethical* manufacturing.

Creating a startup is like riding a roller coaster. For every up, there's also a down. The ups are easy to ride, because who doesn't love to succeed? It's the downs that really get you. It's almost impossible to create a successful business if you are only extrinsically motivated. Most entrepreneurs will quickly realize that you can make a lot more money by going the corporate route. It's the passion—the intrinsic motivation—that will carry you through the rough patches.

▶ WHAT IS THE MOST IMPORTANT ADVICE YOU WOULD GIVE TO FIRST-TIME FOUNDERS?

My general advice for anyone who wants to start a company is this: *Don't.* You think that being an entrepreneur is glamorous? *It's not.* The media biases you, because you only see the top 1% of companies that are out there. In fact, over 90% of startups fail. The odds are stacked against you.

You think that you'll make a lot of money from starting a company? *You won't.* A study conducted at Washington University in St. Louis shows that entrepreneurs on the whole made about 35% less than their corporate counterparts.

You think that you'll have a lot of free time? *Nice try.* Lori Greiner, a notable inventor and entrepreneur, says, "Entrepreneurs: The only people who work 80 hour weeks to avoid working 40 hour weeks."

Are you still reading after all of the bullshit I just fed you? *Great!* Now, I can share the traits and attitudes that I've seen among the most successful founders.

Angela Duckworth calls it "grit." Carol Dweck calls it "growth mindset." At the Haas School of Business at UC Berkeley, we called it "questioning the status quo."

I call it "never settling."

There was one particularly memorable period when we first started Maderight, which we've internally named the "dark days." To provide some context, we used to own and operate a men's clothing brand in New York before we started Maderight. Maderight was just an idea that we had in our heads and we decided to apply to Y Combinator with it. For those who don't already know, Y Combinator is a highly competitive, early-stage startup accelerator based in Silicon Valley that produced companies like Dropbox and Airbnb. We weren't really sure how it happened, but we ended up getting into Y Combinator. I believe we were the first and only company to get accepted based only on an idea. It was the opportunity of a lifetime, so we decided, *why not?*

After the in-person interview in California, we flew back to New York to sell all of our personal possessions, terminate our leases, close up shop on our clothing brand, and permanently move to California— all in the span of one week.

During our time at Y Combinator, we were getting more paying customers than most of our colleagues—even the ones who had been running their businesses for several years.

Just three months into our new business and we were on top of the world. Everything was going in our favor, and it seemed we could do no wrong. Toward the end of the program, the most notable venture capitalists partnered up with Y Combinator to host office hours and coach each of the companies on how to raise a successful round of funding.

In the first hour, a venture capitalist told me, "There is no way you're going to be able to raise money in [Silicon Valley]. You should just raise money from your friends and family if you can."

In the second meeting, an hour later, I wasn't even able to finish telling the VC my business idea. He was more concerned about what he was going to have for lunch that day.

These were supposedly the "friendly" investors—the investors who'd donated their time specifically to help us. I thought to myself, *How will other investors react when I meet with them and it's not just office hours?*

We didn't worry, though. We still had Demo Day, where we would get to pitch our business in front of over 500 investors. In some circles, Demo Day is infamously known as the day when money is thrown around like candy with no due diligence needed.

The partners at Y Combinator call it "the most leveraged day of your company's life." I practiced my heart out:

Write pitch.

Update deck.

Practice.

Get critiqued by Y Combinator partners.

Repeat.

I did this for eighteen hours a day, three days straight.

The big day finally came. We had given up our clothing brand, moved across the country, and worked seven days a week for the past three months for this moment right now. Five hundred investors stood in front of us. We were going to be the next Airbnb!

About twenty companies were scheduled to present before us, so I nervously practiced in the back room while watching the other presentations on a television screen. Those were the longest hours of my life.

Finally, it was our turn.

We nailed it! I gave the best presentation I've ever given in my life. How many investments did we get that day? Zero. Zilch. Nada.

What about some of our closest colleagues who also presented that day? They were oversubscribed. Some had raised over $2 million.

After that day, we *could* have given up. Most people *would* have. But we are not most people. We are entrepreneurs, and to succeed we must never settle. Never settle for "no" as an answer. Never settle for letting things just be the way they are.

Over the next month, we reached out to every relevant investor we could find. We ended up getting meetings with over 100 of them. Ultimately, we raised that round of funding and are much stronger as founders for having endured the "dark days."

Remember: You don't fail until you decide to give up.

CHAPTER ELEVEN

YEHIA ABUGABAL
Oncologist and Founder, International Cancer Research Center

>>>> ABOUT YEHIA

Yehia Abugabal is an Egyptian oncologist and a visionary entrepreneur. He founded the International Cancer Research Center (ICRC), a comprehensive multidisciplinary research center, located in Cairo, Egypt. Yehia recruited a faculty of prominent experts in medical oncology, radiotherapy, radiology, pathology, and surgery. The ICRC is a highly collaborative environment that facilitates informal interactions among researchers.

Yehia is also a respected speaker who works to foster the science of oncology, spread awareness about cancer, educate patients, and mentor young doctors in Egypt and the Middle East. His work has been featured on television news. *Forbes* magazine recognized him as one of the top thirty most influential people, rising stars, and change-makers in the world. In 2016, ArabianBusiness.com named him one of the one hundred most influential Arabs in the world. The American Chamber of Commerce called him one of the "Stars of Egypt."

Yehia Abugabal has been named to *Forbes'* 30 under 30 in healthcare.

The idea of marketing can be overwhelming for some, especially for those who have little or no experience with it. It is crucial that you read as much as you can about the needs of your field and plan your marketing strategy before you jump into the field.

When I first started my organization, I faced the same challenge other startups face—I had a small staff and a limited budget. We were trying to fight our way into the limelight while competing with the well-known giants in the health-care industry.

When my team and I outlined our marketing approach. It was less about a single marketing strategy and more about a spirit that would differentiate us from traditional marketing practices. We learned that many of the principles of marketing are designed for huge firms and well-established companies—for selling a product, not for working in the health-care system. So we needed a new and unorthodox marketing approach to give us a kick, not only in a crowded market but in a developing society that doesn't pay much attention to cancer research.

I realized I needed to define a brand and an identity for my startup. After all, marketing is an important tool that is available to everyone who invests in it, especially emerging companies aiming to shape their image in the mind of the consumers.

As a health-care startup, the sector that I would serve was composed of different groups—companies in the industry, individuals seeking care, and so on. I had to reach out to pharmaceutical companies and gain their collaboration in the fields of research, education, as well as awareness. I needed to connect with the general public, and cancer patients specifically, so I could encourage them to take an active role in my organization, share in the clinical trials, attend awareness seminars, and believe in the message I am trying to deliver. I also needed to gain the support of government entities and NGOs so that we could collaborate.

Our marketing strategy had to be different. It was born out of necessity. We started with only three people working on our marketing efforts, a limited budget, and limited resources—especially compared to our competitors. Basics, like graphic design teams and advertising consultants, were a luxury. We had to find a way to achieve maximum impact with limited resources, so we created our own materials. Our team mastered design software so they could create appealing printed material and we reached out to connections for support creating promotional videos.

We had to be innovative and proactive through our marketing campaign to highlight our unique approach to fighting cancer. We shared our greatest strengths and how we use them to serve the public, promoting our message using cheap and accessible tools, including Facebook, Twitter, viral videos, and email marketing. We considered any and all marketing strategies as long as they produced results. Our goal was to become a major player in our field as quickly as possible and scale up all over the Middle East.

We used several marketing strategies at once, and some were successful. We excelled at relationship marketing, which focuses on creating a strong link between the brand and the customer. Through collaborative work with the American Society of Clinical Oncology, European Society for Medical Oncology, European Society for Surgical Oncology, and others, we were able to build strong trust within the health-care community and reach out to a much larger population.

Our organization acted as a leader rather than a follower in a very competitive field. We created markets and developed innovative health-care products that meet the needs of our consumers.

These are the various marketing strategies we used to successfully promote our company:

- **One-to-One Marketing:** Marketing to customers as individuals, using personalized marketing efforts.

- **Real-Time Marketing:** Using the power of technology to interact with customers in real time.

- **Viral Marketing:** Delivering messages on the Internet, propagated and shared by the public.

- **Digital Marketing:** Leveraging the power of Internet tools like email and social networking to support marketing efforts.

- **Offering Exceptional Services:** Offering twenty-four-hour technical support to our entire research network and accessibility to our strong collaborators, a valuable service to researchers and the public, both of whom have limited resources.

- **Going to Them:** For us, distance is not an obstacle to delivering our message. When it comes to research, we have connected distant parts of Egypt with a strong network and cloud that is monitored 24-7. We have created awareness campaigns that cover all of Egypt using our mobile cinema to show educational videos. Using our mobile mammogram unit, we drive anywhere we are needed to deliver life-saving screenings.

The best marketing tool for my company was one-to-one marketing. It was imperative that we take a personalized approach to meet the needs of every hospital, medical institute, and even the public. This builds trust and a strong connection in a very competitive field.

Press and media coverage are an integral part of any marketing strategy and we have gained their trust over the years as well. When we host an event, after contacting an agency specializing in public relations, we send them an email describing the event, its mission and objectives, and inviting them to take a part in it. We hold press conferences prior to the international conferences that we host, to gain more coverage. We invite the media to attend the conference, and a press release is sent to all the major news outlets. After several successful projects and events, we've found the media is chasing us for the up-to-date and the new-in-the-field information on research and cancer awareness. This kind of press coverage builds enormous trust in the public. People are now more willing to participate in our events and spread our message.

In competitive markets, a startup can easily get lost in the crowd. The challenge we faced, and that any startup faces, is standing apart from competitors. Using new, unusual, and bold marketing techniques is the best way to show what makes your business unique.

CHAPTER TWELVE

>>>> ABOUT COURTNEY

Courtney is an engineer by training and an entrepreneur by nature. After leaving her job as a power systems engineer at NASA to work for her own startup company, she uncovered a passion for building startup communities and encouraging women to pursue careers in tech and entrepreneurship.

Courtney cofounded the Akron-based clean energy startup Design Flux Technologies while an undergraduate in Electrical Engineering at the University of Akron. In 2016, while serving as chief operations officer, Courtney was named a *Forbes* "30 Under 30" in the category of Energy. She has also been called one of the "Top 40 Under 40 in Cleantech" by Midwest Energy and one of *Crain's Cleveland Business*'s "Twenty in Their 20s." She also received the ComEd Female Founder Prize in 2015 through the Clean Energy Challenge.

After spending seven years with Design Flux Technologies, Courtney decided to commit her career to supporting founders full time. Today, she is utilizing her talents in relationship building and advocacy to create an up-and-coming startup ecosystem in Northeast Ohio. She does this through her work as executive director for Launch League, a nonprofit organization that seeks to increase startup success by establishing connections between founders and local resources.

Courtney loves sharing her stories of founding a clean tech company, especially with young entrepreneurs and women in tech. She travels around the globe speaking on the topics of entrepreneurship, women in tech, and clean energy.

Becoming an entrepreneur doesn't have to be planned. The first thing I did to plan for my startup was to not plan at all. You heard me: I didn't plan for it! I actually never aspired to be an entrepreneur—neither of my parents ran companies or small businesses, and I wasn't studying business in school—I was an engineering student. When I was growing up, I was told to find a good job that pays well. So you could probably say that all of the odds were against me starting a company—until you realize that success in starting a company has nothing to do with getting the right degree or having a certain upbringing. It has everything to do with *you*.

When I was in college, I discovered a passion for extracurricular projects. In my freshman year, I was heavily involved in robotics and all sorts of nerdy things. What I came to realize over the course of those projects was that I had certain skill sets that fit well with the entrepreneurial mindset. I tried my best to do co-ops and internships at the highly sought-after companies. I worked for Lockheed Martin and NASA, but I didn't find satisfaction in those work environments. I loved working in fast-paced, challenging environments with small teams and truly passionate people. Those environments gave me energy; they were where I thrived. I knew then that I wasn't cut out for corporate America—and maybe that's how you feel, too.

So how did I start my company? One research project I worked on in college was with a local startup. I was developing a subsystem for that product, something called a battery management system, a tool that prevents batteries in electric vehicles from catching on fire. One day, my faculty advisor came to my teammate and me and asked if we'd like to pitch at a business plan competition. "That battery management system you're working on is a lot like a product," he said. I looked at my soon-to-be cofounder and thought, well that's crazy! We're engineers, and we know nothing about starting a company. But we thought about it and decided, *Hey, what's the worst that could happen? We try and get rejected?* So we went for it. It was the night before the application was due, and neither of us had a clue about business plans or pitching.

We were scrambling to Google-search terms like "profit margin" and "EBITA"—"What the heck is that?" we'd say. Much to our surprise, we, two electrical engineers, got selected as finalists in this pitch competition. Our pitch was horrible. It looked like we were defending a master's thesis rather than pitching a product. Even though we didn't win, the competition was the spark that started us off. People came up to us after the presentation and said, "You know, that presentation was pretty bad, but you might just have something with that product."

After that, we started down a chaotic and nonlinear path to starting a company. Although the Internet has an infinite supply of resources or checklists like "Top 10 steps to start your company," you'll find that there is no catch-all guide that will give you the perfect blueprint for your company. Since we started this company as students in college, we had to first navigate the complex ecosystem that is a public university. Issues of how to handle intellectual property, research facilities, and more bombarded us. As helpful as the university was, we opted to spin our company out and develop and patent our technology on our own. There are so many reasons that this choice was a good or bad one; all I can say is that it's best to ask around, and ask often, about what other people in your area would do. If you're going to start a company, you must have no shame in asking for free help, and boy did we ask for help!

After about a year of trying other pitch competitions and navigating the spin-out process, we added our first teammate—we desperately needed one. He had master's degrees in law and business and an undergraduate degree in finance—the perfect fit to balance us out. With his help, we were able to enter an industry-specific competition called the Clean Energy Challenge. Since ours was a clean tech startup, we had a lot more luck seeking out awards that were clean tech–specific rather than going for more general contests where there was too much competition. The Clean Energy Challenge is where we raised our first $10,000. We felt like kings, holding our big check, grinning from ear to ear.

We worked nights and weekends and traded our hobbies for the startup. We obviously couldn't afford to pay ourselves or quit our jobs (and we didn't have the guts to drop out of school), so we made the startup work by bootstrapping. One of the great things about starting a company in college is that you have the chance to graduate and get a regular job if all else fails. Although we were able to make it work on a part-time basis, that didn't come without sacrifice. Even after we received additional funds through a local grant, we couldn't go out and start spending money on fancy office equipment or payment for cool tech conferences on the West Coast. Startups usually aren't as glamorous as TV makes them seem. We budgeted every penny and lived like, well, college kids. Some of us lived together and worked out of our houses, and most of us worked part time or found unique work situations that allowed us to support ourselves financially while having enough freedom to focus on the startup. We learned the importance of mentors and how folks are usually willing to help a young startup, especially when you're in your twenties.

THERE'S NO SECRET FORMULA TO STARTING A COMPANY

We learned some valuable lessons along the way too. When first starting out, no matter how many training courses you take or YouTube videos you watch, you'll never see the next challenge coming. We found that, as much as folks like to pick apart business plans and focus on the "business model canvas" or the next big fancy tool for business planning, there's very little actual value in following a plan other than having one ready for pitch competitions and funding applications. Remember when I said our business wasn't planned? It's still true today!

We had much more luck when we got out into the industry and finally started to talk to customers, respond to their feedback, and quickly alter course if needed. I've been through over fifty different versions of my pitch deck. I change it every time, constantly reevaluating the message based on feedback from customers.

FALL IN LOVE WITH THE PROBLEM, NOT YOUR SOLUTION

This philosophy was one of the biggest reasons we succeeded in our early days, in fact. A few short years after we started, we realized that there wasn't a market for our technology. The battery management system we started with has far too much competition overseas. We had to swallow our pride and start with a new concept. When you're a student, sometimes it's easy to start with a cool technology, rather than a problem that actually needs to be solved. I tell students now, "Fall in love with the problem; don't marry the solution." Make sure you're solving a problem first, and don't get too caught up in your tech. We learned this lesson the hard way, and even though we had to throw away our original technology, the lessons we learned were invaluable to our future as a young startup.

When creating a hardware startup especially, one of the most critical elements is proving that what you have invented actually works. This was a challenge for us with such limited funding, so we had to be creative to prove our technology. Hardware is expensive! And sometimes, making something brand new looks the same as making something that nobody wants—at first. As cool and revolutionary as we thought our new software-defined power management product was, we struggled to see the same excitement from our customers. We wondered why at first, but then we realized that what we were doing was similar to shoving an iPod in somebody's face in the eighties. Nobody had a clue what our product was or what they would need it for. When we told people we could completely get rid of their battery chargers and power inverters, they looked at us like we were crazy. We had to climb that mountain incrementally, and we are still fighting to prove ourselves. How have we overcome this skepticism? We've established credible partners and worked with local universities for third-party validation. We're raising awareness by speaking at international venues about our vision for the future of the battery industry and working on getting our ideas published in articles and credible journals.

It's no joke: the first steps to starting a company are probably the least defined and most critical. From my experience, this is also where my teammates and I learned the most, and if all else fails, we've gained an incredible amount of knowledge for the next go-round.

KEY TAKEAWAYS

- Starting a company isn't always planned.
- You can only learn what you love by doing it—I found I loved entrepreneurship by *being* an entrepreneur and giving it shot.
- There's no secret formula for starting a company. You have to be ready to try different approaches and adjust as needed.
- Make sure you start with a problem or need, not a solution in search of a problem to solve.
- People love to help young entrepreneurs, but you have to ask for help.

- Have a business plan ready for fund-raising reasons, but focus your time on enacting and adjusting the plan more than on perfecting the plan.

- It's important to prove the value of your product with partners or third parties to gain traction.

➤ HOW DO YOU SUPPORT YOURSELF WHEN STARTING A COMPANY— FINANCIALLY AND PERSONALLY?

If you love what you're doing, it's not work. You're young. You're in college or you just graduated. All of your friends are buying houses or going on month-long vacations to Europe and here you are with a startup. You're probably not pulling in a six-figure salary. If you are, I'm jealous, and maybe you should be writing this chapter rather than me.

This was where I was at in college. I weighed the options and possibilities of how I could support myself while starting a company. Initially, I called upon some wizard-like time management skills to help me manage my coursework in college, a co-op with NASA, and a startup. And when I say "wizard-like," I have to admit, that's a bit of a stretch. Sometimes it's just a matter of thinking outside the box and asking questions. For me, I decided to slow down in my coursework and take an extra year to graduate. As for getting my job at NASA, all I did was apply, but I knew that my time spent in extracurricular projects helped to differentiate me from my peers. There wasn't any magic there, just doing things differently. Sure, I didn't to get to graduate with my buddies, but because my startup was my true passion, I had to make a decision about what I cared about more, and the startup won.

Something always has to give. Aside from lightening my workload at school, I also negotiated a part-time co-op. Usually these sorts of part-time possibilities aren't advertised, but I knew what I needed to sustain my startup, so I asked. It is amazing how many people will give you answers when you ask questions.

When it came to the living situation, I bunked with my cofounder and split living expenses. Even in Northeast Ohio, where we have one of the lowest costs of living imaginable, expenses can be challenging when you're starting a company, so we saved as much as we could. When it came to finding a location for our startup, one that wasn't in our garages or basements, we negotiated a deal with a local business accelerator. They already offered very affordable space, but we negotiated a special rate by exchanging services from our team to complete a project they were working on in the building. This arrangement helped us save a significant amount of funds that we could then throw at our rent.

IT'S OKAY TO ASK FOR (FREE) HELP

We've recently identified more and more law firms that are willing to work with startups and give them a break on services. Often, firms might give a 75% discount on services, and when, or if, you're successful, they'll come back to collect what is owed plus an additional fee for sharing in the risk with your startup. This is one of those things I'm kicking myself for not knowing of before, but at least I can share the information with you now.

We learned quickly not to underestimate the power of in-kind services as well. Many local in-kind service grants are easy to obtain, because there is not much competition, and they have relatively easy application processes and significant payoffs. We received a variety of grants like this, from $55,000 in market-research services to $50,000 in industrial design services, which we used for a prototype.

We also saw more opportunity to bootstrap and really stand out in our startup ecosystem by staying in Northeast Ohio. We had a well-established network here, which is one of the biggest contributing factors to success for an early startup. Startup success is all about who you know, so network, network, network. There are many different factors that will affect what location you choose, but for us, it made sense to stay local for our early years so we could use the network we had already established to raise funding more easily and find resources.

Finally, when it comes to work-life balance, I've become a fan of scheduling "me" time. Whether it's waking up earlier so I can get to the gym at a set time every day or strategically not scheduling meetings before 9:00 a.m., I've found ways to optimize time. Working from home has also paid off for me. I find I can squeeze in work much more easily if I can cook at home while on a conference call or front-load all my emails for before 8:00 a.m. and respond to them after 8:00 p.m.

BOOST YOUR SOCIAL LIFE IN A STARTUP COMMUNITY

I've found great ways to have friends in my local startup community. A few years after we got started, we discovered a local startup community called Launch League. Launch League (www.launchleague.org) is designed to bring founders together so they can network, build relationships, and help each other out. I've found that being part of a founder community not only helps balance my social life but has also led to some pretty awesome business opportunities and great connections. There's an element of accountability to a startup community as well—if people know what you're struggling with, they'll check up on you. This accountability can be especially motivating when you're navigating a tough time and thinking of quitting. I've even found ways to help support myself by helping other startups as a consultant. When you're around an open-minded, flexible group of people, opportunities tend to pop up when you least expect it.

When I first made the decision to leave my full-time job, I turned to my network. When I made another career-transition more recently, I did the same thing. I can't emphasize enough how important it is to get out there and meet people, even if the benefit isn't apparent at first. And sometimes you don't know how they will fit into your life until a certain situation arises. The key is to stay in touch with people and take time to listen to their stories and what they do. Through my network, I found a part-time sales gig that allowed me to work from home, and therefore gave me a lot more time for my startup. Later, the consulting firm I worked with actually came to my startup offering to help us with some software development. Even though we couldn't afford their services, I guess I made an impression on their CEO and he remembered me years later. At the moment when I was looking to leave NASA, he messaged me out of the blue on LinkedIn and asked if I had availability for some part-time work. What timing, I thought! That connection led to a great work opportunity that allowed me to support myself and gave me the time and flexibility to work on my startup.

KEY TAKEAWAYS

- You will have to make sacrifices of your time, but hopefully you love what you're doing so much that it feels like a hobby more than a chore.
- There are definitely ways to save money on rent, for you personally and your startup; you just have to get good at asking questions!
- Keep an eye out for startup-friendly services; you can save a lot of money up front this way.

- Location can be part of your strategy, so be careful to evaluate all aspects of the place you decide to launch your startup—not just the funding environment.
- To help with your social life, try to plug into the startup community.
- Never underestimate the importance of your network.

CHAPTER THIRTEEN

STAFF SHEEHAN
Founder, Catalytic Innovations & Former CEO, Dream 8, Inc.

>>>> ABOUT STAFF

Stafford W. Sheehan is a scientist and inventor, the founder of Catalytic Innovations (http://cat.aly.st/), and was CEO of Dream8, Inc., up to its acquisition. His technologies are used by energy and manufacturing companies around the world to reduce global carbon dioxide emissions and improve their impact on the environment. These technologies include processes for non-fossil-fuel generation, carbon dioxide capture and conversion, and coatings that improve energy efficiency in metal refineries. He received his PhD from Yale University in physical chemistry, which he pursued after his first startup's exit and a pivot toward renewable energy technology development.

Staff Sheehan has been named to *Forbes'* 30 under 30 in energy.

B leary eyed, I looked up at my glowing laptop screen and the half-finished presentation. It was nothing I was proud of, but the sun would rise soon, so it would have to be enough to get the job done. I could hear my coworker, Aaron, snoring lightly on one of the beds behind me. He and his wife had had a baby only a few months before, so this was likely the most sleep he would be getting in a long time. As I shuffled through the slides, I realized that we were missing a few diagrams and figures—I would need help from the rest of my team to pull them together. That work would have to wait until later in the morning, I told myself. It was not important enough to wake up Aaron early.

We were in a hotel room in San Francisco, on the opposite side of the country from our homes and families in New England. These were the final two days of a course, called I-Corps, designed by the National Science Foundation to help bring scientific discoveries to market and stimulate the economy. The program was designed to teach scientists how to talk to potential customers and perform market research, so that we could build businesses around our patents and discoveries using a structured process based off the scientific method. The idea was to speak to us scientists using our own language: by formulating a hypothesis, testing the hypothesis with experiments, and drawing conclusions based on the data from those experiments.

The assumption was, of course, that scientists speak a language different from the one everyone else speaks. This assumption was an example of a solid hypothesis.

Over the last two years, several of my coworkers and I engaged in programs like this to answer one question—an extremely important one, one necessary to answer before starting a company—How can we make money with our product?

Figuring out how to make money is not as straightforward as finding the right price to sell a product or finding out who your first customers will be, even though those are both important parts of it. We needed to find out what about our technology was compelling to our customers, and how we could package it so it would be irresistible to them. In these business-related courses, our teachers called that "addressing the customer's pain point."

Imagine you just invented a new type of piston, like you have in the combustion engine of your car. For the sake of this example, this invention is more efficient and aerodynamic than the ones we have in our cars and generators today. Say you want to start a business around that technology. Do you make a bunch of pistons and sell them to engine manufacturers? Do you design a new engine around that piston, then build that engine, and sell that to car manufacturers? Do you design an entirely new, more efficient car and sell that to end users? How difficult is it to break into these markets? Which model would make a more compelling story to investors? Do the customers you identify as your early market really care about your product?

These are the types of questions that needed to be answered before we were able to answer the most important question of how we could make money with our product. My coworkers and I had developed very specialized catalysts, materials that are added to chemical processes to make them faster and more efficient and use less energy. This technology is so broad that it could be applied to hundreds of different chemical processes, such as bleach production, wastewater treatment, production of renewable fuel, metal refining, and many others. We could have written a business model around selling our products directly, licensing our technology to others to use, or building out a larger solution in which our technology is a key component. On top of that, with so many different applications and accompanying business models, we found ourselves in such a complex market that there was little chance we would be able to get it all right the first time around.

Not that there is anything wrong with not getting it right the first time. In the real world, it's not that odd to take a long journey to find the best market for your skills or inventions. Around the turn of the millennium, three entrepreneurs in Oakland started a company called Savage Beast Technologies. They had developed a new kind of software that helped users find music they enjoyed. They hired a modest number of employees and filed for a patent on their technology. They tried licensing models, paid services, and other ideas to bring their invention to customers, but none of them seemed to work. Before they knew it, they had run out of funding.

Although most other startups would throw in the towel and quit after failing to find a way to make money with their technology, this company was not ready to give up yet. After convincing their fifty employees to stay on board, and taking on personal debt to keep their organization afloat for two years after they had run out of capital, they launched a free radio service. This new type of Internet radio used their algorithm to match users with music that the users themselves selected through likes and dislikes. They had finally found a concept that struck a chord with customers. Today, we know this company as the provider of one of the most popular Internet radio services in the world, Pandora Media.

Just like Pandora, we were trying to find the best product to make money with our technology. In our case, this meant finding the chemical process where our catalysts' attributes were needed the most. We had to identify whether the value propositions that our technology brought to the table addressed something that was painful to our clients. For Pandora, the pain point they addressed with their ultimate product was the terrible music played on the radio. My coworkers and I had embarked on these journeys to find our "bad radio."

This is how I found myself sitting in my hotel room in San Francisco, at quarter to four in the morning, reviewing the notes from hundreds of interviews that I had conducted with clients over the years. I was a brief five hours away from standing on stage and presenting the latest hundred interviews that had taken place in the six weeks prior. I flipped to a slide with the logo of one of the potential customers we interviewed, a company manufacturing electrolysis equipment for hydrogen generation called Hydrogenics. We first engaged this company in 2014, sent them materials, and committed quite a bit of time to building up our rapport with them. Then, one day, our contact at the company evaporated. Despite calls and texts, we never heard from anyone at Hydrogenics again. A quick Google search revealed the cause: in the weeks since we last heard from them, investors gave the hydrogen generation market a bleak outlook due to the low price of natural gas. This resulted in a drop in their stock price, which began trading at $31 per share, down to $14 per share. Many of their employees had been laid off, and with other recent failures in their industry, it was looking like an increasingly unstable market to focus on as early adopters for my technology. No painkiller could have fixed that; they had been eviscerated.

Since the price of failure is high in capital-intensive companies where physical products are manufactured, we emphasized activities like this—talking to potential customers by emailing, cold-calling, flying out to meet them, and showing up on their doorstep, or any other means necessary. Our mission was to identify their problem—no matter how eager they were to keep it from us—and how it could be solved by our technology. Our I-Corps courses and mentors provided plenty of pressure to collect this data, and often our instruction was along the lines of "Do whatever it takes, and don't take no for an answer."

I flipped to my next slide—pictures of the mountainous countryside of Switzerland and the marshy, green windmill-speckled farmlands of the Netherlands flashed before me. Much of my market research took me to Europe, where our technology, our materials, and our systems for sustainable chemical processes are more desirable than in the United States. Environmental laws here in the United States are relatively lax, whereas there is increasing pressure from governments and communities in Europe for companies to be more environmentally friendly. Attempting to speak to customers in Europe was tricky; I repeatedly disappointed my mentors and had learned to take no for an answer. More often than not, the customer and I lacked a mutual fluent language. I found out on the second day of one of these trips that I had planned poorly.

Sometimes when you find yourself at a low point, the only thing you can do is take a break. While on a train ride, as luck would have it, I met a language teacher fluent in German, English, and French. If I'd had my nose glued to my laptop working, I would never have met this person. The language teacher became my translator, traveling with me on a few of these visits with customers, helping to lower the language barrier. Even when the client spoke English, it was nice to have someone who could lead off with their native language, warming them up to the idea of an American asking them all about their business.

I scrolled down to my next slide and came to our most recent pivot. I proposed a change in direction for our product development toward wastewater treatment, based on client feedback and the volatility we experienced firsthand in the hydrogen market. While major pivots in product direction may be discomforting, history tells us that well-executed ones help build great companies.

Around the time of World War II, a small textile equipment manufacturer in Japan, with clients around the world, felt that he was in an unstable market and needed to change his company's direction. He spent years performing customer interviews and assessing consumer demand before making his decision. When he ultimately decided to pivot, he used the expertise in compact mechanical engineering that he had gained from designing looms to build small combustion engines. As our loom salesman predicted, shortly after the end of the war, there was a collapse in the Japanese cotton market, which, had he not pivoted, would have been a death sentence for his business. But he was ready with his engine and a compact motorcycle frame that addressed Japanese consumers' need for affordable transportation. Thus, Michio Suzuki changed the name of his Suzuki Loom Works to become the Suzuki Motor Corporation that we know today. His success taught us to always think from your customer's point of view and provide what they need—a crucial lesson in market discovery.

As the sun came up, I put the finishing touches on my presentation and scribbled down a few buzzwords I should remember to say during my talk. I closed my laptop, popped an aspirin to help me fall asleep, and lay down to get a couple hours of shut-eye before the next big day.

▶ HOW DID YOU DEVELOP YOUR PRODUCT?

Like many doctoral students in the sciences, my experiments never worked. I had spent years of my life trying to build a device, and in the end, found out that it would never be used in the next century—a costly lesson to learn. I had made the decision to go to graduate school to pursue a doctorate in the sciences, embarking on a project to make renewable fuels.

The most important component of any device capable of performing such a chemical transformation is the catalyst. Naturally, I decided to study those. I found out that even the ones that we thought worked well did not work at all, in the self-correcting process that is science. Between searching for purpose in the work that I was doing and wondering whether I would ever graduate, I found that the lessons I had learned from my earlier experiences as an entrepreneur could help me figure out both.

In 2003, I built basic websites and engaged in rudimentary network and database programming in Perl and PHP to make money while I was in high school. I met a few other freelance programmers online, and we eventually pieced together a startup company. Back in those days, it was tough for someone so young to get customers to hire you, so I had to employ a vast arsenal of tricks to find out exactly what my customers wanted. First, I would do research on the Internet to understand their ecosystem, find out who they responded to, who their current service providers were, and learn as much information about their job as I could to stage an approach. After that, I would call them—sometimes being completely honest and telling them that I was trying to sell them my company's services. Before long, I found out that this was not the most effective way to go about it.

Instead, I found that calling or messaging them while pretending to be a confused corporate customer, irate regulator, or sometimes even a superior from within their own company, would wrestle out the information that I was seeking, so I did just that. To support these inquiries, I found that calling the corporate customers, regulators, and partner organizations themselves to gather information helped make my improvised persona seem more legitimate. In no time, my teenage self had stumbled upon a way to interview my potential customers without their knowledge to gain a better understanding of their needs and infrastructure. With the data from these interviews, I could time my arrival and skills as a service provider to exactly address their pain.

I turned my graduate school research into a product by falling back on these skills, albeit with slightly less deceit and more straightforward questioning. But for you to know what I am talking about, you must understand what my product is, and so we must go back a bit farther than 2003.

Around three and a half billion years ago, the first bacterial compounds on Earth developed the ability to perform photosynthesis. Photosynthesis is the process that plants and bacteria use to create different chemical compounds using the energy in sunlight. All the oxygen that we breathe comes from photosynthesis, as well as all the hydrocarbons we use as fuel. Life on our planet depends on and derives its energy from photosynthesis.

Photosynthesis, as you learn in grade school, is the conversion of carbon dioxide and water into hydrocarbon chemicals using sunlight, the fundamental process enabling life on our planet. In nature, plants use photosynthesis to convert carbon dioxide, water, and solar energy into chemical energy by creating sugars and other complex hydrocarbons. This process effectively stores the energy from the sun in the chemical bonds of the sugars. Photosynthesis has been supporting the Earth's ecosystem and balancing carbon dioxide concentration in our atmosphere for billions of years, having begun well before human beings evolved.

In the last century, human beings have harnessed byproducts of photosynthesis, such as fossil fuels, to provide the energy required for modern life. Doing so has released millions of tons of carbon dioxide (CO_2) into the Earth's atmosphere, CO_2 that had been previously sequestered into the fossil fuels by photosynthesis over the course of millions of years. This release of CO_2 is having a noticeable and mea-surable effect on global climate and atmospheric CO_2 concentration.

Regardless of whether you believe in anthropogenic (human-made) climate change, imagine our planet as one big chemical experiment. Any scientist could tell you that drastically changing the concentra-tion of one component in the experiment can have catastrophic, unpre-dictable effects on the system overall. Since we do not have an extra planet as a back-up experiment, do we really want to take the risk? Of course not.

To counteract this potentially catastrophic atmospheric CO_2 increase, scientists around the world have been attempting to mimic the natural processes that oxidize water into oxygen gas and sequester carbon dioxide into the chemical bonds of carbon-based compounds. One of the major hurdles toward doing so is the effective use of CO_2, and the other is the efficient oxidation of two molecules of water into oxygen gas.

I received my PhD in studying efficient ways to do this reaction, by making new catalysts that could perform these chemical transfor-mations with as little energy wasted as possible. These materials are esoteric, and not many people would know what to do with a lump of catalyst, so I followed the same lines of inquiry that led my previous company to find its customers in determining how to develop these chemical materials into products .

I partnered with engineering and chemical companies to iden-tify opportunities for these materials and began my inquiries all over again. Luckily, Google and the Internet are much more advanced today than they were in 2003. Calling different engineering companies, oil companies, and any company that uses electrolysis in their processes, I worked my way up from talking to the junior engineers to their superiors and discovered the Achilles' heel in their processes. If my technology, or a derivative of my technology, could solve their problem, then I would be one step closer to finding out which product I needed to develop. Every time I received help from a young engineer or someone on the bottom of the corporate totem pole, I complimented them to their superiors. Flattery and helping someone get a desired promotion form allies in an industry where they are needed for progress.

I cannot pretend that my organization has found our optimum product yet; we are still very much in the thick of it and trying to develop as much as the next startup. The road to finding a product and making sales is difficult, but so is the initial discovery of the technology that drives product development. If it were easy, someone else would have done it before, but luckily no one has made our catalysts.

In chemistry, catalysts are a material, typically in the form of a powder, that is added to a chemical reaction to make the reaction proceed faster and more efficiently. But catalysts alone are not a product; selling a catalyst is like trying to sell a car engine in the mass market. Some people, mostly specialists, would purchase an engine without a car, but your average consumer is looking for the whole car, engine included. I learned this lesson from talking to my customers, so my company develops integrated solutions around our catalysts for wastewater treatment and CO_2 emissions reduction.

For the latter of those, there are three major fossil fuels that we use to power our planet and contribute the most to CO_2 emissions: coal, oil, and natural gas. Both coal and natural gas are burned in boilers or power plants, while oil is burned in a much more distributed manner in the internal combustion engines of our cars or homes. In power plants, CO_2 exists as a byproduct in the flue gas that is sent up the power plant's smokestacks. There are currently no technologies that utilize carbon dioxide flue gas in a cost-effective manner, and the emissions typically end up in the atmosphere, increasing our global atmospheric CO_2 concentration and further contributing to world-altering effects caused by this change in our atmosphere's chemistry.

In the same way plants that use photosynthesis operate, we built systems around our catalysts for CO_2 that take these emissions and catalytically transform them into ethanol and other hydrocarbons. Ethanol itself is a potent fuel and an additive in all of our gasoline. Next time you find yourself at a gas station, take note of how much of what you fill your car with is ethanol. One of our goals for this product is to replace fossil fuel–derived ethanol with renewably derived ethanol, synthesized from the CO_2 flue gas being pumped out of fossil fuel power plants. We found from talking to our customers that a distributed method of ethanol generation was more desired than an ethanol-generating catalyst, so we developed one of our products to fill this need.

Our other catalysts help oxidation chemistry occur more efficiently, like what algae and trees use to make the oxygen on our planet. Rather than just selling this material, we put it in a new kind of catalytic converter, kind of like the one that you have in your car. A catalytic converter changes all of the harmful emissions in your car's exhaust into less harmful compounds but does not change the air being blown through your car itself. Our wastewater treatment technology transforms the harmful emissions in wastewater by transforming them into less harmful compounds but does not heat up or change the properties of the water itself. It's a wastewater catalytic converter, another product we found our customers cared about. And that is the most important thing when developing a product: more than the technology, more than how much money you throw behind it, and more than salesmanship, it is making sure that you don't find yourself in a situation where nobody cares about your product.

CHAPTER FOURTEEN

TARUN GANGWANI
Cofounder and Head of Product, Grok

>>>> ABOUT TARUN

Tarun Gangwani is an award-winning product developer and software designer whose work has been used by millions of people around the world. Tarun has been featured in major publications, including the *New York Times*, *CIO.com*, *Tech.Co*, and *Forbes*. Throughout his career, his focus has been solving real human problems with state-of-the-art technology, from cloud computing to artificial intelligence. Today, he works to bring these two capabilities together with Grok, a platform that helps businesses save time and money by reducing application downtime and proactively resolving IT incidents.

Tarun enjoys writing about technology trends and product design, meeting inspiring people, and having new experiences through travel and culture. On the side, he is an avid coffee enthusiast who roasts beans from all over the world. A proud Indiana University alumnus, Tarun has degrees in cognitive science and human-computer interaction design. He and his wife reside in California.

Tarun Gangwani has been named to *Forbes*' 30 under 30 in enterprise tech.

E very entrepreneur dreams of creating a product as successful as the iPhone, so it helps to use Apple's success as a blueprint for how to deliver great solutions to the marketplace. In 2007, the world tilted slightly on its axis as Steve Jobs introduced what has become the standard for all phones today. Apple was the first company to truly figure out the smartphone category because it had a relentless focus on the user experience, it utilized technology as a supporting mechanism to solve user problems, and it thought about scale from day one. Even after ten years, Apple has maintained its success due to its keen awareness of the market and prescient development of the iPhone application ecosystem. Many consumers who purchased an iPhone went on to purchase a MacBook laptop, an Apple Watch, and Apple TV. While competitors were able to achieve parity with Apple's offerings, Apple sustained an advantage because it thought not only about the core products but also about the spaces between them. Apple has provided the gold standard of product design, development, and execution, and the company has certainly influenced the way we think about product.

Entrepreneurs must deliver compelling solutions, like the iPhone, in highly competitive markets. Smaller companies lack cash, human resources, and the time to deliver equally killer innovations. Incumbents in a market can easily dedicate a few resources and spin up a team to squash smaller companies from being a competitive threat. These same battles are waged in every industry for every product category, which also means all small companies will struggle in a similar way, regardless of what they wish to deliver. Buyers are also aware of the pros and cons of choosing a startup instead of an incumbent. Switching costs from one ecosystem are extremely high—how often have you flipped from an Apple product to the analogous Microsoft or Google product or vice versa?

As a result, our product development strategy consists of not only creating experiences that delight customers but also of taking into account the inevitable competitive pressures our offerings will face.

Creating a well-designed product requires focus on end-user *needs*, not just wants. Throughout our approach, we consider both the big picture that our offering exists in and the little details that keep people excited about returning to our service. As customers adopt our product, my team and I celebrate our successes, but remain vigilant under the continued pressure to differentiate, scale thoughtfully, and stay focused.

IDENTIFY USER NEEDS, NOT NICE-TO-HAVES

The Internet offers a diverse and complex set of offerings for every industry. Products not only compete for your attention, but they also have to convince you that you *need* what they have to offer. In just a few seconds, someone has to find your website, gain interest in your product, and then decide it is worth spending hard-earned cash on. As an entrepreneur, winning each sale is euphoric because of how improbable it can be for someone to buy your product, even *after* you optimize funnels, convert a click ad, or do something else to get them in the front door.

Entrepreneurs should seek every opportunity to directly interact with prospective customers, to uncover their needs, and build products they cannot live without. Businesses within a shopping mall use the windows of storefronts to convince you to purchase products, and it's the same on the Internet. While shopping at the mall or online, you usually pass by several products because the businesses could not convince you that the product was an absolute necessity—you figure you can always get it later. On the other hand, you don't usually pass up a product you *need*. Products like these solve a **pain** point you have, are **presented** in an appealing way, and are offered at a **price** you can accept. I use these three *Ps* as a framework to market the products I create, as any one of them can demote a product from a *need* to a *want*.

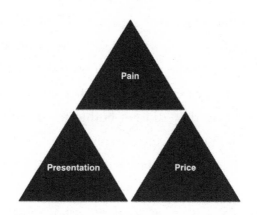

PRESENTATION

The first homepage for Grok, a startup where I ran product, seemed to actively turn people away, because it used too many fancy words, making the product too difficult to understand. Our company sought to improve businesses' mobile and web applications so they fixed their own issues without requiring humans to intervene. We likened the process to homeostasis: when a change occurs in your natural environment, your body responds automatically to the change. For example, your pores close up when it gets cold outside. To create our solution, we used state-of-the-art artificial intelligence algorithms and custom automation capabilities. The application monitoring and analytics space contains many competitive solutions, so we put our IP and biological vision front and center.

When I spoke to prospective customers, I could hear the confusion in their voice: "What's homeostasis?" They even apologized, and I could tell they felt *bad* about it. If anything, I felt bad for making people feel like they did not remember high school biology class. The problem was that we were so excited about differentiating our solution that differentiation became the centerpiece of our content strategy. At first, Grok failed the **presentation** test—prospective clients could not understand what we sold, so they did not bother to consider the price and had no idea what pain point we were solving.

My team and I went back to the basics and reoriented our messaging to highlight the core user pain points we were resolving, instead of the underlying technology we used. Our main homepage headline read, "Maximize custom satisfaction by eliminating [app] downtime." We learned that presenting our solution as a direct answer to pain would guide the reader to learn more about our product. We added content related to industries and use cases that helped potential customers understand how Grok works to help mobile and web applications run efficiently. Once we communicated that we could provide greater value than everyone else, using real metrics and examples, we allowed people to look under the hood at our AI algorithm and automation platforms. The result: we saw a double-digit percentage increase in page views and many more developers signed up for free trials.

PAIN POINTS

To understand the pain points we hoped to solve, I spent many hours speaking with customers about their businesses, picking out little details that would help me understand their current tools and processes. We heard that monitoring dashboards provided too much noise, and customers would get frustrated and burned out when having to manage their applications in the cloud. Using demos and other collateral, we would address prospective client pain points head on, making our offering the obvious choice. In many cases, clients will pay a premium above other alternatives for tools that solve their pain points, even if other competitive offerings have a better user interface or support.

PRICING

Pricing can be difficult to nail down the first time. A deep understanding of the conditions you seek to improve can help you find the initial price range where your product belongs. Prospective Grok clients would rely on humans constantly monitoring applications, so we framed our pricing around the money saved by freeing up people's time to focus on more important problems within their business. In this case, our offering was a cost saver, rather than a revenue generator. Companies can use either the difference of cost savings or revenue generation to set a solution's price and then explain the value of your offering, rather than letting customers get too focused on absolute numbers.

REMOVE BLOCKS THAT LEAD TO FAILURE IN ADOPTION

When I first searched for the words "monitoring solution," I saw hundreds of products, many of which are thoughtfully designed and highly scalable. The best products shared the same characteristics: they were easy to get started (great onboarding), easy to use (great UX), and it worked with the tools people trust (great integration). These three qualities are critical to succeed in a world where too many choices can actually inhibit decision making.

A great onboarding experience can build brand awareness and create customer stickiness. When you purchase an iPhone, the pristine packaging exudes exclusivity and class—making you feel like part of an elite club. Apple takes significant care in designing the box, as it knows it has become an iconic part of the brand. The concept of packaging-as-brand is the same reason the jeweler Tiffany uses distinctive blue boxes to this day.

Once an iPhone buyer carefully pulls off the shrink-wrap, a black slab is revealed that looks like a uniquely designed, custom gift. From there, the onboarding experience moves to the screen, where a software wizard meticulously walks them through steps to get to know the product and set it up to their liking. People can embed their personal tastes into their phone, which simultaneously makes it easy to use and difficult to part with later. This difficult-to-part-with feeling is reinforced when a user's contacts, emails, and photos are uploaded to the device (and Apple's iCloud) in minutes. In the end, customers appreciate Apple's attention to design, and they grow to expect that same experience in the rest of the Apple ecosystem.

Software as a service (SaaS) products like Grok are not excused from having an analogous onboarding experience, and we continued to look for ways to improve the first experience of any new feature that was presented to the user. Grok users, developers of cloud applications, want an experience that enables them to try the product quickly and then allows them to look under the hood for further details later. Our SaaS delivery model means developers can sign up for a free trial in seconds, use a sandbox dataset to try the platform in minutes, and integrate with the tools they use every day to really kick the tires in under an hour. If a developer wishes to learn more about our IP and way of thinking, we provide ample documentation beyond the initial onboarding experience.

As we continued to roll out new features, we would release blog posts that introduced why each capability mattered to the user, emphasizing how we were solving their pain points with each release. Each new version of our product offered more ways for companies to leverage our solution to solve their problems, which we knew would make the solution indispensable to them in the long run. Even though Grok isn't a physical product, like the iPhone, it still emulates the steps of opening a package to create a seamless onboarding experience.

Products with great user experiences delight customers at every opportunity, and well after the onboarding phase. Some tasks a user takes within a product may take a few seconds (on an iPhone, setting a photo they took as the background) and others several minutes (configuring email). Some tasks are for specific users (downloading podcasts), and others are more generally applicable (setting an alarm). *All* of these tasks should have a great experience that speaks to a product's brand and the needs of the user. Each task might require its own mini-onboarding flow that helps someone understand how that particular product feature works. These are typically not as-over-the-top as the initial set up, but they still matter.

Grok's more complex tasks required additional guidance to ensure a great user experience, and we exploited these lengthier interactions by writing engaging copy and providing transparency wherever possible. When a user specified which application they wished to monitor with our product, we provided an *easy setup* feature to auto-discover the application metrics we thought would be most important for Grok to analyze.

If a user had an advanced understanding of how their applications perform, they could specify the metrics themselves using a simple table interface. Developers could start an embedded *guided tour* within our product to bring up a brief, step-by-step wizard that would overlay on top of the product's user interface. This contextual, just-in-time experience gave us a chance for our product to have a voice and build trust with the user.

Most products that come from startups are required to have some initial integrations with a larger, more established tools to build brand recognition and promote growth. When the iPhone was first released, its mapping capability was powered by Google Maps. YouTube was preinstalled. Today, Apple charts its own maps and has its own video sharing service. Thus, at the beginning, Apple focused on its core competency in device manufacturing and platform design while leveraging partnerships to capture a larger mindshare and to build consumer trust. Integration with services can be the core value of a product: Slack, SaaS messaging, and collaboration tool for teams, gained explosive growth by integrating with most every available SaaS application that existed. It became an indispensable tool for small and medium businesses, because it stored several communications around the artifacts from other platforms, making it difficult to leave—creating stickiness.

Grok was designed to integrate with companies that build tools our users trust, and we would use each integration as a brand-building opportunity. From the beginning, we imbedded programmatic hooks into all aspects of the platform (i.e., APIs) to enable developers to write their own mini-programs (a custom *integration*). This allows Grok to work with the other solutions developers use to maintain operational excellence. Our team went further and built these mini-programs for developers as well, providing them free for users of our product. Many of these programs worked with other highly successful companies that are incumbents within their spaces. When Grok discovered a potential application issue, it could trigger a notification to ServiceNow® to let teams know that something was wrong. Upon creating these integrations, we would write a quick blog post about it to share with our audiences. The promotion of an incumbent company like ServiceNow® would draw readers from that user base, meaning more people would be exposed to the Grok platform itself. This practice, known as partner marketing, was both a way to help our user base via integration and to promote the growth of our product.

RAPIDLY TEST IDEAS AND METHODICALLY WORK THROUGH SUGGESTIONS

The world changes fast, as do the tastes of users, the jobs they need done, and the demands they have for tools they leverage. In the old days of software distribution, CDs were released annually to provide updates to the latest operating systems. Now companies use the cloud to push updates on a regular basis. Advanced web companies like Facebook and Netflix test new ideas every second for finely tuned segments. Given the speed of the market today, startups should quickly, but carefully, adapt to user feedback by rapidly testing ideas. As Erik Bernhardsson said, "The speed at which a company innovates is limited by its iteration speed."[11]

To test ideas, companies should constantly measure user behaviors and app performance metrics to get a sense of how a product is used and where people are struggling through the experience. Every

---

[11] Erik Bernhardsson, "Iterate or Die," March 1, 2016, https://erikbern.com/2016/03/02/iterate-or-die/.

click, screen, and data point can be monitored to understand the pain points users have when employing your service. When Apple provides the wrong directions to users within their mapping app, the company makes it easy to for users to report the issue and improve the service. Apple also generally measures the performance of every iPhone it ships, learning when their phones crash (suddenly fail and then restart). These measurements are used as a benchmark for their annual operating system releases where they aim to fix most of these issues.

When building Grok, we used a combination of open-source tools and monitoring products to understand which aspects of the product were resonating with customers. We gained our most valuable information by using this data to conduct further surveys and analysis with current and prospective buyers. We measured the total time users spent on our marketing site and their bounce rate—the percentage of users who left the website right after visiting the homepage. These two metrics provided the first indication that our content strategy was not resonating with our target user base, which led to the marketing site changes discussed earlier. We confirmed this point by talking with users, either by cold-calling them or following up from tradeshows we attended. As we gathered information, we pushed updates to the site and continued to use quantitative and qualitative measures to confirm our changes were making a positive impact.

Prospective Grok buyers typically had great suggestions for improvement for our core product, but I had to weigh them against suggestions from current customers and other work that was in the pipeline. In general, if a prospective buyer's requests were easy to implement and release, then it was worth taking the little extra time to build a capability that could result in a major deal and additional revenue. Meeting these requests may even mean hiring people to build the additional functionality, but this expense can be justified if you see more buyers in the pipeline requesting similar capabilities. Throughout the testing process, a continued focus on user goals will guide you to the features that must come soon, as opposed to those that can wait for a later day.

Building either a physical or a web-based product requires focus and patience. When successes arrive they should be celebrated collectively as a team. Product managers are responsible not only for the actual product that's shipped but also for the well-being of those who helped make the product happen. Each customer that puts their hard-earned cash into your company has validated your team's hard work, so take the time to appreciate your team and your customers! When a customer hits a snag, recognize that issues happen and that you can quickly fix bugs without losing rapport with them. In other words, be fast to admit the problem *and* to fix mistakes.

Most startups will never achieve the same success as the iPhone, but most startups can be successful at solving a user problem and bringing joy to a person. Great companies like Apple have set the bar high for startups to deliver innovation, but a product's greatest successes are relieving a user's pain from having a poor experience with another product or when the user can go home earlier every day. Once a company can provide these experiences repeatedly at scale, they too will have a seismic impact on the world.

➤ HOW DID YOU DEAL WITH COMPETITION, AUDIENCE, AND TRENDS?

Companies contend in a global marketplace, so true dominance and market share come to those who first emerge in one market and then scale to multiple markets. However, with the emergence of the cloud, startups can enter a market faster than ever before. An incumbent's mistake can quickly lead to a disruptive event for the established firm.

During my time at IBM and then growing my own startup, I witnessed product offerings move through three distinct timeframes within their lifecycles. Companies can navigate a competitive landscape within these three timeframes:

1. **Early**—from business conception to first delivery

2. **Mid**—from first delivery to notable market share growth

3. **Late**—from notable growth to having majority share within a market

EARLY-STAGE GROWTH

Early-stage companies are charged with identifying their core competencies and considering which markets they believe have the most potential for initial growth. The Internet and cloud have made it easy to test multiple ideas based on what a team believes are most impactful for the markets they wish to enter. Early adopters of services will invest in technologies that fill a need or solve a critical pain point they have. Once a company identifies these needs and exploits them by creating an innovative yet usable solution, it will most likely see some growth, regardless of competitive pressures that may exist in the market.

When my cofounder and I started Grok, we leaned on our core competencies in cloud computing and automation to deliver a product that satisfied the needs of a specific audience of application developers. We knew that large vendors delivered solutions around the monitoring space, but few echoed our personal experience in this space and our particular IP to solve the problem. Initially, we targeted companies within the cloud hosting market by pointing out how different we were from related services, but eventually we learned that starting from the *similar* pain points we solved would more effectively capture our audience's attention. Instead, we championed our core competencies by showcasing how we work with the ecosystem of tools developers trust. Today, Grok has captured market share because of our ability to disregard an "us versus them" mentality.

Another way to launch a new product is to grow it within an established company. Growing a product within an established company has its benefits and challenges, each of which are a function of the time and budget set aside to nurture the product or service. When we first conceived IBM's cloud platform Bluemix, the company was seeking to make a major play in the cloud infrastructure and management spaces and deliver an offering to compete with other large cloud computing vendors such as Amazon and Microsoft. IBM has many more resources to grow a product, but the company is also under intense pressure to succeed, with shareholders hoping to see expedient returns on their investments. To move with speed, the company leveraged its loyal customers and successful products as channels for growth. With a few testimonials and early successes in hand, the offering could scale to more clients who prefer to see results before adopting a nascent offering.

MID-STAGE TRACTION

When companies have products that move to the mid-stage of growth, they begin to look beyond their initial target market for opportunities in other populations with similar needs. At this point, a mid-stage company has successfully validated its product or service offering. Unfortunately, this makes the market more attractive for competition, and more entrants can emerge who will attempt to latch onto the company's success. To thrive, businesses must not only pick the right adjacent markets to enter but they must continue to directly address substitutes who try to take the share they worked hard to accrue.

Facebook's methodical growth provides a great blueprint for founders to analyze when growing their business into new markets. After dominating Harvard, Facebook opened up its social network to a few more colleges, requiring an .edu address to sign up for the service. Facebook latched onto the needs of college students (e.g., relationships) and used that as leverage to markets with related concerns. After studying a college population for about a year, Facebook expanded to schools of all levels, eventually opening up to entire countries. With each new market, Facebook expanded the product offering with new capabilities that addressed the specific needs of the additional populations while still innovating its base product. With each step, Facebook carefully listened to and gathered data from new audiences and constantly iterated its product to provide value and remain relevant.

With Grok, we charted out the next stages of growth, anticipating the needs of the customers within new market segments even in the earliest stages of product development. As head of product, I conducted several interviews with prospective customers, comparing similarities and differences with a solution like ours. To understand our next market segments, we researched the monitoring and automation tools they use every day. Our product roadmap stayed true to our core offering but expanded to offer integrations with these new tools as appropriate for our new audiences.

Organizations larger than Grok can leverage their established brand within markets they inhabit to ensure prospective customers of their willingness to grow a product. IBM has over one hundred years of experience as a technology vendor, so its move to the cloud provided a natural extension of what it offered to existing customers. For example, customers who already used IBM databases hosted on servers were presented with a seamless opportunity to connect to cloud databases. Customers could manage all of their IBM assets through one established relationship, rather than needing to shop around to other providers.

It can be cumbersome to make changes to your core product offering during this mid-stage because the initial product validation and your early users motivate your company to stay the course, especially as customers adopt your offering for critical business needs. As IBM's cloud solution Bluemix continued to grow, user interface changes needed to be carefully evaluated and tested with existing clients as well as prospective clients. The team established a "sponsor user" program, which signed on a select portion of customers to try product enhancements before the enhancements were released to the general public. Programs like the sponsor user program provide a safe space for mid-stage companies to test potentially radical product roadmap departures. Most customers enjoy being a part of such programs, as they get to influence the offerings and provide thought leadership as well.

LATE-STAGE ESTABLISHMENT

Companies in the late stages of growth will seek sustained competitive advantages, but despite their impressive success, they should remain cognizant of new entrants. Companies at this scale should consider how their core business can be broken down to achieve optimizations within various areas of the initial offering. Each part of the business will face its own competitive challenges and opportunities, but the overall growth of the entire business should not be lost. Integrating with other companies can transform complex products into differentiated offerings that share resources among them, so it benefits businesses if they understand their products as a suite of offerings, rather than as one monolithic concept.

As Amazon created its dominant e-commerce platform, the company observed that its cloud computing infrastructure innovations could be provided as discrete services for other companies to leverage as well. This idea birthed Amazon Web Services, the most dominant cloud computing as a service provider in the world. Amazon, initially a web store, has since created new units within several areas, including cloud computing, artificial intelligence, mobile devices, and even shipping and freight management. Amazon recognized that the core competencies within the teams they developed to solve their own problems could be spun off as companies that a conglomerate could manage. To sustain growth of the larger company, Amazon has expanded and bundled several incentives of the individual units within its *Prime* offering, providing lock-in to many of its services at an afford-able yearly price. This diversified dominance in several industries will keep the company relevant, even if the individual units succumb to disruptions by emergent threats.

When I worked at IBM as a designer, I saw firsthand how the company transformed its business by creating organizations around core team competencies. IBM hired thousands of new employees within a singular, common design unit *before* deploying them to the company's various units within Cloud, Watson, and Mobile segments. The benefit of bringing employees on as cohorts is the lasting relationships they have during their journeys within the company, which leads to knowl-edge sharing about the markets they will support. Additionally, my exposure to designers with different skill sets helped expand my own, which enabled me to jump onto new products that needed someone with a diversified set of skills.

It is both more exciting and more challenging than ever to build and sustain a business, thanks to increased access to emerging tech-nologies. Within hours, startups can conceptualize, build, and ship an idea to thousands of users. The Internet has made it easier than ever to research and analyze companies and find unique points of differ-entiation that can be used as an entryway into a market. I consider competitive analysis and market research a core part of my role as a startup entrepreneur—not just at these early stages of my company, but in the later stages that are, hopefully, to come. My goal will be to continue to focus on the unique user needs within each target market we enter, ever wary of assumptions about the desires of customers who I hope to delight with my products.

CHAPTER FIFTEEN

JOEY PRIMIANI
Founder and CEO, Superfuture Labs, Previously Backplane and Cortex

⟫⟫ ABOUT JOEY

Joey Primiani is an entrepreneur, designer, inventor, and digital artist. Passionate and creative, his web designs have been called "ingenious" by Fast Company, "charming . . . incredibly unique" by Mashable, and "simple and brilliant" by TechCrunch. Named to *Forbes* list 2016 of "30 Under 30" and *Business Insider*'s "25 Under 25 Hot Young Stars in Silicon Valley Tech," Primiani founded his first web development and design company at the age of eight.

A young leader in the field of user experience design, behavior design, and gestural interfaces, Primiani created many mobile and tablet applications as an intern at Google, Yahoo!, and Revision3 by the age of nineteen, where he focused on building beautiful, intuitive products that half a billion people around the world use on a daily basis.

As the creator and CEO of his second venture, Cortex, funded by i/o Ventures, Primiani created a patented technology for a content-sharing application utilizing radially distributed menus that became the fastest-growing sharing platform on Chrome and was ultimately acquired in 2012. A critic's favorite, Cortex has been called "insanely fast and beautifully built" by Mashable.

In 2011, Primiani cofounded the company Backplane, a platform that allows like-minded people to connect across their shared interests. It raised $18.9 million Series A, funded by Lady Gaga, Eric Schmidt, Google Ventures, Troy Carter, Sequoia Capital, Greylock Partners, Peter Thiel Founders Fund, Ron Conway SV Angel, and more. Joey created Lady Gaga's official fan community website, LittleMonsters. com. Viewed by millions on a monthly basis, it is a place where fans can come together and share their artwork and stories, as inspired by Gaga.

Currently, he is the founder of the Palo Alto–based mobile startup studio Superfuture Labs, whose mission is to advance humanity through technology, art, and design. Superfuture is the creator of popular iOS and Android mobile apps such as Life, Sketch, Kiwi, and Spaces. By adhering to design principles, the products are both tool and toy—beautiful, simple, fun, playful, and friendly.

He serves on the boards of the fashion technology company Studio XO, the collective consciousness app Entangled, the Q&A website IceBreak, the virtual reality company Retinad VR, and the remesh and astronaut training facility Star Harbor Academy. He often lectures and writes about entrepreneurship and technology.

Joey is an advocate of transhumanism, the singularity, space exploration, commercial astronautics, STEAM Education, arts and culture, fashion technology, sustainable living, animal welfare, human rights, effective altruism, artificial intelligence, and intelligent clothing.

When building a company, it is important not to create one for the sake of creating a company. It is most effective to close your eyes and imagine what the ideal future looks like, and then build what is missing today, to create the world you would want to live in.

You can easily do this by closely observing your own behavior throughout the day and seeing what you can optimize or make better. There is a significant chance that if you build a product that you love and use on a daily basis, there are many other people like you who would benefit from the same. The best companies are often built by founders making something that provides value, that they could benefit from, something they, themselves, would like to use.

CHAPTER SIXTEEN

LOUIS-VICTOR JADAVJI

Cofounder, Wiivv

⟫⟫⟫ ABOUT LOUIS-VICTOR

Louis-Victor "LV" Jadavji is an entrepreneur focused on wellness and 3-D printing. LV cofounded Wiivv in the summer of 2014. Wiivv has since raised $8 million in venture capital and now has a team of thirty people in Vancouver and San Diego. Its inaugural product—a custom fit 3-D-printed orthotic insole—is the most successful consumer 3-D-printed product of all-time. LV believes that Wiivv's custom wearables will one day usher in the era of bionic human beings. He was selected by *Forbes* as part of its "30 Under 30" list in the field of Manufacturing and Industry and is the youngest on the list at twenty-two years of age.

STUMBLE UPON GREAT IDEAS

During my teen years, I started seriously considering what my career could look like. Playing pro basketball crossed my mind. Overall, I felt best suited to be a diplomat—I was a good speaker and personable—and my family agreed. It did not cross my mind to pursue an entre-preneurial career—that is, until I was met with a problem that affected me. As a vegan and an athlete, I needed to know the ingredients of my meals when eating out. The goal was to avoid compromising the proper calorie, carbohydrate, protein, and micronutrient intake required to perform as a competitive athlete for the sake of my vegan diet. My first startup built an app for that. After a year of learning how to do things, the startup folded as a result of our lack of experience in most aspects of growing a business.

During my sophomore year at Claremont McKenna College, I developed a passion for 3-D printing after attending the Kairos Global Summit in New York. At the summit, Autodesk and General Electric demonstrated the possibilities for the technology—everything from 3-D-printed imitation body parts to jet engine parts were on the display that day. At the time, I had a venture importing compressors for natural gas vehicles from China to the Midwest and was also driving a 1991 Saab Turbo 900—a cherished gift from my father—which had some parts that needed replacing. Being interested in cars, a close friend and I figured, "Wouldn't it be great to 3-D print parts for vintage cars?" And so we did. Our customers included the car restoration shows on the History Channel, and it was fun to try to engineer solutions for them. Materials available for 3-D printing didn't work well enough in some cases; nonetheless, I learned all I could about the 3-D printing industry, reading every industry newsletter and attending the Inside 3D Printing Conference in New York in the spring of 2013.

Successful entrepreneurs often say that one idea leads to a better idea—and this was the case for me. Due to a high-jumping injury from my high school days, I wear foot orthotics. They were—and still are—expensive, poorly designed, complicated to get, and sometimes inaccurately made. In late 2013, I had to get refitted for orthotics and was prepared with a few questions for my foot doctor. "How are these made?" I asked. "How does the cost balloon so much, and what are your margins?" I learned of the intense labor involved, and the oftentimes silly number of redos and unhappy customers. What made things click for me, however, was that the set of recommended materials for most foot orthotics was easily replaceable with materials readily available from a 3-D printer, which I knew because of my exposure to the material sets from printing car parts. Thus, my work with car parts—my first idea—led to 3-D printing orthotics, which was a better idea. For this reason, I encourage keeping your ears tuned for better ideas germinating from original ones. Some entrepreneurs ignore important opportunities because of tunnel vision and the refusal to let go of original ideas when better ideas come along.

The new idea was bubbly! Foot pain. Solve foot pain. Solve centuries of ill-fitting footwear. Make the solution mobile accessible so that all could access it. Why not make this my focus?

In the fall semester of 2013, I collaborated with a close friend on an end-of-semester project involving 3-D printing orthotics as a case study. I made connections with foot experts around the world in the process. Continuing to foster an idea that I cared about as earnestly as this one was a challenge while still studying at Claremont McKenna College, so I planned to drop out after my junior year. Instead, I moved to Mountain View, California, to work for Atlassian Software in San Francisco during the second semester of my junior year, which was within the scope of a special program of Claremont McKenna's, but based in Silicon Valley.

➤ WHAT ARE THE BENEFITS AND DRAWBACKS OF COFOUNDERS, TEAMMATES, AND MENTORS?

PLAN GREAT RELATIONSHIPS

While Atlassian was a great company to work for, it was not my first choice when contemplating a move to Silicon Valley. You see, back in the spring of 2013, at the Inside 3D Printing Show in New York, I met a fellow alumnus of Claremont McKenna College, Shamil Hargovan, who, at the time, was leading the charge for Hewlett-Packard's foray into 3-D printing out of Sunnyvale. I sensed that Hewlett-Packard could shake up the industry and fuel tremendous innovation, so I was keen on maintaining the relationship. We got along very well, and I wanted to work with the innovation team behind HP's 3-D printing, yet we could not determine a good fit for me at HP.

Then we had dinner. Three times. Shamil told me, "One cup of tea, I know you. Two cups of tea, you're my friend. Three cups of tea, let's work together." That was the most helpful cue ever. He was open to my idea to create a seamless experience for orthotics and insoles—going from mobile scan to 3-D manufacturing—and we discussed how the idea could be expanded to different kinds of footwear and even cover the body with perfectly matching wearables to enhance human biomechanics.

In the waning days of my stay in Mountain View, I needed to see Shamil one more time. He was in Australia visiting family. I extended my trip until his return. We had our final meeting and shook hands on a partnership for Wiivv, the universal platform for body-perfect (our word for "custom") gear.

Beyond planning my relationship with Shamil, I had a map of my desired "Mastermind Group," a concept espoused by Napoleon Hill, author of *Think and Grow Rich*. It included the names and roles of all the individuals I dreamed to have involved with Wiivv in some way. There were roughly twenty people on this map, and I had met only five or six of them. Today, 90% of the group is involved. The few who aren't involved were not worth including after all. Again, luck has something to do with it, but planning years ahead who you want in your circle helps get the universe working for you.

As my story shows, perseverance pays off very well. I continue to believe that you can forge a special relationship with anyone in business if you make a true show of passion for your beliefs and ideas. That self-assurance is contagious and makes the realization of grand schemes seem like a possible feat. This attitude was very helpful when I had to convince my parents that I would leave school in the third year of a four-year program. I sent them an email with my thoughts and plans confidently laid out, and that email helped turn their opinions in my favor. Before that email, my conversations with my parents on this subject weren't easy. To improve things, I made it a habit to speak as if what I wanted was already mine.

If you have an idea that energizes your soul like Wiivv did mine, do not wait for a more convenient time to pursue it. After that email to my parents, I compromised and agreed to finish the semester I had started. A month after, a competitor burst onto the scene with a whopping $7 million in funding and Founders Fund backing. Founders Fund— my dream fund—had backed a competitor because I compromised. I remember tearing up at the news while walking down University

Avenue in Palo Alto. I felt like I was losing months in school while my competitor gained momentum. Since then, I think we've made up the ground we lost.

It's a big world. With six billion people, someone else is likely thinking the exact same thing you are. While being first to market is not necessarily the key to success—in Wiivv's case, we're doing swimmingly—in new industries, like 3-D printing consumer goods, it helps because of the novelty you'll have. Funds will back the original startup with the big idea, but not the next one. Press will cover the first heartwarming story, but not the next one. Narratives get old quickly. You want the narrative on your side so you'll have an easier time with funding and public relations. If you can avoid it, don't be second.

MANAGE EXPECTATIONS

The most important thing I've learned to do in my young entrepreneurial career is to *manage expectations*. It sounds simple; however, it's a hard-earned skill to be forthright about the execution risk of getting something done. Without that skill, I wouldn't consider myself a principled entrepreneur. So work at it.

It feels right to be *credible*, for my words to carry weight.

It's important for entrepreneurs to be acutely aware of stakeholder expectations. The companies you found will need varying levels of inputs and resources. We are human. We can execute beautifully, but we cannot always make miracles happen. This gap between fair expectations and stating that you can defy the laws of gravity is the biggest lie you will tell people repeatedly. In many cases, it can be your undoing.

In my first business—the nutrition app—despite having a hot product, we thought we could bootstrap ourselves to huge success in a highly competitive marketplace—restaurant recommendations. That lie cost us.

In my second business—a natural gas compressor idea—we promised ourselves huge success building a business importing heavy industrial equipment and machinery while still pursuing our college degrees. That lie cost us dearly.

In my third business—Wiivv—the time and cost it would take to *create* a new market was underestimated. We've successfully adjusted, but that gap caused us to prematurely rush into a market that is typically adverse to change, when our marketing budget was still lumpy. This cost us in bets that did not meet a threshold for brand awareness and precious startup time experimenting with growth-hacking techniques.

In the aftermath of these undoings and close calls, I often wonder why I would repeat this pattern over and over again. Sometimes it's a combination of a bit of ego and trying to make people happy. Take, for example, how easy it would be to delay a moment of truth when there are still millions in your startup bank account. Picture yourself there. I've played this mental game with myself. There are investors around the table. You have fresh financing, and fresh expectations, and also fresh risk to match those fresh expectations. In situations like these, I would love to have the clarity of fair expectations, whether they are expectations for recruitment, burn rate, go-to-market strategy, and so on. And when things don't work out—again, playing this in my head—I would hope to never again delay a moment of truth in hopes that a miracle may happen. I'd just be doing so to please people, after all. And the irony is that I would have a higher risk of disappointing and losing on a trusting relationship.

To beat your ego, I highly recommend reading the book *Ego is the Enemy* by Ryan Holiday. To beat the people pleaser in you, what follows will help. Realize the irony that when you try to please, you will lose your credibility eventually. What will people think of you then?

You see, when people have different expectations for a business, it can be a recipe for discord and failure. The more variations there are to juggle, the more likely you are to play the people-pleaser role. People pleasing is a big mistake, so the key is to have one set of expectations that you have to meet to keep everyone on the same page. If later employees and investors join the fold, then you can stick to the same rules of play—and they can fairly judge your good credibility. I've had close friend entrepreneurs tell me about horror stories of stakeholders who continually change their expectations. This behavior is self-serving: by changing expectations, they are pitting you against your close partners and all the stakeholders who have kindly ascribed to the expectations that were set at the beginning.

How do you measure success for a startup? Ask yourself: Did you accomplish what you set out to accomplish? Did that message stay the same among the people you kicked this off with and all new stakeholders coming in? What I'm saying is, if you always have a fixed point of reference, you can avoid playing the people-pleaser with insufficient resources to make everyone happy.

Close friend entrepreneurs taught me how to mitigate this execution risk. First, be truthful with yourself as to what's a realistic expectation—ask, "What's your code?" Second, come to an agreement with your partners on those expectations at the onset of your business. Finally, have every single person who comes into the fold ascribe to the same expectations. Let's look closer at each of these steps.

STEP 1: WHAT'S YOUR CODE?

With your family and friends, define success from this venture to the next and what would be a neat conclusion to your career. What's really important? That you tired yourself out in your twenties, but had a billion-dollar valuation and enriched yourself for a relatively small $5 million? Or that you extended your entrepreneurial career with good lifestyle habits and you retired a billionaire? Your expectations for yourself, and how they adjust when seen in the context of your whole life, are really important to set once and for all. *Think and Grow Rich* by Napoleon Hill is a great book to read at this moment in the cycle.

STEP 2: WHY IS THIS ONE WORTHWHILE?

With your business partners or cofounders, figure out what success looks like for this particular venture. Jot it down in numbers. Sign off on it. What do you want the company to exit for? What do you each want to make individually? This thought process is critical because sometimes selling the company for more money (and taking more capital to get there) means a lesser financial outcome for any of you. Who do you want to exit to? This is also critical because exits sometimes come with golden handcuffs, such as being tied to a corporate job for years. Ending up in a VP role at Google or Facebook could be exciting, but at other companies, not so much.

STEP 3: WHY WOULD SOMEONE HELP YOU?

With your early employees and angel investors, figure out what personal success means for them. Your first engineer may want to buy a house by the water for a cool million earned from this company when he hits forty. Ask yourself, can his wishes be fulfilled with the trajectory you've mapped for the company and the equity you intend to give? Think about it. If you've realistically defined success in your niche as selling for $50 million in five years, and you're giving the employee, who is now thirty-eight, a small part of 1%, then your employee's expectations are out of whack. Don't ever sit there and say it's possible and hope he or she buys it. If you do, sooner or later, this person, who could have been instrumental to your long game, will never want to work for you on any other venture. Again, think about the math. Does it line up with expectations? Some entrepreneurs, like the founders of Buffer, have been brutally honest with public charts on equity allocation, and it serves them well.

Then there are your early investors, your first few board members—the list goes on and on. You simply cannot make all these people happy if everyone has different expectations. That's why you stick to the expectations you had at the onset, except in the rarest occasions where you believe all your stakeholders are aligned and no grudges will be held. In doing so, never *ever* move the goalposts.

By making sure that we're all aligned on the desired and realistic outcomes, we're already working toward an honest reflection of the inputs necessary to be successful. By now, you probably think I'm talking about money. If so, let me point you to the most valuable resource: your team's time.

It's a fast world of venture capital money, and raising millions can feel good. Sometimes, though, because of those millions, the expectations you ascribed to your business get lost, the same expectations you had when you made your sales pitch to those investors. If you're moving the goalposts—changing expectations—because you ascribed unrealistic expectations to your business to get funding, it won't be long before things go awry. I attend many founder meetings between startups, and the above is all too common. At Wiivv, we've learned from the past, and from mistakes made by fellow entrepreneurs, and have grown very good at making a compelling but realistic case for the growth prospects of our business. Staying honest about expectations has saved us tremendously and allowed us to maintain credibility with all our stakeholders.

The following is the typical scenario we strive to avoid: the goalpost is the time to execute on budget. The minute you raise venture capital funds, you're on a clock. Every milestone is a brick you need to build your business. If you're catching yourself skipping milestones because you argue with yourself and your board that they're not necessary, that's far worse than trying to play catch-up.

The minute you start missing milestones, you start adding more people or resources to your current task. Ironically, this is killing your chances of succeeding because your runway is shortening to please the current expectations of your stakeholder group. To see how this *doubly* kills you, take a look at Brook's Law. Brook's Law states that adding engineers late to a project actually makes a project come in later.

When making goalpost decisions, get the facts, then make the decisions alone with *only* your one set of expectations in mind. It's good to get used to making fact-based decisions on your own and quickly. Have a personal code, stick to it, and make managing expectations with integrity part of that code. You'll also make faster decisions as a result.

With people, you'll find it's sometimes faster to build a relationship when you're showy and you exaggerate likely outcomes, but being principled and cultivating a relationship over two to three years pays off in the long run. People will trust your integrity and be willing to consider anything you throw at them, in this venture and the next one.

Learning the importance of managing expectations with integrity took a lot of introspection. This is something I want to take seriously, and I hope other entrepreneurs who I work with will take it seriously as well.

CHAPTER SEVENTEEN

⟫⟫⟫ ABOUT ROSE

Rose is the cofounder and CEO of Six Foods, a company that makes Chirps—healthy, delicious, and sustainable foods with insects. (Her cofounder, Laura D'Asaro, is also featured in this book.) She is a *Forbes* "30 Under 30" in Social Entrepreneurship, an *Elle* Impact Award winner, an Echoing Green Climate Fellow, a MassChallenge Gold Winner, a Harvard Dean's Design Challenge winner, and a TEDx speaker. Rose worked in strategy and marketing at Abercrombie & Fitch and Microsoft. In college, Rose managed HSA Cleaners and the Harvard Shop through Harvard Student Agencies, managing an annual budget of $1.5 million. She also has a passion for education and sits on the board of an education nonprofit, Wema, Inc., in Kenya. Rose is a graduate of Harvard College and plans to matriculate to Harvard Business School in 2018 as part of the 2+2 program.

There is an ongoing debate in the entrepreneurship community about the importance of cofounders. Investors are more likely to invest in companies with multiple founders, rather than one founder, because there is strength (and more skill sets) in numbers. I know that if it weren't for my cofounder Laura, I would not still be working on Six Foods, a company that makes food out of cricket flour. Starting a company is one of the most stressful and isolating experiences. One day, your manufacturer could drop you out of the blue, and you could have no products to sell. Or you could spend all your life savings on your idea only to find out that no one wants your product or service. If I didn't have Laura to bounce ideas off of and to share in my misery, then I am not sure I could have withstood the stress of entrepreneurship for so long.

Despite the sunny image Laura and I give off in public, we are like any other cofounder team with our fair share of problems. Many of our problems stem from the fact that we are inherently different people. I grew up in a very strict, traditional Chinese American household. As the only child to my immigrant parents, I felt a lot of pressure to fulfill my parents' expectations. Until the age of twenty-two, I was almost the perfect immigrant child. I studied hard, got into Harvard, and got an amazing full-time offer to work at Microsoft. On the surface, I was your classic consultant, banker-type professional.

My cofounder and college roommate is completely the opposite. Laura grew up in Seattle, Washington, to parents who encouraged her to explore her most creative and wild ideas. Every Halloween or school spirit day, Laura made her own elaborate costumes. I'm talking about covering her entire body in red, orange, and yellow streamers and tying her hair to fifty helium-pumped balloons, so that she could *be* fire. In high school, she decided she wanted to raise money for cancer, so she crawled the world's fastest mile and raised $5,000 for cancer research. The depths of her imagination were allowed to flourish, and no one ever told her "no."

We have very complementary skillsets, but because we see the world differently, we sometimes argue. I am the practical business-person, and she wants to explore all the possibilities and crazy ideas. Sometimes I am frustrated because she can't see that her ideas don't generate sales. Sometimes she is frustrated because she thinks I am stifling all the fun. Our fights can escalate so fast, suddenly we are screaming at each other, and Laura is crying, and I am so mad that I cannot sleep at night.

We have been through four years of college and three years of running a business together, and in that time, these are the top three lessons I have learned about having a cofounder.

LESSON 1: PICK SOMEONE WHO CARES MORE ABOUT THE COMPANY AND MISSION THAN ABOUT HIS OR HER OWN SUCCESS

If you worked with Laura and me from day one, you would question why we are still working together. From the beginning, we have dis-agreed. Laura wanted to create a food truck that sold bug food to the local community. She loves community projects that bring people together, where she can be close to the lives she's affecting. I wanted to create a consumer packaged-goods company because I wanted to be in every grocery store in the nation. My thought was that the only way we could make a difference in the world with our idea was to scale the company globally. That way, people would actually start to rely on insects as a protein source.

Laura wanted to create an insect burger, because she believed that was how we were going to create change immediately. The whole idea was that if people could eat insect meat instead of animal meat, we could dramatically decrease carbon emissions, water usage, land usage, and more. While Laura's idea was on-point, the simple fact was that no one in America was ready to eat an insect burger three years ago. I was convinced that our company would shut down within months of creating an insect burger because we'd find that there was no market for our product.

This year, Laura spent many hours selling our product to a summer camp. I was so incredibly mad at her for spending her time selling to a summer camp and not to retailers. My thought was that the only way we could scale was by, first, getting into as many grocery stores as possible and, second, by showing positive results in those stores, so we would get into more stores. I believed that any time not spent on that goal was a waste of time. Laura disagreed and continued to pursue this summer camp. A month later, they placed an order for ten thousand pounds of Chirps and fed over 300,000 kids cricket chips. I was so wrong. Laura furthered our mission significantly with one sale, because we helped educate 300,000 kids about sustainable eating, which is our goal.

We have had fundamental disagreements from day one, but the reason we are still working together and flourishing is because we have the same goal. It has never been about being right or wrong. We both put what is best for the company first. Even though we sometimes disagree about what strategies to use, we know that staying together and working through our issues is best for the company. Therefore, we are always able to work out problems. You can always get more money or pivot if your idea is not working, but if the team is not working, that's the end of your company.

LESSON 2: DEFINED ROLES BETWEEN COFOUNDERS CAN HELP MITIGATE A LOT OF PROBLEMS

Since Six Foods was just Laura and I from the beginning, she and I had to run everything in the business—marketing, sales, finances, operations, actually packing the orders and shipping them out, etc. However, when we both did everything, we kept stepping on each other's toes, and decision making took twice the time. For example, something as simple as writing an email newsletter to our customers took days, because Laura and I would keep editing each other's drafts and disagreeing about the messaging of the newsletter. I also remember the early days when we applied for different grants and awards. We would stay up until 5:00 a.m. the night before the grant was due, and by 3:00 a.m. we were shouting at each other because we couldn't agree on how to answer the questions.

After a while, it became apparent that we did not have the capacity to do everything together, so we divided the business duties. I was in charge of marketing, finances, fundraising, and partnerships, and Laura was in charge of operations and sales. At first, we were happy that we were able to divide tasks; it felt like we were finally able to get more done. However, over time, it was readily apparent that Laura did not like being in an operations role. She is not a detail-oriented person and she often will miss small details. However, in the case of operations, small details could mean the difference between an order of one hundred and an order of one thousand, or it could mean sending an order to the wrong state. Laura felt like she was set up to fail in her role, yet we needed her in that role because we did not have the money and resources to hire someone else.

For a year, Laura and I continued to fight internally, and she struggled personally in the business because she felt like she was constantly failing or about to fail. Every day she woke up in a state of panic, because she was afraid of all the mistakes she might potentially make that would ruin the business. Another problem was that Laura was not interested in taking on any of my roles. Therefore, we were stuck in our positions, and both of us were on edge and constantly fighting. The fighting and tension were so constant that we didn't know if it was caused by the mismatch of roles or a fundamentally toxic partnership.

One year later, I can confidently say that we are not a fundamentally toxic partnership, and most of our problems arose from the mismatch of roles. We have hired two part-time operational team members to take those responsibilities away from Laura, so that she can just focus on sales. Ever since that switch, we are much happier, and Laura feels again like she is contributing to the business and succeeding on a personal level.

LESSON 3: IF NOTHING ELSE IS WORKING, TRY COUPLE'S COUNSELING

It is very natural for cofounders to have conflicts; put any two people in a room for years and I guarantee they will fight. However, when you put two people with very different viewpoints and skill sets together, there is a greater chance for conflict. Sometimes, the best partnerships are the fieriest partnerships. From the beginning of my partnership with Laura, we've had advisors who've gotten to know us personally and we've turned to them when our conflicts become too much to settle between the two of us.

About a year ago, Laura and I hit the low point of our partnership. We had worked ourselves to the bone for years, and we were burned out. On top of that, Laura was unhappy in her role, and I felt like I had the weight of the entire business on my shoulders. Every interaction between us led to tension and earth-shattering fights. We admitted to each other that we were the source of each other's unhappiness. We worked with different advisors who listened to us and tried to help mediate. However, what Laura and I lacked was a tool kit to reverse the toxic cycles we had developed with each other over the years we had known each other. We knew what our problems were, but we didn't know how to fix them.

One advisor suggested we go to couple's counseling. At that point, we'd exhausted all other options, and we were willing to try anything. I am so glad we listened to that advice. An unbiased healthcare professional helped Laura and me communicate our pain to each other in a common language, something we'd had trouble with in the past. The best part of the counseling sessions was that the therapist gave us exercises we had to practice that helped bridge the gap between us. For example, Laura is very much a feelings person, so she doesn't hear facts and rationale until she feels supported or can understand my feelings. Therefore, before I disagree with her using facts and rationale, I learned how to say, "When this happened, I felt . . ." I had to learn to establish common ground with Laura before we could move toward an understanding. Because we were so invested in our relationship and business, we were able to work through our deepest issues. Now, I'm happy to say that we are so much happier, and we are on the same team, with only a few spats now and then.

Ultimately, founding a company with someone is almost like getting married *and* having a child together immediately. You pour your energy into raising this baby and, most likely, your partner will sometimes disagree with how you go about it. Their points of objection will frustrate you, break your heart, and shatter your ego. Meanwhile, you are probably doing the same thing to them. Any partnership where you are building something you care about with someone else is hard work, because there are two minds and two hearts that have to align. However, when they do align, that's when the magic happens. Just remember to choose someone whose heart is in the right place, create separate roles, and try couple's counseling if all else fails!

▶ WHAT IS THE MOST IMPORTANT ADVICE YOU WOULD GIVE TO FIRST-TIME FOUNDERS?

I was starting my last semester of college when my college roommate and now cofounder, Laura, sent me an article about why we should all eat insects. Several years ago, she had been studying abroad in Tanzania when she saw a street vendor selling fried caterpillars. She was horrified by the food choice, but also intrigued. As a vegetarian, she didn't know how to think about insects—should insects be considered vegetarian or not? In the end, she decided to buy the fried caterpillar (when in Tanzania, right?) and before she could think about it, she put it in her mouth and bit down. Her first thought? *This tastes like lobster!* It actually makes sense because insects and crustaceans are closely related.

When she got back to the United States, she started researching— why are people eating insects in Tanzania and not in the United States? She found out that insects are one of the most sustainable protein sources. For example, it takes two thousand gallons of water to make a pound of beef, but only one gallon of water to make a pound of insects. On top of that, insects are even more sustainable than some plant proteins, like soy protein. In terms of health benefits, insects like crickets have more protein and 33% less fat than beef, and they are a complete animal protein with all nine amino acids.

Laura was ecstatic! As a vegetarian, she had found the sustainable, complete protein source she had been looking for her entire life. She sent me an article about why the world should be eating insects, because I guess that's what you do when you have a crazy idea. It just so happened that I had recently returned from Beijing, China, where my friends had dared me to eat a fried scorpion. I'd had the same reaction Laura did—this tastes like shrimp! So when Laura sent me the article, all I could think was, *why aren't we eating insects?* So we set out to find a way to make bugs appealing to Americans.

Along the way, we have learned many lessons. I want to share with you three of the biggest ones: (1) the more you fail, the more likely you are to succeed; (2) your idea is not that special, so don't be afraid to tell people about it; and (3) entrepreneurship is not right for most people, but everyone should try it at least once.

LESSON 1: THE MORE YOU FAIL, THE MORE LIKELY YOU WILL SUCCEED

For us, failure started from day one. Our first experiment in figuring out how to make bugs appealing to Americans was to fry up crickets in our dorm room and feed them to our friends. Our friends freaked out! One of the guys even fell out of his chair from pure shock. However, our friends' reactions didn't stop us—in fact, we took it on as a challenge. We continued to experiment with insects in the kitchen, changing their form, taste, and texture. We even found a Michelin-star-trained chef to work with us pro bono, every week, after hours, in the kitchen to understand how to create an insect food that people could get behind.

We finally figured out that the best way to get Americans excited about eating insects would be to put them in a form that is not scary. We created cricket flour by drying crickets and milling them into flour. Then we put the flour in America's favorite snack food—chips! We called them Chirps Chips. We took our idea to investors, because we needed to raise money to actually make cricket chips. Generally, most investors politely told us we were crazy. One investor actually said to us, "I have been an investor for ten years, and this is the worst idea

I have ever heard." His words will be forever burned into my brain. Some people might have given up right then and there, but we refused to let him bring us down. We decided to prove him wrong.

Because we couldn't raise any institutional investments for our idea at that point, we had to find another route to raise the funds we needed to prove out our idea. We launched a Kickstarter campaign and, to our surprise, we raised $70,000 in thirty days, making us one of the most well-funded food Kickstarters ever. We used that money to make cricket chips. It turns out that you cannot make a chip in your own kitchen, because you need to cook it at temperatures up to 700 degrees, and each chip has to have consistent texture and flavor. Therefore, we needed a manufacturer who could make our chips for us. We ended up calling more than four hundred manufacturers—we got more than four hundred "nos" before someone said "yes."

Since creating our first chip, we failed a thousand more times. Once, we printed the wrong labels on our chips and we personally had to unlabel and relabel ten thousand bags of chips. For a while, we focused too much on operations and not on sales. We failed in other ways, too. Each time we failed, we could have ended our business right then and there—some of our failures were so big that it didn't seem like there was any rational way to keep going. One of the things that kept us going was that we knew we had survived other massive obstacles in the past, so we always kept pushing in the face of challenges. The great thing about the failure process is that each time you fail, it gets a little easier to manage than the time before, because you already survived all the other failures. In the end, if you fail enough and survive, you will eventually begin to grow.

LESSON 2: YOUR IDEA IS NOT THAT SPECIAL, SO DON'T BE AFRAID TO TELL PEOPLE ABOUT IT

There are two big mistakes entrepreneurs make: (1) they think their idea is special, and they operate in stealth mode because they are afraid their idea will be stolen, and (2) they are afraid to show people unfinished ideas and work, because they are afraid of criticism. Both are deadly mistakes. The truth is, if you have an idea, chances are someone else has thought of the same idea already. The difference in ideas comes down to execution. Take Facebook, for example. Before Facebook, there was Friendster and Myspace, and many other social networks in development. What set Facebook apart in its success and growth was its ability to test its idea and change what did not work.

When we first created our cricket chips, we decided to use black beans in our recipe to make our chips healthier. Black beans turned the chip purple, so it looked like a healthy blue chip. Had we not shared the idea with anybody else, we would be a failed company today with a purple cricket chip. When we created the purple cricket chip, we put the picture on our Kickstarter campaign and our website to test how people would respond to it. Everybody asked us, "Is your chip dark because of the crickets?" We found that consumers were scared to try our chip because they thought they could see the cricket in the color of the chip. Therefore, we changed our recipe from black beans to navy beans, which made our chips yellow, a more "normal" color for chips. After that, we never lost sales from people who were afraid to try our chips due to the color.

Also, in the beginning, we came up with many theories about who would be eating our chips. We assumed vegetarians would eat cricket chips, because Laura is vegetarian. It turns out, most vegetarian thought-leaders did not know what to think about eating crickets, so they were unwilling to endorse the idea. Then, we thought maybe outdoorsy people would like to eat cricket chips, because they care about the environment. It turns out that outdoorsy people won't bring cricket chips on their outdoorsy activities, because the chips get crushed in their backpacks.

We could have invested lots of time, energy, and money in the wrong idea if we had not immediately tested our assumptions with our consumers. Because we asked for feedback from our customers and pretty much anyone who would listen, we were able to fix our wrong assumptions immediately. This saved us the little time, money, and energy we could spare to focus on the right idea and approach. In the end, success comes in part from getting to market first, but more so from getting to market in the right way.

LESSON 3: ENTREPRENEURSHIP IS NOT RIGHT FOR MOST PEOPLE, BUT EVERYONE SHOULD TRY IT AT LEAST ONCE

The last three years have been very difficult, with many emotional ups and downs. I live in San Francisco, one of the most expensive cities in the world, on an annual salary of $22,500. For years, my cofounder and I worked over one hundred hours a week, manually labeled tens of thousands of chip bags, and called hundreds of manufacturers before finding one who would make our product. I have been kicked out of manufacturers' offices, laughed at, told by investors that my company is the worst idea they have ever heard, and more. The list goes on.

However, I have also learned how to build a product from scratch and I have learned how to sell a product—a product that no one believed would sell. I have learned how to put together a balance sheet. I have learned how to ask other people for money and how to convince people to give me free products and services when I have no money. I have learned how to give a talk and have the audience in the palm of my hand. I have learned that I am emotionally stronger than I ever believed I was. This list goes on. Now, Chirps Chips are in hundreds of stores, and we are shaping the future of food by changing the eating behaviors of people from the ground up.

Did I mention that I am only twenty-five years old? I plan to stay an entrepreneur for life, but if I don't, I am so much more prepared to take on the challenges in any industry and career, because I have learned to crawl my way from nothing to something.

Entrepreneurship will be the one of most humbling and challenging experience of your life, but it will only make you stronger, wiser, smarter, savvier, and so on. Not everyone is foolish enough to want to stay in this stressful career; however, the experience will make anyone better and stronger. So if you have an idea, just go for it. What do you have to lose? More importantly, what do you have to gain?

CHAPTER EIGHTEEN

SERCAN TOPCU

Cofounder and Chief Marketing Officer, Tembo Education

>>>> ABOUT SERCAN

Sercan Topcu is an award-winning marketer whom the United States Citizenship and Immigration Services has deemed as having extraordinary ability in his field. He is the youngest Turkish citizen to receive the O1-A Visa, an extraordinary ability visa given to only the top professionals in their industry. He's the only social entrepreneur from Turkey to be selected for the 2016 *Forbes* "30 Under 30." He is also the only Turkish citizen to make it to the finals for the world's largest social entrepreneurship competition, the Hult Prize, in 2015. Sercan is the cofounder and chief marketing officer of Tembo Education, which makes education accessible to children worldwide via mobile phones.

Sercan has been with Tembo Education since day one, developing and executing marketing and branding strategies. With his contributions, Tembo Education has been selected for the MassChallenge Accelerator in Boston. Tembo presented at the 2016 Global Entrepreneurship Summit and the 2016 Social Capital Markets Conference. Tembo has also won the Sustainable Florida Small Business Award and the John W. Henry Foundation Social Impact Scholarship. Sercan is honored to be a part of such a great team, and he is excited to see the impact that his work with Tembo Education will have on the lives of children worldwide.

If I could go back, I would have gathered more information on successful social enterprises. I strongly believe that we will see more and more social enterprises emerge. The nonprofit and NGO mindsets are becoming antiquated. For me, it is crucial to understand that making money and doing good are not mutually exclusive. People often believe that if you are making money, then you are doing so off the backs of underserved people. Though it is important to always keep people honest in their work and to question their motives, this negative assumption is far from the truth.

Underserved populations still pay for services and products. Though they do lack a certain amount of comfort that comes with having a higher disposable income, they still do have disposable income. The issue is to address a need at a level that they value. But a true social enterprise provides value while being able to create incentives and positive externalities. This means you have to create closed-loop-cycle business models where no value is lost. This is why I believe not every social enterprise makes sense.

Tembo Education fills a need that is, unfortunately, very dire. The need is not as flashy as some other social issues, and it certainly does not get as much coverage. However, it is the key to solving many of the challenges we face today and will face in the future. We make high-quality early education accessible to children worldwide, via mobile phones. What sets us apart is our business model, which got us many accolades. The business model you create as a social enterprise speaks to your intent. We made sure we created value across the chain, period. A great example of this is how we value the parents and the caregivers who are enrolled in our program. We know that whether our customers are in an emerging market or in an emerged market, they appreciate financial returns. In emerging markets, we have established such returns for our customers by providing them airtime—phone minutes and texts—for their success. Most of the emerging markets still use pay-as-you-go systems and do not have long-term contracts like we do here in the United States. In markets that have already emerged, we provide returns to our customers by giving them monetary incentives such as gift cards for their success.

Incentives are so crucial in the social value you provide. From a business standpoint, incentives create stickiness. They increase retention and decrease attrition. What is more, for your business partners, stickiness can even mean reduced churn rates and increased market share. From a customer standpoint, incentives give them the power of choice. They allow customers to direct the extra financial value and put it in food, water, health care, or energy—whatever they need most. I remember a conversation I had with Vinod Parmeshwar, director of global human resources at Oxfam. We were talking about how to set up models to give more value to people. I was thinking of all kinds of products, services, and resources, which led to more and more challenges with regard to their execution. But Vinod gave me an example of how Oxfam gave people more value for their money and gave them the power of choice, meaning Oxfam allowed the people themselves to decide how to use the money Oxfam gave them.

It might seem a bit out there, as most of our customers have not had any real form of education in doing a value analysis or that might sound judgmental. It is a question of trust. How do you trust those you serve to make the best financial decision given their circumstances? What Oxfam observed was this: people directed the money to exactly what they needed, time after time. In believing that I knew better how to provide resources to underserved populations, I suffered from a common problem, sometimes called "White Knight Syndrome." I was trying to decide what would be better for them. I did not appreciate the pure, raw entrepreneurial skills people developed from living in those conditions. But Vinod did. Because of his knowledge, his model has helped hundreds of thousands of people. Following the lessons he taught us, we were able to create value that is beyond just one thing. Giving the power of choice to our customers allowed us to create positive externalities that reach beyond our business. That is what the heart of a social enterprise should be about.

BE ADOPTABLE, BE LOCAL!

If I could go back, I would save more funds to stay with the locals more. Since we are a mobile technology company specializing in education, it may seem like we do not differentiate according to region and culture. That is not true for us, just like it is not true for any other company. Adapting your products and your services is crucial for longevity. Even more importantly, being adaptable allows you to customize and individualize your offerings to serve your customers better.

Another positive outcome of creating an adaptable platform is being more flexible and able to use local resources. As we all know now, empowering local institutions and businesses creates a whirlpool of positive impact. This is exactly what we have done at Tembo Education. We made sure our educational activities are culturally adaptive. This adaptability is what led us to have high acceptance and penetration rates in the market.

My favorite example is an activity we have in the program where the student must make a circle walk, run, and march around. Instead of making people use a certain tool as a prop, we stated that they could use anything they have that is circular. The results were not only amazing but also showed us how innovative people are all around the world. We had individuals use their husband's belt, an old tire, and some even used a stick and mud. This example also relates back to the importance of giving the power of choice to the people. We gave users choice, and depending on their culture and resources; they came up with solutions that are not only adaptable for them individually but also culturally.

It is also important to note the small but constant iterations and adjustments we did to create a culturally adaptable platform. Our platform was possible because we were able to immerse ourselves within the cultures of our customers—which in turn was made possible thanks to our international partners and relationships. Working with local organizations gave us access to connections that would otherwise be almost impossible to make. Some of these connections are in fact higher-ups in governments. On one occasion, we made a connection because we chose to work together with a highly regarded church on the ground. Working with them not only gave us access to an invaluable network but also helped us increase our reach and get to market faster.

HOW DO YOU FORM PARTNERSHIPS AND RELATIONSHIPS?

There is no cookie-cutter method. Forming relationships definitely takes time, but more than that, it is important to vet the organizations you work with. For Tembo Education, we identified our potential contacts by simply going through a ton of research and articles. We set aside the names of the organizations we thought we could build mutually beneficial relationships with and contacted them. We not only read through articles, but we also looked into the resources they used as well. It was a meticulous process. If you do create an adaptable platform, then I strongly suggest that you work with local organizations—they will be crucial for your on-the-ground operations.

CHECK OUT THE O1 VISA

If I could go back, I would have applied for my O1-A Visa earlier than I did. I am a Turkish citizen living in the United States. I chased an H1-B Visa for years. However, when you are a successful entrepreneur, you have another option called an O1 Visa. To be eligible for an O1 Visa, you must meet three out of eight success metrics. You can find the details on the United States Citizenship and Immigration Services website.

In my experience, the O1 Visa has been a blessing. I am currently able to work with as many companies as I want to, as long as they accept me as an independent contractor or as a corporate-to-corporate consultant. Was it hard to obtain? Yes, it definitely was. Obtaining the Visa required me to be the only Turkish entrepreneur listed in *Forbes* as a social entrepreneur, the only Turkish representative at the world finals of the Hult Prize, and many more honors that came from hours of sweat and tears.

When my friends and peers from other countries ask me what makes the United States different, I tell them it is the way Americans define hard work. Personally, I learned the true meaning of hard work in United States. I was a door-to-door kids' book salesman in West Virginia. Another time, I had to quit my job as a campaign manager to pursue my entrepreneurial goals; this required me to be a commercial cleaner for months to make ends meet. What struck me the most was that these seemed to be totally logical steps to accomplish my goals. I can easily say that no friend or family of mine would have allowed me to be a commercial cleaner in Turkey. You might think this would be a good thing, but it actually is not. Family pride and self-entitlement are the major reasons why I would never have such a job in Turkey. However, here in the United States, that cleaning job was just another step to keep climbing up the ladder. Here, that type of work is considered hustle; it is considered hard work. The culture of stepping out of your comfort zone, the pursuit of happiness, these are what make this country extraordinary, and I am thrilled that this country considers me extraordinary as well.

The best way to go about attaining an O1 Visa is to talk to an immigration lawyer. It is worth the consultation fee. This visa does not affect your company's legal structure, and, to international eyes, it gives you more credibility.

There are many other types of visas that an international entrepreneur in the United States can apply for, but not as many that garner the respect of an O1 Business Visa.

➤ WHAT ARE SALES AND MARKETING TACTICS THAT HAVE WORKED FOR YOUR COMPANY?

Word-of-mouth marketing is still king! If I could go back, I would create more supportive tools for our word-of-mouth (WOM) marketing. I utilize a combination of traditional and new-media strategies to promote Tembo Education. Depending on the market, the culture, and even the season, the effectiveness of each marketing medium changes. However, we found out that WOM marketing is always a very reliable resource for promoting your cause. In our case WOM turned out to be the most effective tool in emerging markets. In fact, while our executive team was located in the United States, our personnel located in the slums of Lagos, Nigeria, were able to recruit ninety-three new home educators to our program within three months, simply using WOM.

It is also important to note that if you are going to utilize WOM, you need to establish credibility. I used a mix of successful traditional and new-media strategies to further establish the credibility of our brand. The traditional marketing strategies mostly consisted of print media, such as flyers, brochures, and even Tembo identification tags for our recruiters. The new-media strategies mostly focused on social media presence but also included call-to-action videos.

MORE EVENTS, MORE PROMOTIONS!

If I could go back, I would have done more research on more events. Tembo Education is a social enterprise. It is a mobile education platform. We serve low-, middle-, and high-income individuals as well as schools and organizations. It would be foolish to think that one marketing tool would be the single best tool for our company. However, the most important marketing tool for our company is attending events. We are able to create a strong network by attending events such as competitions, networking luncheons, and even accelerators. Events allowed us to position ourselves right in front of our end users, both individuals and organizations.

The events we participated in consisted of gatherings that allow us to showcase our organization's vision, mission, and its traction. I recommend all businesses try to identify events that are beneficial to their mission. To decide which events your company should attend, consider three factors.

1. Consider whether the event will help your company with its focus. The event shouldn't be a distraction or spread your resources too thin.

2. Consider whether the event will benefit the company's call to action, such as funding, recruitment, etc.

3. Consider whether the event can give you press attention.

For us, having a big core team—five cofounders—did present some challenges. Answering these three questions allowed us to always stay on track and utilize every opportunity. These events ranged from something as small as being featured at a local dance studio opening to something as big as being a world finalist at the largest social enterprise competition in the world, the Hult Prize.

The dance studio opening happened at a time when our marketing department was focusing on creating mutually beneficial relationships with local organizations. Therefore, attending this specific studio opening met all three criteria. I was able to get us presentation time and a bistro, which allowed us to showcase Tembo Education and attain contact information of significant individuals. Another reason we chose to attend was that the event also hosted a famous local NGO that provides free food to underserved children. The local NGO brought press attention that benefited us. More than that, as both the NGO and Tembo focus on children, we were able to create a strong relationship, which continues to flourish today.

The Hult Prize competition issued a challenge focusing on early education for the year 2015. The challenge fit perfectly into how we wanted to maximize children's potential. In addition, it gave us access to an accelerator and a network of world leaders. Lastly, having beaten all the Ivy League schools and ending up as the only US team in the world finals, we gathered substantial support and press attention.

Therefore, if you are looking to gain press attention and promote your company, the most effective and collaborative manner is to identify events to attend. Select events that are related to the vision and mission of your company as well as the goals and objectives you have identified for that time period.

EMAIL MARKETING

Email communication is another critical part of how we promote and brand ourselves. The key for a successful email conversation is to create a concise and straightforward email with a clear call to action. Though writing a straightforward email sounds very basic, it can get a bit convoluted when you are trying to shape the email to its respective subject and recipient. We found using a communication funnel to be very effective. Every contact related to a future possibility is made by our CEO. He then forwards the conversation to the respective department head. For example, if the email is about marketing, exposure, media, promotions, business development, and branding, then I am the one who carries on the conversation.

At Tembo, we pride ourselves on our transparency and communications, and it is no different when it comes to handling email threads. After our CEO forwards us the respective emails, we blind copy him on the thread. This procedure allows everyone to be on the same page, so we make an informed final decision. Staying consistent with an outline is also crucial for your company's email marketing. We have an e-newsletter, and we found out that by staying consistent we were able to attain higher readership rates than others in the industry. Another factor that contributed to readership rates was including an actionable item that is relevant to the audience. These could be trustworthy industry articles that feature action steps that would be helpful for your audience, interesting documentaries that relate to your audience, or even Kickstarter items that you believe will provide value to your audience.

Creating your e-list with the right contacts and the right audience is all about providing your audience with easy access to your sign-up platform. Don't just put a form on your website; make your sign-up form available at the right place at the right time. Achieve this by doing usability and cursor studies on your social media channels, your e-newsletter, your website, and mobile platforms to see where your audience clicks next, when they click, and how long they stay on a page. Doing such studies will give you information about where each tool's highest points of attractions are. Utilizing these points for inbounding emails will make the process smoother and easier for your audience. Lastly, make sure you have a sign-up form readily available at the events you attend.

MARKET RESEARCH MAKES YOU STAND OUT!

If I could go back, I would keep better track of all the market research data to use it as a bank for future reference. Success on social media is, again, determined by the call to action. Social media might be very useful or it might be a distraction as a vanity metric. At Tembo Education, we have a wide range of social media channels. For our company, Instagram and Snapchat are about better connecting with our audience and helping them visualize what Tembo does and, more importantly, why. Facebook and Twitter, though, are more about business. Facebook is a great tool for generating buzz and Twitter is great for real-time collaboration. I have seen firsthand how much impact both Facebook and Twitter can have. The key is doing your market research right before utilizing these channels.

Facebook ads are incredibly useful. After consulting other companies, I have discovered that the shortfalls others experience with Facebook ads usually stem from jumping to conclusions. More often than not, companies set their ads with interests and tags that they think their audience will fit into. Keep in mind, they are not just guessing interest and tags; these companies use them because they have gathered those interests and tags from their interactions with their audience, which is not a bad idea. However, the challenge is to go one step further—I suggest identifying what else is common among your audience. A perfect example of this was when I was setting up an ad for a bakery. Besides the usual interests and tags that I identified, I found out that more than 80% of my client's audience also liked Disney. Just this small addition—Disney fans—increased the ad's organic viewership another 26%, its shares another 30%, and its clicks by about 15%.

Twitter is the best tool to use while attending events and competitions. You can connect directly with decision makers and arrange follow-ups. Again, to make sure you leverage as much as you can, it is best to research key persons of influence. Identify their tweeting habits, such as the topics they choose to associate themselves with, the articles they share, and the language they use—whether formal or informal. Make your contact a couple of days in advance. Like and retweet some of their tweets, which will associate you with your business. Make sure to spread your likes and retweets to make your engagement more organic. Show what you learn from them, what you appreciate about them, and how you can create value for them. Organic engagement will not just happen with tweets, so some market research has to go into visiting their website and other social media channels to get a deeper view of who they are. This research has proven to get engagement back, which will allow you to arrange follow-up meetings and communications, in turn allowing you to steer the conversation toward your goal.

It all comes down to which media channel will promote your company best. Most of the time, the best choice will be a combination of channels. To figure out which channels are most essential and create the most return for your business, you have to be in touch with your audience and end users, which means you have to operate. So the best way to promote yourself is to keep making an impact in the lives of your target audience and tracing how the word gets around.

CHAPTER NINETEEN

SARAH GUTHALS
Social Engineer and Entrepreneur, GitHub's Social Impact Team

>>>> ABOUT SARAH

Sarah Guthals is a social software engineer and entrepreneur focused on providing kids everywhere with access to high-quality computer science education. Sarah grew up in a low-income household, the daughter of a single mother who was an immigrant and a fourth-grade teacher. Sarah's upbringing taught her the importance of learning and education and inspired her to dedicate her career to design products, software, and companies that focus on kids with similar backgrounds.

After receiving her BS, MS, and PhD in computer science from the University of California, San Diego, Sarah cofounded ThoughtSTEM, cocreated LearnToMod and CodeSpells, and wrote many books for kids about creating digital artifacts with and without code. In 2016 she was named one of *Forbes* "30 Under 30" in Science for her work in computer science education. In May 2016, she joined a large software company, GitHub, with the goal of creating a professional experience for kids under thirteen to create, share, contribute, and collaborate on digital artifacts from all around the world. She continues to work with UCSD to develop online and in-person courses on how to teach computer science in K–12 schools. She also promotes the next generation of builders through books, videos, and mentoring.

'm one of three cofounders of a startup that began as a tutoring company and is now a software company. Our primary goal was to teach high-quality computer science to children ages eight to eighteen. We focused first on in-person workshops and after-school programs. We then moved into the software space by developing a website where kids could get similar instruction at home or in school. I cofounded the company in 2012 and left in 2016. The most important things that I learned in those four years were about people: my cofounders, my employees, and my mentors.

FINDING THE RIGHT COFOUNDERS

When serial entrepreneurs told me that choosing a cofounder is like choosing a spouse, I thought they were being facetious. They weren't.

When you choose a cofounder, you are choosing someone who will be with you when you are at your weakest—when you are at your poorest, most tired, and most vulnerable. You are choosing someone to be there when you fail and to share in your glory when you succeed. You are choosing a partner, someone to be your equal, someone who you will have to trust with *your* vision. Choosing a cofounder is not easy, and I highly recommend working with potential cofounders before making that commitment, even if it is on a nonbusiness project. You need to learn who they are, how they work under pressure, and how you work with them under pressure.

Before I tell you my story, I want to reiterate that this is *my* story, and mine alone. My cofounders may tell the story differently, and I completely respect them for that. I don't actually know how they truly feel, so when I say things such as "they thought" or "they felt" it is my interpretation, not their actual feelings.

I met my first cofounder in grad school; let's call him Greg. In retrospect, we actually weren't great together. We had worked on research together in grad school, on a program that taught kids to code through the metaphor of magic and spells.

In our first year of working together in grad school, Greg and I didn't always agree on how to build the software. It felt to me as though he didn't care much about testing it with actual students. Or at least he didn't care as much as I did. This difference in opinion caused problems early in the development of our software, but they were alleviated when he started working on other projects, and I basically became the owner of the coding-as-magic project. It was always a strange relationship between us because we had very similar roles and expertise and were both pretty stubborn. So both of us were "right," but neither of us would concede to the other.

You don't want to add this kind of relationship to the stress of a business. However, we were blinded by respect for one another and by the desire to build something great, so when Greg suggested that we take my weekend tutoring sessions and turn them into a full-fledged company, I excitedly agreed.

Our third cofounder was Greg's girlfriend; let's call her Sandra. Sandra was also a PhD student at our university, but in biochemistry. She had the focus to figure out all of the legal and financial jargon so we could follow all of the state and federal laws, while maneuvering within the rules of our university, and come up with a plan to actually make money. Phew! The roles were divided up as such: Greg was chief executive officer, I was chief technology officer, and Sandra was chief operating officer.

On Halloween of 2012, the IRS accepted our paperwork and our company was formed. As a young grad student, only twenty-three years old, I really thought I knew a lot. On one level, I realized I had a lot to learn, but I was also stubborn.

I felt as though Greg didn't trust me enough to make decisions for our company. Greg, as the CEO, had a very specific vision that he wanted to see brought to life. If my ideas conflicted with that vision, Greg and Sandra often voted against them. Another issue that shows our stubbornness was that Greg and I had stopped meeting and talking to avoid conflict. This meant that Greg would spend weeks developing his ideas and plans and then present them to Sandra and I. Sometimes Sandra would already know about them. This lack of communication meant that by the time I heard about a pivot, or an idea, it had already been thought through. Even if I happened to agree with the idea over-all, I wasn't given the chance to go through the same thought process as Greg. Thus the lack of communication also created a lack of teamwork and ended up hurting the company.

In retrospect, I needed a partner who was willing to work through issues until they were resolved. Greg and I worked through issues until one of us didn't care anymore. This problem-solving style would end up being one of the reasons I left my company in 2016.

In the end, I do think stubbornness is a useful quality in an entre-preneur. You have to believe that you and other people should invest time and money in your vision, idea, and company. However, it is just as important to be able to learn and grow from your experiences and the experiences of others. It took me about two years to learn to convert stubbornness into drive and to embrace being wrong.

➤ SHOULD COFOUNDERS DISCUSS EVERYTHING OR TRUST EACH OTHER TO MAKE DECISIONS SEPARATELY?

I think that there should be a bit of both. If a decision pivots the direction of the company, or costs money, then everyone should be involved in the thought process *and* in deciding whether to pursue it. However, if a decision is a minor day-to-day thing, then maybe it can just be documented and shared. This is a conversation my cofounders and I should have had early on. We always expected to talk about everything, but when communication channels began to fail, we stopped talking about anything. Expecting to talk about everything is unrealistic, especially as your company starts to grow.

Not only were Greg's and my visions for our company different, our visions for our personal lives were also different. We should have agreed, up front, what the expectations were for number of hours worked, holidays, and weekends, and made sure that those expectations were negotiable considering major life changes. We should have made sure we were comfortable with what we were agreeing to. And most importantly, we should have addressed what would happen if someone was able to work significantly more than someone else. When we started, I worked 6:00 a.m. to 10:00 p.m. every day, including weekends, and I barely took off holidays. I was on email every moment, unless I was sleeping. This lifestyle was *not* sustainable, and when I started living a more sustainable lifestyle, it became a point of conflict between Greg and I. I was interested in getting married, buying a house, and having children—and I did two of these while working at my startup. Greg and Sandra were fine with dating, renting apartments, and not having children yet. This put us at odds regarding our roles within the company as well. I wanted to work about sixty hours a week, while they were happy to work more than eighty hours a week.

I wanted to make sure that we were all earning at least half of what we could make in the industry, about $60,000. They were okay with us making significantly less, about $30,000. The personal side of life is just as important, I would argue, even more important than the business side. If you cannot agree on the level of sacrifice you're willing to make, it can make business decisions difficult.

Working with Greg and Sandra was, by no means, all bad. In fact, I wouldn't take any of it back. By working with strong-willed cofounders, I learned *a lot* about myself as a person, a team member, and an entrepreneur. The most important thing I learned is that when you are starting a company, it is likely that your time will already be spread extremely thin.

It was absolutely critical for me to decide which battles *needed* to be fought and what was worth my time—both socially and within the company. In the end, if we had to make a decision between my idea and Greg's idea, I was okay either way, as long as I didn't think there was an actual problem with Greg's idea.

Being flexible can be a useful skill in any relationship. You cannot always change someone's mind, so you should learn how to accept that someone doesn't agree and be able to continue forward toward a common goal in spite of that. Similarly, if my husband wanted to go camping and I didn't, I needed to decide whether the trip was something important (a family get-together) or just something for fun. If it were important to him, I would go.

Another skill I gained was the ability not to react right away, to buy myself more time. At first, not reacting was difficult for me. When something negative happens, if you give yourself time to think about what happened and how it actually affects you, you can save yourself a lot of arguing and discussion. Staying calm not only helps you avoid unnecessary conflict, it also helps when good things happen, too. When something good happens, there is always the chance that you will overcommit yourself. If you give yourself time to think about whether you want to commit to something, you can evaluate the benefits without experiencing the pressure and excitement of being offered an opportunity. This skill is important when talking with investors as well. As a cofounder, you will come across a lot of people who think they know the "solution" to the problem you are trying to solve or who think your approach is completely wrong. You will have to learn how to accept criticism and give yourself the chance to decide how you want to react. In some instances, you can give yourself a few days. In other instances, you can only give yourself a matter of seconds. Giving yourself those few seconds of silence allows you to react logically instead of emotionally.

Finally, I learned to make sure each cofounder and/or core team member has a clearly defined role. When you are first deciding to start a company, each important managerial role should be clearly defined. All roles that need to be filled should be assigned to someone. If there isn't a current team member to fill a role, then the role's responsibilities should be written out, along with a timeline for finding a person to fill that role. If two cofounders have similar expertise, then they should defer to each other based on roles. For example, being the CTO, I would defer to my cofounders on business-related decisions and they would defer to me on technical decisions. Though roles will help determine who should be making what decisions, it is also important for every key member to be included in the decision making. Just because a person is the CEO doesn't mean he or she should be able to make all of the decisions on their own.

LEARNING TO BECOME A MANAGER

Though finding the right cofounder(s) is critical to your success, hiring the right people and cultivating the right environment for your employees is also extremely important. Learning to become an effective manager can be difficult. In particular, it was important for me to listen to my employees and determine what they needed from me, not just what I needed from them.

First, you have to hire your team. Determining whether someone is going to be a good hire during a short interview, with a résumé in hand, is not easy at all. It really takes practice. We were very lucky in our business, because all of our employees started by teaching our weekend workshops. Our company ran two workshops every Sunday with fifteen to thirty children. We promised a 1:8 mentor-to-student ratio. Mentors were typically undergraduate or high school students who had some experience or interest in teaching children. Coding wasn't a requirement, because my expertise was teaching people to code. Each mentor that we hired went through six hours of training spread over the course of one week: two hours each day on Monday, Wednesday, and Friday. I taught them our curriculum and some of the "gotchas" that they would probably run into while teaching. I also taught them a bit about interacting with students and their parents. Following the training, each mentor was required to shadow an existing mentor or me and to learn how we ran things. Then they would work hourly as a mentor. This process allowed us to vet each of our employees and eventually assign additional tasks (e.g., creating new curriculum) to ones who were doing really well.

However, for some of our projects, we didn't always have this "internship" opportunity. For example, we wanted to hire a small team of coders to develop a new curriculum and interactive website from scratch. None of our current mentors had the expertise we were looking for. For this project, we tried to take a similar approach to our mentor hiring. We hired three interns for a short project and told them that there could be opportunities for future work after they completed their project. This move allowed us to see how each employee worked without committing to them for a long-term appointment. We found, coincidentally, that out of every three employees, one always seemed to shine. Though this isn't a hard and fast rule, it is a rule of thumb that I continue to use when I have new projects. We found some of our very best employees using this internship process and we offered them full-time positions within the company.

Still there were times when we had to hire someone for a full-time position based only on a résumé and an interview. In these cases, providing prospective employees with scenarios seemed to help me vet them. Asking them to delve deeper into their previous projects and describe how they saw their potential and future role in the company gave insight into who they were and who they wanted to become.

Whether I was able to vet my employees or had to hire them based on a résumé and interview, I took it upon myself to ensure that they succeeded. Once every couple of months, I scheduled a meeting with my employees in which I gave them feedback on their performance and I asked them to give me feedback on my management of them. I gave them at least a week's heads up, so that they could come prepared, and I asked them to tell me what they needed from me. These meetings were semicasual; I invited them to coffee and paid for it. We chatted and they had all the time they needed to discuss anything with me. After I talked with each employee, I had a meeting with the entire team and discussed some of the issues that were brought up and how I planned to address them. In some cases, I gave specific examples, and in others I kept the situation general (so as not to embarrass an employee).

I learned a great technique for running these one-on-one meetings from one of my best teachers. It is called "Keep, Quit, Start." Ask employees what they want you to keep doing, what they want you to quit doing, and what they want you to start doing. Now, as the manager, you are not required to do what they tell you, but the questions open up a dialogue. For example, one of my employees asked that I stop changing their projects month by month. I couldn't stop doing that because we were in a three-month stretch where we were reprioritizing the company's focus and I couldn't predict when I would have to change their projects. But this feedback allowed us to have a dialogue about the problem—mainly that they felt like I was asking them to do work that I didn't care about, because I was switching projects so often. It seemed like busy work, not an actual contribution to the company. It was important that we discuss the significance of work they were doing for the company. From then on, I made sure that my employees understood *why* they were switching projects and *when* they would be able to work on their original projects again. This new understanding made our working relationships seamless and allowed them to feel confident in their contributions, even if the project changed.

Though I encourage you to read books and watch talks on effective management practices, it's also important that you listen to the people you are managing and reflect on what you liked about people who have managed you in the past. The most important thing to remember about management is that it is also a learning process. Not everyone thrives under the same management style. Learning what your employees need from you can help you get what you need from them.

LISTENING TO YOUR MENTORS

Peers (cofounders) and mentees (employees) are only two-thirds of the equation. My goal, in any situation, is to learn. And when I started my company, I had the perfect opportunity to learn from people who had started companies before me or who were older and had their lives together. Mentors don't have to be people who are doing exactly what you want to do. You can find mentors in all walks of life. Mentors have a quality that you are interested in emulating; they are people who can help you become your best you—not a copy of them.

I have many mentors who help me in many aspects of my life. The importance of having mentors who can guide you in different ways is critical to a well-rounded success. My mentors include

Irene Esper: My mother, Irene, has and always will be a mentor to me. She always grounds me and helps me figure out what is important in life overall, not just in my career.

Kris Zsebo: My mother-in-law, Kris, is a successful biochemical engineer who, throughout her career, has been the CEO, director, manager, and more for a number of companies developing new treatments for various illnesses. As a female immigrant in a male-dominated field, my mother-in-law dealt with a lot of issues that I eventually ran into. It was important for me to learn from her how to be strong, because I was working in similarly male-dominated fields—computer science and entrepreneurship.

Beth Simon: Beth has been my mentor since I was an undergrad. She was my first computer science professor and she was the first person who introduced me to the field of computer science education. Not only is she a mentor to me in my professional field but she lives a happy life and gives her personal life equal importance to her professional life.

Jennifer Argüello: Jennifer is a UCSD alumna who has had many different roles within the technical industry. She was an entrepreneur, developer, technical project manager, program manager, founder, consultant, and advisor for a variety of social impact and technical companies. From Jennifer, I learned a lot about lean startup and what is important when you are learning to work for yourself, either as a founder or a consultant.

Finding mentors who can offer you guidance in all aspects of your life is critical to success. That often means finding more than one and adjusting who is mentoring you based on your goals at that time. It can seem awkward to look for mentors, but you will find that if you listen to those around you and learn from what people have to say, mentors are everywhere. You do not have to have a formal conversation about someone being your mentor, though I have acquired some in that way as well. Simply being available and eager to listen, learn, and contribute is what makes a good mentorship relationship.

➤ HOW DO YOU SUPPORT YOURSELF WHEN STARTING A COMPANY— FINANCIALLY AND PERSONALLY?

I had a wild four-year startup ride in my mid-twenties. I had to make a lot of decisions and sacrifices to start a company without a piggy bank of cash.

BEING A GRAD STUDENT AND STARTING A COMPANY

When my cofounders first reached out to me with the idea of starting a company, I was a PhD student in computer science, living in San Diego, making about $24,000 a year. I was in a committed relationship with Adrian, my then boyfriend and now husband, who was also a PhD student making the same amount of money. We lived in a one-bedroom apartment near campus, we were both making payments on our Toyotas, and we had two of the most precious kittens ever, Luke and Princess.

Our life was pretty simple; we ate pasta most nights and didn't go to restaurants too often. We didn't have the financial means to invest in a company, but I had the personal drive to put in the work. My two cofounders invested about $2,000 for our startup costs, which they would get back when they left the company. We decided that the rest of our money would come from our customers.

I don't think this financial structure is typical for twenty-first-century startups. Typically, you see early startups pitching to venture capitalists and raising funds from friends, family, and investors. In the early days of our company, my cofounders and I decided to focus on a product that could make us money with very little up-front cost, other than our time spent teaching in person. In addition to teaching, we concentrated on student-focused funding opportunities that could help us with early costs. We participated in a program called MyStartupXX for female entrepreneurs. We were awarded a small investment and given mentorship throughout a summer. We also received funding from the National Science Foundation (NSF) through their I-Corps program, which helps researchers turn their research into a profitable company. With small grants like these, and with mentorship from those running these programs, we were able to sustain our initial costs of creating the company and hiring our first few employees.

As investors will tell you, a startup isn't just about the money and product, it's about the people. So it's important that I explain how we, as people, started our company. My mother is a fourth-grade teacher and for my entire life I was surrounded by education, learning, and teaching. I have a younger sister, and when I was little, I remember playing school with her. I would create curriculum, teach her a lesson, create homework for her, and then grade it. I loved all aspects of teaching—even the grading. I also loved building and problem solving. I loved solving mysteries and reading riddles. Even though I wasn't the most creative person in the world, I loved creating.

So in my second year of college, when I discovered that I could be a computer scientist who did research and built software, curriculum, and pedagogy on how to better teach computer science, I had found my calling. My PhD work was focused on computer science education—the teaching and learning of computer science for novices, children in particular. In the fall of 2012, I started teaching children to code on weekends, just for fun. I met them at their houses or at my university, where we built and created code and discussed the process and concept of coding. It was so much fun! During this time, I was also working on an iteration of a video game that I codeveloped, where kids as young as eight could run around an enchanted world, acting as wizards, and solving the problems of the local gnomes with the use of magic spells (which were actually code).

When my future cofounder, Greg, saw me teaching kids on the weekends, he was inspired to create a company, and that is why we started off by teaching kids to code in person. We already knew that there were parents who would pay for this kind of education because they were paying me to do it. Even better, we now had a group of parents who could give us insight into our customers and help us get the word out to other parents. From that point on, the work was a balancing act—we had to find ways to get enough customers to pay all of our costs (materials, renting space, hiring tutors) while also saving money so that we could pivot to a scalable, more profitable product by the time we graduated and needed to be paid through the company.

We were all very lucky, because as PhD students in the sciences at our university, we were all paid $24,000 per year, and our tuition was covered. As long as we were dedicating enough time to our research, and we were making sure that what we developed for the company was **not** something that we developed as part of our research, we could legally earn our PhDs and run our startup simultaneously. This dual-work arrangement meant we didn't have to worry about living costs while creating a startup. Coming from a low-income, single-parent home, I didn't have family startup funds to finance me through this endeavor. Without the support of my university, I could never have been a part of this startup.

Supporting yourself financially is not the only thing that matters in life. It is also critical to support yourself mentally, emotionally, physically, spiritually, and whatever other way that isn't as easy to calculate. My cofounders were dating when we started the company. The fact that they were working on the company while also spending time with their significant other made it a lot harder for me. I had to find time to conduct my research for my PhD, run a startup, and have a healthy relationship with Adrian outside of work. Though I was only twenty-four, Adrian and I had life plans as individuals and together that we wanted to plan for.

THE FIRST TWO YEARS OF RUNNING MY COMPANY WERE HARD

There is no way around it. I didn't sleep a lot. I had a number of ailments that were hard to control (e.g., migraines, asthma, insomnia, nightmares, and fibromyalgia). I wasn't home a lot. I hardly saw Adrian, and I slowly fell into a deep depression. I woke up around 5:00 a.m. every day and often got to school before it was even light out. I would work until around 10:00 a.m., when everyone else was starting to stroll in, and took a short break for coffee. Around noon, I tried to have lunch with Adrian, though it often didn't work out because I had meetings or way too much to do. I didn't leave campus until around 8:00 p.m. and when I got home I worked while eating dinner and watching some TV. I tried to be asleep by 11:00 p.m. I did that every single day, except Sundays, when I ran our in-person coding workshops all day.

I ran myself ragged like this for the first two years. By then, we were finally able to hire and train enough people that we didn't have to be at the weekend workshops, so I started taking Sundays off. On any day off, I essentially slept all day. It was hard, not just on me, but on Adrian. We lived together and saw each other every day, and while he wanted to support me through this crazy adventure, we didn't even have time to relax and have a conversation together. During this time, I leaned a lot on my cofounders and other PhD students whom I could talk to online. I also leaned on personal interactions that were meaningful, but that didn't require a lot of commitment. I do not regret this time at all because it worked out in the end, but I hope that by my writing this, other cofounders can take time before, during, and after starting a company to figure out what is valuable in their lives—which can change! The first two years of our startup were financially, emotionally, physically, and mentally difficult. I didn't mind the financial difficulty so much because I was pursuing my passion. I now know that my emotional, physical, and mental well-being are more important to me than anything.

STARTING MY ADULT LIFE

When I graduated with my PhD in 2014, I was able to pay myself $60,000 per year through my startup and I managed to reduce the hours that I worked to a more manageable schedule of about sixty hours per week. Those were still twelve-hour days, but I didn't work weekends, and I never worked when I got home. Without the looming deadlines of school, I was able to focus more on the priorities of the company and my own life.

The year after I graduated from school was spent recovering my sanity and health. First, I recovered my relationship with Adrian. We ended up getting engaged and married because we were able to communicate effectively and spend time together. I then worked with many doctors to control my long list of medical issues. The fact that it took me one year to normalize myself meant that I had pushed too hard for too long. I don't tell this story to come across as a martyr, and I don't tell this story as a cautionary tale of what everyone *must* go through to start a company. I tell this story as an example of my path to create something that I could proudly call my own. It *does* take blood, sweat, and tears to start a company—but only the amount of blood, sweat, and tears that you are prepared to give.

Now that I have left my company, I have the perspective to think about what was good and bad about the experience for me. The single thing that I regret about the entire adventure is not checking in with myself often enough to ensure that what I was doing was still aligned with the life that I wanted. There is one reason I give for leaving: the company was beginning to focus on an online product for the purpose of acquisition and less on the education of individual students. Because of this pivot, I wasn't willing to risk the life that I wanted to live for the company. I wanted to buy a home and start a family with my husband, so I needed to find a workplace that could allow me to do that, while hopefully still teaching children to learn coding. I was able to find that sort of work, luckily, but I was prepared to put my family first until I could find it.

ARE YOU LIVING THE LIFE YOU WANT TO LIVE?

When you start a company, only two questions really matter: are you living the life that you want to live? Are you preparing for the life you want? These questions matter both financially and personally. Are you okay with not being able to earn a lot of money at first while working long hours? Are you okay not having the stability of a job with an HR department, raises, healthcare, retirement plan, and vacations? Are you okay with the potential failure of the company? Before starting a company, outline the life you think you want to live and make sure that this endeavor is on the path to achieving that life. As you work to build the company, constantly check in with yourself, and anyone else who it might affect, to make sure that the answers are still aligning.

LIVING AN ADULT LIFE WHILE TAKING RISKS

As I mentioned earlier, I ended up leaving my company in 2016. I joined another company that is still considered a "startup" but has over 500 employees. At my new company, I have stability because I know that it is unlikely the company will go under or disappear. I have benefits, a 401(k), and vacation time. I'm never expected to work more than forty hours a week, and I am never expected to be available on the weekends. The best part? I have managed to find a position building software that encourages kids to learn to code! Even better? I get to focus on low-income, minority kids. Because I have the support of a successful company behind me, I can focus on having a real social impact without worrying about finances. That isn't to say that we didn't worry about social impact at my startup, but when you have to pay people's salaries, pay rent, and purchase the pencils you're using, there is only so much you can do "for free" for your customers. I got my new position because of my PhD work and my startup. I designed this role for myself. All of the work I put in during the first twenty-eight years of my life led me to this point. I approached a company, helped them start a new project, brought my expertise to the table, and now I work with brilliant people to make a dream a reality.

Leaving my company was an interesting transition. Personally, I didn't want to "sell out." I didn't want to leave just to make more money or have more stability, though writing that now sounds like a very reasonable reason to leave. I wanted to make sure I didn't ever lose my passion for helping kids learn to code. Leaving wasn't an easy decision. My cofounders and I spoke privately about it. I mentioned a few of the things that were important to me. First, I needed to be able to make a steady income, barring anything crazy like we run out of money. Second, I needed to have a steady schedule. Third, I wanted to have creative decision making.

My cofounders agreed to a steady schedule but disagreed on a steady income and creative decision making. They wanted to lower our personal incomes to alleviate pressure on the company. I liked this idea, but being an adult with financial responsibilities, it was difficult to plan on reducing my personal income by half (which is what my cofounders wanted to do). Also, our CEO wanted to have sole decision-making power on the future of our company and products.

Now, I am willing to have sleepless nights, and I'm willing to not make money—if I get to see my dreams become reality. But to sacrifice to make *someone else's* dream a reality didn't make sense to me. It was important that I was a part of the process to *create*, not just build. As a computer scientist, I am lucky enough to be in a field where, if I want to be a builder, I can apply to work for amazing companies like Google and Microsoft and make six figures. I wanted to *create*. So when my personal life goals and my business life goals were being compromised, it didn't make sense to stay.

Before leaving, my cofounders and I wrote up a separation document that our lawyers reviewed. Essentially, I left with no claim to the company (other than having it on my résumé) and I would "sell back" my shares for an extra month's pay to help give me time to find a new job. Additionally, I would receive the rights to some of the IP I created (clearly outlined in our separation document). This was something I could agree to and we departed on good terms. I still wish them all the best. I hope that what they continue to build and sacrifice for becomes something that changes our world—and I will be proud to have been a part of it.

The most important thing I learned when I became an adult is that you have to be comfortable with the decisions you make. When I was younger, it was much easier to make decisions that I could change later. They seemed like life-altering decisions (which major to choose, which university to go to), but all these decisions were much smaller than quality-of-life decisions. The interesting part about becoming an adult is that you have to *decide* what quality of life you want, what is important to you, and what you're willing to sacrifice to get it. If having money is important to you—that's okay! You just have to make sure you set yourself up for a career where you can make a lot of money and you might have to be willing to sacrifice some free time. If freedom to travel and explore is important to you—that's okay, too! You just have to make sure that you have some way to support yourself financially, and you might have to be willing to sacrifice some financial goals. I have my PhD in computer science and my sister is pursuing her BA in art. We both want *completely* different things in life. I want the house and kids and she wants to be a nomad. She is successful. I am successful. Being successful in a nontraditional job (e.g., entrepreneurship) doesn't mean being superhuman; it means creating the life you want and making the sacrifices you're willing to make to achieve it.

CHAPTER TWENTY

DANNY ELLIS
Cofounder and Chief Executive Officer, SkySpecs

>>>> ABOUT DANNY

Danny is the cofounder and CEO of SkySpecs, a company developing software and services for enterprise drone deployments. His fellow cofounder, Tom Brady, is also a contributor to this book. Danny earned two degrees in aerospace engineering from the University of Michigan. After graduation, he and his cofounders were presented with the opportunity to forgo the usual engineering career path and instead join an incubator at the university to attempt to commercialize the autonomous drone technology they had been working on during graduate school. Danny turned down job offers at SpaceX and Northrop Grumman to give the startup path a shot. Four and half years later, in 2014, Danny was recognized by *Crain's Detroit Business* for their "20 in Their 20s" award, recognizing twentysomethings to watch in metro Detroit. In 2016, *Forbes* included him in their "30 Under 30" in the category of Industry and Manufacturing. Danny and his team began working on drone technology eight years ago, long before drones fascinated the world. Danny is a Techstars alumnus and current mentor. He is passionate about helping other startups succeed, particularly ones that involve some form of hardware.

START WITH TWO FOUNDERS

First-time entrepreneurs should start their company with two founders. Not one, not three, and definitely not more than three. Exactly two. Although my cofounder, Tom, and I had been given this piece of advice by many mentors from the very beginning, we stubbornly didn't listen and chose instead to figure it out the hard way.

Tom and I met during the summer of 2008 when we were both working on internships in aircraft hydraulic systems in Kalamazoo, Michigan. We were both pursuing degrees in aerospace engineering at the University of Michigan, both interested in creating new technology, and both extremely bored with our jobs as test engineers. We spent most of our summer hanging out in a test cell, watching monitors, while numbers ran across the screen, brainstorming insane ideas for businesses in aerospace. None of our conversations were ever serious; we never thought starting an aerospace company, especially in Michigan, was possible.

We returned to school that fall and didn't think much more about our conversations of starting a business. A year later, we founded Michigan Autonomous Aerial Vehicles, a student team with the goal of building an autonomous drone for an international competition. Tom and I naturally came together to pursue the idea of an autonomous drone. We had a great time getting to know each other at our internship and both agreed that we'd rather spend our time at the university actually building something.

Why two founders instead of one? Unless you have started a business before, and you are very comfortable being alone, you don't want to start a business by yourself. You need someone to share the pain and excitement with and someone to give you a counteropinion about everything. We are all guilty of fixating on an idea that we think is absolutely perfect and not stopping until we realize, far too late, that the idea is failing. A good cofounder will challenge all of your ideas. And you need to challenge his or her ideas in the same way. This isn't about inciting fights over what is right or wrong, but instead openly considering all possibilities.

So if counteropinions are good, why not have three founders? At SkySpecs, we started off with three founders, quickly added a fourth founder, and then a first employee who might as well have been considered a founder.

Let's take a quick tangent—what exactly is a founder anyway? Does a founder need to be there on Day Zero when you sign your articles of incorporation and send them off to the state? Does the founder need to be the one to put the first dollar into the business? How about the one who comes up with the name or the first logo? Or maybe the founder is the one with the ideas? How about the highest education level? Maybe the highest level of real-world experience?

In practice, the term "founder" describes an executive member of the team, who was part of the original team to develop the core technology, prior to raising a round of funding or hiring external employees. This definition is obviously nebulous, and it is ultimately up to the team to determine who is labeled a founder.

Although no one really has a good definition of founder, the ramifications of giving someone that role can be huge. In the beginning, it may seem like everyone is excited and just wants to make the world a better place, so they don't take their titles too seriously, but these attitudes will change as soon as you gain any form of success or failure. Early on, we had the problem of our technology originally being developed by a student team at the University of Michigan. When we originally pitched the idea of the company, there were many students still working on the project at the university. A few of us had clearly been on the project since the very beginning, and we were going to be the founders of the company, but it was less obvious who else should be involved and to what extent.

Why shouldn't you have three or more founders? Startups have to make decisions quickly. They have to come up with a plan, execute, analyze, replan, and execute again, all while keeping egos in check and thinking pragmatically about the problem. When you have two founders both of you can sit in a room, discuss the problem and various solutions, and come up with next steps pretty quickly, even if you disagree. When you have three founders, no matter the situation, two founders will bond over a decision and the third will be left out. The founder who is left out may change depending on the situation, but making decisions by overruling a founder, two against one, does not make anyone feel good. There is also the risk that the team will pursue ideas because two people are loud and emotional about their opinions.

This kind of faulty decision making is exactly what happened with our team in the early days. Over time, some founders left to pursue other interests, and ultimately we were down to the two original founders: my partner Tom and me. The moment we transitioned to two founders, our team immediately began working better together.

In the beginning, Tom and I strived to have a flat organization. We were warned that this organizational structure wouldn't work and that we had to have hierarchy, but we didn't want others in the company to feel like their contributions meant less to our success. As it turns out, we ended up with a relatively flat organization: two founders in the executive roles and the rest of the team below that. This structure is beneficial for a number of reasons: the employees know who to look to for a final decision, who to ask for advice, and who to ask when they inevitably want a raise. The employees also all feel like we are in this together and that they are just as important as everyone else. The structure is beneficial to the two founders because we can make decisions much faster and then we can get the team behind us.

You should never promote a new hire immediately to the founder level. In fact, you should never promote anyone to the founder level after the company has been formed. This doesn't mean you can't hire more executives later on, but these hires should be far down the road. One of the easiest ways to make an employee feel like their contributions are worth less is by hiring a new employee years after and immediately bringing them above the dedicated employee. This is a guarantee for disaster.

SHARE THE CREDIT; TAKE THE BLAME

Another challenge to almost every startup is properly recognizing accomplishments and successes. No startup is successful without the incredibly hard working team that makes up the startup. Historically you will see all the credit going to the CEO; just think of Steve Jobs, Elon Musk, and Bill Gates. They all receive the credit for their new products, as if they were the ones inventing every new piece of technology. Don't get me wrong, they have done amazing things, but they wouldn't have gotten anywhere without their incredible teams.

This problem is even worse with first-time startups. The CEO or founders immediately get all the credit, since they are the ones in front of investors, on stage at competitions or conferences, and in interviews with journalists. It is very easy for the founders) to automatically take all the credit. This behavior will quickly distance the team from the founders), as the team doesn't see recognition for their continuing hard work. If you're the founder, share the credit with your team. On the flip side, when the whole team messes up, take all the blame. Don't ever throw your team under the bus by blaming them publicly when something goes wrong. This is one of the main roles of a CEO: share the credit; take the blame.

In our company, we were not so good at sharing credit in the early days, and it is something I am constantly trying to improve on. I always look for ways to give recognition to our team. After all, our team is the single biggest contributor to our success so far. Tom and I wouldn't have gotten anywhere if we were the only ones working at SkySpecs. This is a lesson that is often learned after a team gets upset and, in many cases, decides to leave because they don't see the problem getting better. Founders may not even recognize that their team is unhappy until it is too late.

The press will quote and credit the CEO by default. It is the CEO's job to ensure this doesn't happen. Put your team out there to talk to the press. Nominate your team for awards. Find ways to get their names out there, even a little bit, so the world knows what an incredible job they are doing.

MENTORS

Our company has had many struggles—almost all of which we were warned about early on, but we ignored the warnings. Our strong mentor network has helped guide us to resolutions. Our very first mentors were two of our professors from the university. They believed in us when we were freshmen in their classes, when we were graduate students teaching for them, when we started a student team with a very ambitious goal, and ultimately when we founded SkySpecs. They have been with us every step of the way, offering us workspace, resources, guidance, funding, and unprecedented support. Anytime a problem arises, we approach them first. We have had the unique opportunity to stay connected to the university throughout the entire SkySpecs journey.

In 2014, another opportunity fell into our laps: we were accepted into the R/GA Accelerator powered by Techstars in New York City. Techstars is one of the most well-known startup accelerators out there today. Its biggest benefit, by far, is the enormous network of mentors all willing to help their portfolio companies. We dove into the program not knowing what to expect. One thing we did know was that we needed to evolve our business model, focus on technology development, and figure out how to improve our decision-making processes. At one point in the program, one of our mentors asked us to draw our business on the board. The resulting sketch proved that we had no idea what business we were actually in, which forced us to have some very difficult, time-consuming, and energy-consuming conversations with our team. With three founders and four more team members at Techstars, these conversations were made all the more challenging. The good news was that we all realized we had to come to a solution and we were all willing to figure it out, even if it meant going against our personal opinions.

Another mentor of ours made it clear that our flat organization was causing us to move slowly, because we could never firmly decide on a direction for the company. This realization was an important turning point in the culture of our company. Shortly after Techstars, one of our cofounders decided to move on to other career opportunities, leaving just Tom and me as the executives and decision-makers. Not long after, Tom and I were able to secure another round of funding—and then our one and only partner and customer was purchased by a big energy company. This gave us the opportunity to reorganize our team, refocus our mission, and replan our future.

REFOCUSING AND REBUILDING

In the early part of 2015, we decided to take our leadership team to an off-site strategy-planning meeting. We asked an external mentor to join and help guide us through a structured process to figure out what the hell we were going to do now that we had raised an additional $2.75 million. The result? Two days of heated conversation. There were points when we felt like we were completely wasting our time, followed by moments of clarity and direction.

The months that followed the meeting were the most productive, exciting, impressive months of our entire existence. We had finally found what it meant to have a structured, focused, and motivated team all working toward a common goal that was actually going to benefit our customers. This kind of success would never be possible if there were fighting between cofounders, confusion between the cofounders and the team, and lack of decision making by the executive team. While it wasn't easy to lose a cofounder, I have no doubt that SkySpecs is still in existence today because the number of decision-makers was reduced to two.

It's never easy to find the perfect cofounder. Tom and I never planned on starting a business—it just sort of happened. We had spent years together as friends, classmates, colleagues, and teachers. It is not an exaggeration to say that starting a business with someone is equivalent to a marriage. You probably spend even more time with your business partner than with a spouse. You have to face tough decisions together, share good times and bad, travel well together, and find ways to allow each other to focus and thrive on individual accomplishments. You also have to collectively manage a team of people. If you aren't able to work together to get that team of people focused in the same direction, you are going to spend a lot of time and money not doing much of anything.

Tom and I inherently have opposite viewpoints on a majority of topics. Tom is more conservative about spending money and agreeing to pursue an opportunity. I am more susceptible to saying yes to anything that comes across my desk. Together we are usually able to find the best path forward, one that won't distract our team and will keep us within a reasonable budget—in terms of both time and money. By no means has the journey been perfect, but we have learned far more firsthand than we ever could have from a book, and we have managed to keep the company and the vision alive. Perseverance is the most important trait any founder can have. If you are able to push through the growing pains of starting your first company with a cofounder (or many founders), you will be able to find a way to make the business successful.

⟩⟩ HOW HAVE YOU DEALT WITH FAILURES?

"YOU'RE A SOFTWARE COMPANY!"

MVP: most of the world associates these letters with the phrase *most valuable player*, but I want to talk about the phrase *minimum viable product*, a term created by the new age startup community. If you haven't heard this phrase already, you are about to hear it over and over again until you can't take it anymore. The first time I heard MVP in our initial startup incubator, I thought, "OK, this sounds simple enough." The second time I heard it, I cringed. I cannot stand the overuse of buzzwords that have a complete lack of substance. What does it even mean to be an MVP? Mentors and investors will give you feedback to get to an MVP and, often, you will feel like it is hollow feedback—you will feel like it is an easy way of saying, "I don't like your product, but I'd rather give you nice-sounding feedback than tell you that I don't like it." While we believed that we were building an MVP, we didn't truly embrace the concept. We were dealing with hardware—we built drones. We thought the MVP process, which was designed primarily for software-as-a-service products, didn't apply to us.

"You're a software company." This was something one of our first mentors was trying to drive into our brains. Even though, when we first started, hobby drones weren't widely available yet, he warned us that the hardware was going to become commoditized (another word you never want to hear as a startup) and that we needed to capitalize on the software value. Software was easier to duplicate and scale with minimal cost and had been proven, in multiple industries, to be the most valuable component. However, we didn't see a clear path to making our software valuable without the hardware of the drone. It wasn't like the smartphone market where we could just make an app and have millions of people download it. Without the drone, our software was useless.

So what did we do? We continued to design a brand-new drone from the ground up. We built aluminum molds for carbon fiber layups to make the airframe and propeller guards. We designed and fabricated circuit boards. We wrote flight controllers, navigation software, visualization tools, and communication protocols. We spent a ton of time "flight testing" before we could even verify that our software or hardware was working properly. We spent countless hours tuning parameters that weren't even programmed right, essentially meaning they could never be tuned properly. And we banged our heads against the wall for hours, days, and months on end, striving to reach that minimum viable product. It was so elusive, but we were determined to get there. What we didn't allow ourselves to realize was that we were not pursuing an MVP. We were pursuing ten different MVPs all bolted together.

TO PIVOT OR NOT TO PIVOT

Pivot—another startup buzzword that makes me cringe. While we were learning from mentors and incubators, they repeatedly told us that we needed to consider a pivot. They said that good startups pivoted all the time. We heard this advice with the words "Startups keep changing their minds until they get lucky and something sticks." We were not in this to be entrepreneurs. We were in this because we had a love for small flying devices and we wanted to bring this new, innovative technology to the industry. If we pivoted to something completely different, none of us would have been interested enough to stay. We couldn't imagine a world where we were simply a software company and didn't have our own drones.

Our first big failure came in 2013, less than a year after founding the company. We considered a variety of markets that we thought would benefit from drone technology and chose bridge inspection as our primary focus. We set out to talk to potential customers and industry experts, eventually landing in the offices of the Michigan Department of Transportation (MDOT). They were very excited about our technology, but they weren't able to give us money directly. Instead we had to reply to their request for proposals and work through their grant process.

At this point, we hadn't raised any money, weren't paying salaries, and were barely scraping by with enough money to purchase parts to build our first system. We had spent months on this grant proposal and now we had to wait a few more months to hear the results. The grant was scoped for two years' worth of work for $150,000. At the time, we had thought this was an enormous amount of money and it would keep us going. Little did we know that this was not even close to the amount of money we needed to sustain ourselves.

I vividly remember when we received the results of the grant proposal. The grant that was specifically crafted for our technology, and only published because we asked the MDOT to support us, was awarded to someone else. My cofounder, Tom, heard the news first. I was in the middle of teaching a class when he came in with a very depressed look on his face. We had poured all our energy into this grant and got absolutely nothing for it. We were getting very close to the point where we couldn't operate any longer without paying salaries and we had no near-term opportunity for funds. For the next week, we were pretty certain that our short-lived experience as a startup was going to end without anyone ever knowing we existed. We hadn't raised money, hadn't created a product, and didn't have anything to lose if we quietly pushed it under the rug and moved on to corporate jobs.

A BLESSING IN DISGUISE

Who knew that our first big failure would be the best thing that could happen to us? This is one of the biggest lessons that I've learned in going through the startup process: you never know where success is going to come from. Keep your head up, keep your eyes open, and try everything. Shortly after we got word that we weren't awarded the MDOT grant, an advisor suggested that we apply to the Michigan Clean Energy Venture Challenge (CEVC), a university-sponsored business competition with a focus on clean energy. The grand prize was $50,000. We laughed, having no idea how we qualified for a clean energy competition. His suggestion: change our focus from inspecting bridges to inspecting wind turbines. Our focus on bridges was arbitrary anyway, and we didn't have anything beyond a concept, so why not make the change? We replaced all the pictures of bridges in our pitch deck with pictures of wind turbines and did preliminary research on the wind market to put together our case.

We had competed in a few smaller business competitions and won $10,000 here and $10,000 there, including the student portion of the 2012 Accelerate Michigan Innovation Competition, but we still didn't have a great understanding of our business. The CEVC took place over the course of two rounds with a semifinal pitch and a final pitch between the top ten companies. We practiced repeatedly for five straight days with a variety of mentors giving us crucial feedback as we frantically rebuilt our deck. The day of the competition came and we didn't feel like we were even close to ready. I gave the pitch, trying to remember all the statistics we had learned about the wind industry in a short time. We kept the other industries in the pitch, including bridges, and simply said that wind turbines were our "beachhead" market—our key market as we were starting out. Surprisingly, the judges felt this was enough for us to be a "clean energy" company, and we made it to the finals.

Next, we moved from a small room of maybe forty spectators and five judges to the Ross School of Business at the University of Michigan, where we presented in an auditorium filled with spectators. I gave a shortened version of the pitch and felt pretty good about it, but I didn't think we had any chance against the other teams. Getting this far in the competition had already boosted our spirits. After having the wind let out of our sails by losing the MDOT grant, we now believed we could succeed in other markets. After many hours of waiting, we filed back into the auditorium to hear the winners. We were hoping to walk away with at least a $10,000 check for third place, which would sustain us for another month or two while we figured out how the hell we were going to raise money.

The award ceremony finally started. The organizers began by thanking everyone involved, and then they announced some category winners for Best Prototype, Most Disruptive, Best Team, Best Pivot, and

Judges' Choice, all for $5,000 prizes. Most Disruptive and Best Pivot! If these weren't the epitome of the buzzwords that I hated in the startup world, I'm not sure what else would be. I didn't even want to win these awards because they went against everything we were trying to do. Then they announced the category prizes and we didn't win those either. They arrived at the second-place prize for $20,000 and, again, we didn't win. At this point, we felt a little depressed knowing we were going to walk away from this effort with nothing more than a pat on the back.

At last they announced that SkySpecs was the first-place winner, with a $50,000 dollar prize! We couldn't believe it. They presented us with one of those giant checks with our name on it and we got our picture taken with everyone on stage.

We had never seen this much money in one place at one time. We had no idea what we were going to do with it or what the future held for us. This "pivot" to wind turbine inspection had paid off. Now we had to see if we could really turn it into a business. After winning this competition, the state of Michigan funded us to go to the American Wind Energy Association conference in Chicago to meet with customers and experts in the wind industry. We barely had a CAD model put together, but that didn't stop us from throwing together a booth and setting up meetings as if we would be ready to launch later that year. This conference led to us forming industry partnerships and diving headfirst into the wind energy industry.

FAILURES CONTINUE

Winning the CEVC and forming partnerships in the wind industry, in late 2013, led us to raising our seed-round of $600,000 from family and friends. This was both incredible and nearly detrimental. A group of engineers with absolutely no business experience had defied the odds and raised enough money to hire a team, find a warehouse, and buy enough material to build a small fleet of drones. We graduated from school, began paying ourselves very modest salaries, and jumped into business full time. Lack of funding is one of the hardest parts of being in a startup and is usually what ends up killing most startups. Here we were managing a seemingly enormous sum of money with our heads down in development.

At this point, we were still committed to building absolutely every aspect of the drone. We used our funding to set up manufacturing, print more circuit boards, and buy expensive sensors to put on the drone. The problem with winning this business competition and then successfully raising money was that it seemed to validate our approach of building everything. Our advisor was still reiterating that we were really a software company, but we refused to believe it. We were dead set on building and selling drone hardware.

We spent so many late nights and all-nighters in our one-room warehouse. I can't even count how many carbon fiber layups failed because our process changed almost every single time. We frantically wrote and rewrote new flight control software while we rushed to do flight tests. Very little of this process was scientific. Instead of following theory, we followed the guess-and-check process over and over again. As time went on, the team grew frustrated and investors began to ask us when we were going to start making money.

In the summer of 2014, we were looking at the very real possibility of running out of money and having very little to show for it. During our initial fund-raising, we made a big mistake: instead of raising more money the first time around, we actually asked some of our investors to put in less than they wanted, because we were trying to hold tightly onto our equity. Taking less money than was offered proved to be one of our most naïve mistakes, one that almost cost us the company. When you have money on the table, take it!

We were looking around for other sources of funding and ended up applying for a National Science Foundation Small Business Innovation Research grant. Surprisingly, we were awarded the grant with our very first application. This grant brought in $150,000 for a year of work to further develop sensing for automated flight. We were very excited that this grant could at least cover some of our costs while we continued to figure out how we were going to raise another round. Unfortunately, this grant wasn't completely lined up with our eventual business plan and ended up being more of a distraction. It did help contribute to our overall traction, and definitely helped us in our eventual fund-raising, but looking back, the grant's work wasn't worth the amount of money awarded.

Around this time, DJI, the Chinese drone company that is known for their easy-to-fly Phantom drones, was becoming very popular with hobby and prosumer drone users. More drone companies were popping up, offering services for real estate, photography, delivery, and even inspections, all with $1,200, easy-to-fly systems. We weren't anywhere close to a productized system ready for customers and we were already losing market traction. These hobby drone flyers were typically flying illegally and weren't doing anything more than collecting pretty videos, yet they were doing business. One weekend, a few of us on the team decided to figure out what was so special about these drones by buying one of the flight controllers. We wired it up, taped it to one of our existing custom-built airframes, and took it on a flight test. Simultaneously, the rest of our team was getting ready to flight-test our custom-built controller. We set up our custom drone, took thirty minutes to debug some code, and then attempted a takeoff. The drone hovered, somewhat stably, about two meters off the ground, but was unable to perform any maneuvers. Right next to it we had the same airframe, motors, and payload, except the flight controller was the taped-on DJI. Without any setup or tuning, we powered up the motors, took off, and flew around the field with ease. It was immediately clear that we shouldn't be re-creating a flight controller when one already existed and worked brilliantly.

As engineers, it is incredibly difficult to take a product that you've been working on for years and throw it away. Engineers have an innate drive to carry their inventions and their products all the way through to the end, but we were entrepreneurs, not just engineers. An entrepreneur should look at the product and ask, "What can we throw away to get to an MVP sooner?" We still had not realized that this was the question we should have been asking. After some debate, we finally decided to swap out our custom flight controller for the working, off-the-shelf flight controller and to move on to building the unique aspects of our product: the automated flight. One step closer to an actual MVP!

A SHORT MOVE TO THE BIG APPLE

While we were working through the grant and setting up another fund-raiser, we were miraculously accepted into a Techstars program in New York City. We had no idea what to expect or whether Techstars was the right program for us, but we were running out of money fast. We didn't have a clear direction for the company and we couldn't think of a better plan forward, so in early October 2014, we moved seven guys from Ann Arbor into a four-bedroom apartment on the Upper East Side of Manhattan.

We packed up a U-Haul and drove the ten hours from Ann Arbor to New York, realizing only when we got there that a U-Haul does not belong in Manhattan. We were accustomed to having an enormous space for all of our equipment. Now we were being forced to cram into a tiny apartment and a small office with ten other companies. These changes forced us to reassess what was truly valuable and what could be left behind.

We went through the very rigorous Techstars process of meeting dozens of mentors, refining our business, tearing our business down, and building it back up again. Every day we questioned what we were doing and why we existed. This process made us think very critically and face the brutal truth that we really didn't have a way to make money any time soon. The realization caused tensions to rise within the team, and the reality set in that some drastic changes needed to be made. Nothing changed overnight, but this constant feedback from mentors eventually guided us to make some major changes.

Two weeks after moving to New York, Tom and I flew home to compete in the annual Accelerate Michigan Innovation Competition with a top prize of $500,000. Techstars highly discouraged us from taking a week off from the program to go to the competition because one week out of fifteen is a significant portion of the program. We left anyway. This same competition had awarded us third place in the student portion two years prior. We needed the money—we were trying to figure out how to afford living in New York while paying seven people and finishing Techstars.

The semifinals of the competition were held on a Wednesday. I pitched a new business model that we had conceived only a week before. We were still focusing on the same markets as before, but we had a much stronger focus on software for collision avoidance for industrial drones. Our mentors loved the change of focus and thought it was our best pitch to date.

The following morning, we found out that we had made the top ten and would be pitching for the grand prize that evening. Furthermore, we noticed that we were the only company in our category, almost guaranteeing we would win the $25,000 category prize. We were stoked that this trip back to Michigan would land us some cash and justify the short hiatus from Techstars. That evening, I went on stage to give a shorter, five-minute pitch. I hadn't given this particular pitch very much attention and had to wing it. Fortunately, the videos we put in the presentation were powerful, making it easier. Plus, there was pretty much no pressure—we were certain we had already won some money.

Three hours after pitching, we sat down to hear the results. First the category prizes, eight in total with our category last. When our time came to take the stage and accept our $25,000 prize—someone else was announced. What could this possibly mean? Was our final pitch so bad that they decided to reconsider our category altogether? Or did this mean we took second place with a prize of $100,000? We sat in our seats nervously as they continued the event, drew raffle prizes, thanked sponsors, and finally got to the second-place announcement. Tom and I looked at each other, saying, "Let's make sure we look happy that we won second place instead of disappointed that we didn't win first." After all, the second-place prize was four times the amount we thought we had won just a few minutes before. Drum roll . . . "Second place goes to . . . Cribspot." I will never forget the look on Tom's face when we heard that we didn't win second. He was shocked, considering the possibility that we were about to get first place, disbelieving it could be possible, and hesitant because maybe we wouldn't win anything at all.

The moment finally came: "First place goes to SkySpecs!" The rest of the night was a complete blur. We had just won $500,000, ten times more than the first business competition we ever won. The amount was enough to fund our company for an entire year. Even though we had struggled to figure out what we were building and how we were going to sustain ourselves, we had found a way to impress the judges and get them to see our vision.

Winning Accelerate Michigan for $500,000!

Our home for four months in New York.

I GUESS WE ARE A SOFTWARE COMPANY

Halfway through Techstars, we finally got rid of almost all the fabrication that we were doing and we focused on being a software company. From the beginning, we knew that our automated flight software was what we cared about the most, but we still weren't sure how to deliver that value. We started by coming up with a way to simply sell drone collision avoidance software to current drone users. We compartmentalized some of the software we had built, designed an add-on that could be equipped to a drone, and then attempted to sell it to a small early-adopter group. This plan was short lived. It was very hard to build a product that could easily be integrated to any drone that anyone could use. Early trials didn't go very well and we started to get a lot of questions about how to use the product. This made us realize we needed to do the complete integration. When we graduated from Techstars in February 2015, our plans had changed, but we had nearly as little direction leaving as we had going in.

Not long after coming back to Ann Arbor, we lost three of our engineers, including one who was our chief technology officer, because they all recognized that we didn't have a clear vision for the company. We were three years into the business, had learned a tremendous amount, won over $700,000 in awards and grants, had some early customers, completed Techstars, raised a round of funding, and grown our team, yet we still didn't seem to have a way to make money. We *still* had not developed an MVP. After our team shrank, Tom and I got together to figure out how we were going to move forward. We narrowed our product focus even more; rewrote our pitch deck, strategy, and projections; and made it our top priority to raise a Series A that could regrow our team with an achievable mission.

In November 2015, we raised our Series A with a total of $2.75 million in funding from local venture capitalists. We hired more engineers, our first business and marketing team, and finally put together a plan to get to a real MVP. We set our sights on developing software to complete the first automated inspection of a wind turbine at the 2016 WindEurope conference in Hamburg, Germany. All of 2016 was spent with this goal in mind, turning away any opportunities that didn't improve our ability to hit this goal. For the first time since our founding, our team was 100% behind the goal, the plan to get there, and the work that needed to go in to achieving it. When the time came, not only were we confident that our demonstration would work, but we were done weeks ahead of time. We launched the first public demonstration of a completely automated wind turbine inspection on September 28, in twenty-five-mile-per-hour winds, in front of a group of experts from the wind industry. We had finally reached our MVP!

PERSISTENCE AND FLEXIBILITY

Startups are hard! There is no question that the deck is stacked against you right from the beginning. Failure is a constant part of being in a startup. We ran out of money twice, lost team members, built the wrong products, wasted money on products we threw away, upset customers with products that weren't ready, and still somehow found a way to make it this far. Our team has had incredibly resilient passion, persistence, and perseverance, to the point of delusion. We didn't realize we were failing even when we were close to losing the opportunity to move the company forward. This was probably a good thing at the time, but we also could have made it to our current MVP quicker if we were willing to accept small failures in pursuit of the bigger success.

My advice to all first-time founders is this: be persistent, but keep an open mind. Your first solution will most definitely not be the solution you bring to market. You are going to fail, and fail a lot. Eventually, you will learn enough from these failures to find a success. At Sky-Specs we are not done failing. We are simply quicker to recognize when something isn't working. SkySpecs has found a way to be a successful startup. While we have gotten over most hurdles that kill early companies, now we have to continue to learn from our failures to make a successful company.

CHAPTER TWENTY-ONE

JESSICA HENDRICKS YEE

Founder, The Brave Collection

>>>> ABOUT JESSICA

Exposed to fashion design and travel from a young age, **Jessica Hendricks Yee** was born in Paris and grew up outside Manhattan with eyes glued to the cases in her mother's jewelry shop. Fascinated by indigenous cultures and spirituality, she traveled to Cambodia to teach English. She was mesmerized by the tangled synthesis of the beautiful culture and its heartbreakingly violent past. This small Buddhist country was rebuilding in the wake of genocide and the reality of human trafficking. Combining her love of jewelry and a philanthropic spirit, Jessica was inspired to create a jewelry company to celebrate this unique community and connect courageous women across the globe, so she founded The Brave Collection. The Brave Collection is a Brooklyn-based line of jewelry that is handmade in Cambodia by local, fair-trade artisans, providing job opportunities and donations to programs that empower Cambodian girls and fight against human trafficking.

Jessica and The Brave Collection have been featured in *Vogue*, *Glamour*, and on MSNBC. Jessica was selected as a 2016 *Forbes* "30 Under 30" in Retail and E-Commerce, and she was invited to the White House as one of sixty young entrepreneurs to witness President Obama's speech encouraging support for emerging global entrepreneurs.

In Cambodia, we are creating job opportunities for artists post-genocide, and combining Eastern and Western ideas to create modern products that celebrate the distinct Cambodian culture. The small Buddhist country of Cambodia is home to the largest religious monument in the world, Angkor Wat, a magical city of ancient Buddhist and Hindu temples. The Cambodian people have an incredibly rich cultural history of design and spirituality and an ancient alphabet that is forever minted in the stone walls of the sacred temples. In the 1970s, however, civil war and genocide destroyed much of the indigenous culture and systematically murdered one-third of the population, including 90% of the artists.

Cambodia today is the home of the lowest-paid laborers in the world—miles of farmland is sprinkled with factories where people are often working in slave-like conditions. Cambodians today are strong, resilient, hardworking people, but with a poor education system and a recent history that threatened creative thinking with violence. The opportunities for dignified work are slim, and opportunities to find employment as an artisan are truly scarce. Still harder to find is a creative community that is producing products beyond traditional souvenirs for tourists.

The Brave Collection collaborates with a small artisan group in Cambodia to reinterpret some of the most meaningful parts of the culture into wearable art for a global consumer, thus far focusing on the alphabet and icons of the local Buddhist religion.

Returning home from a trip to Cambodia, I was surprised at how many of my most learned and well-traveled friends were uncomfortable discussing the frightening issues of human trafficking and global poverty. Others felt that the issues were so immense that, although they wanted to help, they didn't have a clue as to where to begin. Through our Brave Bracelets, we offer people an easy, affordable way to connect to artisans across the globe, and an approachable, empowering, and meaningful way to give back.

Our production story is crucial to our brand story. One of the reasons people purchase our jewelry is that they are moved by our efforts to provide job opportunities to artisans who come from disadvantaged backgrounds or suffer from disabilities. In addition to consistent monthly salaries, all of the artisans we work with receive health insurance and stipends toward their children's educations. Our methods of production are more than a technicality; the artisans are part of the DNA and soul of our brand story and the values our clients associate with a brighter future for all people.

Sourcing this production team was not easy, and managing a production team in Cambodia from New York was definitely a challenge. So how did I connect with this team in the first place? And how have I been able to establish consistent quality control with artisan partners in a time zone eleven hours ahead and thousands of miles away? With uncompromising passion and lots of patience.

When I developed the idea for The Brave Collection, I was a recent college graduate with no money, no team, and no experience in overseas production. Luckily, I had a few things going for me: I had an incredibly clear vision for what I wanted to create, the guts to ask for help, and the persistence to keep going until I found what I was looking for.

I knew I wanted to work with a fair-trade production team that was producing products ethically. Fair-trade production, for me, was crucial to my brand story and an absolute nonnegotiable. I had no clue where to begin, so I started from scratch, opening up my laptop and Googling "fair trade production Cambodia." I stumbled upon a small company in the Midwest that was importing ethically produced baskets from Cambodia. A wave of excitement rushed through me as I scrolled through their simple website—this was my first clue. With nothing to lose, I picked up the phone and cold-called the company. A man with a gentle voice answered the phone. "Hello!" I chirped. "My name is Jessica, and I want to produce jewelry ethically in Cambodia! Do you have any advice?"

I was lucky enough to speak to a kind person on the other end of the line, who was touched by my sincerity and desire to make a difference. He shared a bit about his experience sourcing his production team with me and gave me a couple of names of people who were on the ground in Cambodia to reach out to.

Here is my first takeaway: When searching for a production team, you mustn't be shy, but rather courageous enough to talk to as many people as you can who may be generous enough to share some insight with you. If you can find someone who is producing something different than you, this is ideal, because you eliminate the fear of competition and allow the person you are speaking with to feel safe enough to be candid about his or her experience.

A few similar cold calls later, and I returned to Cambodia with a list of names and an unwavering determination to return home with production partners.

I loved the idea of finding women who were in need of work and hiring them to produce for my collection. I soon realized, however, that I needed a team with some experience to ensure proper communication and quality control. Moreover, I arrived in Cambodia with an *idea*, not a flourishing business, so promising people secure employment before having a proven business model or stream of revenue felt like too big of a risk to take. The last thing I wanted to do was make a promise I couldn't keep.

I decided the better option would be to find a small, existing group of artisans, with some production experience but a lack of exposure to the global marketplace to capitalize on their talent and hard work.

After arriving in Cambodia, my first meeting was with a woman named Simone, whom the basket importer had recommended. Simone was an expat who had been living in Cambodia for a decade and knew how to navigate her way through the different artisan collectives that existed, as well as the loopholes and common mistakes foreigners from the West make when trying to collaborate with artisans in the East. I was grateful to have found Simone and spent the next few days with her, traveling throughout the country and meeting with potential artisan partners.

Meeting with different artisan cooperatives, I was surprised to learn how few groups existed and how many of them were strongly tied to a nonprofit or religious organization in the West. The bulk of the organizations that existed consisted of one-room studios that housed five to ten women who were working on handmade crafts. They were being paid a salary by generous donors in the States or Europe to cut felt, fold colored papers, do basic beading, and so on. Then, at the end of the day, they put their wares in a bin on a shelf. In the beginning, they tried to sell their wares, but the market for paper chicken keychains was limited. They had given up, resigning themselves to taking their paychecks with gratitude and limiting their expectations about the value of what they were creating.

I was so disappointed! Sure, it was incredibly noble for individuals and institutions abroad to send funds to women in Cambodia in need of work, but the model was hardly empowering or sustainable. My vision was to create a business with products that met high design and quality standards, products that would be competitive in the marketplace on their own merit, not as a pity purchase.

On my last day with Simone, I felt rather hopeless. She brought me to a small building with a cheerful coat of paint on the walls. I said a little prayer and walked into the studio.

Entering this studio, I was immediately struck by the intricacy and careful attention to detail in the products that were being crafted by hand. I felt a warm, welcoming energy as I was greeted by the bright faces of women who, despite their shy humility, carried themselves with confidence and a simple grace that seemed to come from pride in their careful work. The head of the cooperative was named Nini, and she had worked her way up from mopping floors to being the head of this group of twenty-six artists.

I fell in love with this place. I made a personal connection with the women working there, one that would continue and even blossom as we later built our relationship over email and Skype after I returned to the states.

This group was different. They didn't lack skill or determination; they merely lacked access to a customer base beyond the thrifty back-packers who wandered by their studio. They also lacked exposure to modern design and creative thinking, things that are not taught in the state-run educational system, which focuses on rote memorization of facts and discourages individual, outside-the-box thinking. I believed that, if given the chance, these artists could create pieces that could retail in New York for $100 and compete against top designers. They could do far more than make five-dollar souvenirs.

Herein lies my second takeaway: When choosing a production team, you are truly choosing your most important partner in your business, one that you will be incredibly dependent on and vulnera-ble to. It's imperative that you meet face to face and connect as people and form a bond of trust and mutual respect. Things will go wrong, and then they will go wrong again, and again, and again. Orders will be late, quality will be inconsistent, and mistakes will happen. When things go wrong, you will need a strong foundation to fall back on if you are going to problem-solve as a team and work through these inevitable issues.

Returning to New York, it took about six months for us to get to a point where our quality was consistently high enough for me to feel comfortable sharing the jewelry line with a circle wider than friends and family. Each day of this six-month period was a frustrating, trying, uphill battle. How is an artist who has never left Cambodia supposed to be able to conceptualize the level of consistent quality that would be demanded by top boutiques in Manhattan? In the beginning, I followed my heart, giving in to the instinct to overpraise and overpay for samples that were below my expectations. However, I soon realized that I needed to take on a more tough-love approach, demanding meticulous quality and a strict adherence to deadlines. As cold-hearted as it felt to be so demanding toward artists who were doing their best, it was ultimately the most productive and empowering move I could have made. Our conversation became one between equals, problem solving and collaborating with the same goal in mind, and it allowed us to ultimately produce pieces that spoke for themselves and that we felt incredibly proud of.

My third takeaway is this: Have patience regarding production. The process from inception to completion took exponentially longer than I ever could have expected, but it was well worth the wait. The challenges we solved together only strengthened our communication and level of trust, building a foundation that is still rock solid four years later.

➤ WHAT SALES AND MARKETING TACTICS HAVE WORKED FOR YOUR COMPANY?

The idea for The Brave Collection came when I was teaching English in Thailand during my time at New York University's Tisch School of the Arts. I had lived in New York my entire life and was fascinated by the ways different people lived their lives, how they spent their days, how they saw spirituality, what they valued, and how I could then take pearls of wisdom back to my life in the States.

I had an absolutely dreamy summer in Thailand, falling in love with the warmth and beauty of the Buddhist people and of the beautiful children I taught. At the end of the summer, I decided to extend my trip to visit the famous temples of Angkor Wat in Siem Reap, Cambodia. I had read that Angkor Wat was the largest religious monument in the world—a city of ancient Buddhist and Hindu temples—and I wanted to see it for myself.

Strolling through these magical temples, I realized that the Cambodian people had an exquisite history of art and spirituality, and I developed a deep respect for this beautiful culture. This reverence made it that much tougher to swallow what I learned about Cambodia's history: Cambodia suffered genocide from 1975 to 1979, where one-third of the population was killed, along with 90% of the artisan community.

As a teenager in Cambodia, I saw girls my age and younger lined up in front of bars and restaurants as items to be purchased. Child prostitution on the scale that I encountered there never escaped my mind, even after I returned to the United States. I had never heard of *human trafficking*, and had no idea what I was seeing—I just knew it felt terribly, terribly wrong.

Back home in New York, I read an incredible book called *Half the Sky: Turning Oppression into Opportunity for Women Worldwide*, written by *New York Times* columnist Nicholas Kristof and his wife Sheryl WuDunn. The book shares stories of the challenges and opportunities for women in the developing world, and it helped me to contextualize what I had seen on the streets of Cambodia.

The more I read, the more I learned, until I became the girl at the dinner party spewing horrific facts at my fellow diners, like this:

- Did you know that human trafficking is a multibillion-dollar industry and the largest criminal enterprise in the world?
- If human trafficking was a business it would be on the *Fortune* 500 List above Nike and Xerox.
- One person is trafficked every fifteen seconds.
- At the peak of the transatlantic slave trade, an average of 80,000 slaves were brought over from Africa to the new world. Today, twenty-five times that number of women and girls are being sold into sex trafficking every year.

As you can imagine, when I shared these facts, I was often met with blank stares, uncomfortable silences, and complete disconnect. I could throw out statistics, but I couldn't seem to get my community back home to really *feel* this struggle as I had felt it when it was right in front of me.

My mother owns a beautiful jewelry store. I grew up working at the store and watching the intimate connection that is formed between a metal smith who crafts a piece by hand and a woman who wears that piece each day on her skin. I began to think that perhaps jewelry could act as a tactile connector between my community at home and the community I fell in love with in Cambodia.

I decided to return to Cambodia with the idea of creating a collection that would provide employment in the East, spark conversation in the West, and donate a percentage of profits to support girls and women against human trafficking.

The first item my company made was a bracelet that said "Brave" in the Cambodian alphabet. I brought this sample back to New York with the dream of selling thousands of units. There I was, with an important cause, a dream of making a difference, our first new designs, and absolutely no customers.

How did I turn this personal passion project into a full-blown business as a college graduate with a tiny bank account? My first piece of advice is this: when developing a sales and marketing strategy for a startup, throw your ego out the door! Creating brand awareness and momentum from scratch is difficult, and it's going to require you to be as humble, creative, scrappy, and endlessly enthusiastic as you can be.

No matter where you are in your career when you start your business, there is a lot of value in beginning at the grassroots level. I see new entrepreneurs worrying about getting A-list press and celebrity support right out of the gate, before they have even shared their new business with their closer community. You may feel self-conscious or even worried about coming off as self-congratulatory when sharing your new business with your community, but you must remember that these are people who love you and want you to succeed, and you're going to need their help.

When I first launched my company, I was a twenty-three-year-old living in a tiny sublet in the East Village. I had no money to invest in marketing and no customer base to market to. I needed more than my own sheer determination to get this business off the ground—I needed a community. I went to the one place where I had community in spades: home. I decided to launch my line with an intimate friends-and-family launch party in the suburbs outside of Manhattan, where I had grown up. The launch wasn't the glamorous A-list event I had dreamed of, but it turns out the launch was much better than that. It was a defining moment when I brought together friends and family who believed in me, and I humbly asked them for their support.

At first, I felt uncomfortable asking friends and family to support my idea and to put their hard-earned money toward my products—on preorder no less. What helped me gain the confidence to lean on my community was a piece of advice my then boyfriend, now husband, gave me. He said, "Don't think of this as a favor from your community. Think of it as presenting them with an *opportunity* to be the first ones to get involved in an exciting, important, impactful project that is going to expand and flourish because of their involvement. You are granting them the chance to be part of the American Dream."

He was right. Meekly asking for favors will only get you so far, but exposing your heart and your sincere passion and igniting a feeling of possibility in those around you will do more than get you some initial orders. It will create a movement and grant you your first and most dedicated brand ambassadors.

My first launch party earned me $5,000 in revenue, enough to place my first purchase orders with my production team. The party also got a hundred people wearing my product and spreading my brand story to their friends, igniting a small but mighty ripple effect.

As our company has grown, creating inexpensive but powerful events has been a key component of my marketing strategy. I realized that if I were scrappy and creative, I only needed a few hundred dollars, along with emails, calls, and texts to everyone in my network, and I would be able to fill a room with potential buyers. If I were willing to put myself on the line and speak to the crowd about my vision and why it was important, I could walk away with the revenue needed to build my company and enough new clients to organically spread the word about The Brave Collection in their circles and expand our customer base. It sounds simple, but you'd be surprised at how few small brands utilize this kind of grassroots method to gain momentum.

With the growth I experienced from grassroots events, I was ready to take my product to a wider audience, namely, the press. At that time, there were only a few print publications with a national footprint and getting your product featured in one of those was key. Today, the media landscape has changed dramatically, and if you own a smartphone, you can be an influencer and help a brand garner credibility, clientele, and capital. With so many people to approach, it can be daunting to know where to begin. Focus on building a few strong relationships rather than reaching out to mass lists blindly. Be thoughtful about targeting editors and influencers whose tastes and values are aligned with your brand and who truly believe in what you are doing.

In the beginning, it is tempting to reach out to any and every editor. But here's the thing: getting your hands on a generic press list of contacts isn't rocket science. Anyone with a friend of a friend in public relations can get a spreadsheet with names and emails on it. The result? Editors are absolutely bombarded with emails, often containing pitches meant for another department entirely. If they took the time to read through every email or forward it along to the appropriate person, the magazines would go out of business because their editors would have no time to actually write articles!

On the other hand, receiving a thoughtful, handwritten note through the mail, along with beautiful materials and a succinct pitch that aligns beautifully with the types of stories that an editor is already focused on, is a dream. In fact, by doing so, you make the editor's life easier by doing their work for them—you are connecting them with the inspiration they need to write powerful stories.

For me, it has taken time to meet editors and influencers whom I really click with, people whom I enjoy speaking to on a personal level, people who have become champions of my work, and I of theirs. Yet these relationships—and I can count them on my fingers—are the ones that have made the biggest impact on my company.

The other point about marketing that is a bit counterintuitive is that, just because someone has a large, loyal following, doesn't mean that their fans will necessarily become your fans. There is a wildly successful blogger who fell in love with The Brave Collection and was inspired to call upon her massive network to support our collection. I was over-the-moon thrilled! What an opportunity! How many units we would sell!

On the day of her big blog post, I waited and waited and waited and watched the sleepy back end of our website as one or two measly orders rolled in. How could this be? Her fans loved her for her ultrasleek aesthetic, but ultimately they had no interest in our more bohemian designs.

Compare that experience to this: a journalist with a tiny column released a piece about our line a few days later. To be honest, I had forgotten that it was even happening, as her audience was quite small. While I appreciated the support, I didn't really expect any growth in audience or business to come from her piece. I remember coming out of a meeting to find that dozens of orders had piled up during the forty-five minutes that I had been offline. I couldn't believe it! That *tiny* column produced this incredible return? Why?

This experience was a big learning moment for me. I realize the importance of targeting the appropriate demographic. Even though the well-known blogger had a large following, her fans followed her for the couture trends she covered, not for our ethical fashion under $100. The journalist, on the other hand, had a much smaller audience that was composed of readers who were interested in women's empowerment and sustainable fashion. The reputation of the journalist aligned with our brand values so closely that her fans were our exact target demographic. Her fans were thrilled to learn about and immediately support our products.

The takeaway? Don't be seduced by the big-name celebrities and publications if they aren't an organic fit for your product, and don't write off the smaller blogs and influencers that may have a loyal community of fans that will translate to loyal customers for you.

Lastly, how can you use the tools at your disposal, namely social media, to market your brand story not only to celebrities and journalist but to everyone? The key is to define your mission statement, brand values, and brand aesthetic and to share consistent marketing so that strangers can relate to and interact with your brand in a personal way. To create your "brand bible," begin by mapping out the following:

- Your brand's mission statement, in one sentence.
- Your brand point of view, in two paragraphs.
- Your target customer: define her every value, fear, desire, and idiosyncrasy; truly bring her persona to life.
- Your brand values—don't just define what you *are*; be sure to also define what you are *not* (e.g., aspirational, not snobby; mysterious. not obscure).
- Your brand's positioning—which other brands do you want to be associated with or merchandised next to on a sales floor?
- Your brand's visual inspiration—think outside the box here: the more varied the sources of inspiration, the better. Create the mood board that captures the spirit and magic of your company and its distinct point of view.

Stick to this brand bible in the photos, captions, comments, and tone that you use to describe your brand. Doing so, you will target the right audience for your brand and create a memorable association with your product.

GRACE GONG is the creator of "The Last Key To Success, the secret recipe by founders under 30." She became interested in entrepreneurship though the mentorship of Jinbo Yao (CEO of 58.com, China's largest online marketplace) and Xiangdong Qi (President of 360.com, search engine). She lives in San Francisco.

facebook.com/killergoaway

linkedin.com/in/gracegong

instagram.com/killergoaway/

Twitter: @killergoawayGG

Made in the USA
Monee, IL
13 June 2020